Advance Praise for

Beyond Satisfied

"Kenneth's book is every bit as essential for teaching men how to pleasure women as the *New York Times* bestseller *Come As You Are* is for teaching women about their own capacity for pleasure."

—**ZHANA VRANGALOVA**, PhD, NYU professor of human sexuality; sex and relationships researcher; speaker; writer

"Kenneth Play taught my body everything it knows about squirting."

—**WEDNESDAY MARTIN**, PhD, #1 *New York Times* bestseller and author of *Untrue*

"Kenneth Play is a sex ed Renaissance man. He distills information from complex arrays of sexual knowledge, psychology, physiology, and neuroscience into a fine sexual aperitif, a tonic for those who want to transcend limits and discover their own exquisite sexual tastes."

—**JIM PFAUS**, PhD, IF, neuroscientist; sex researcher

"Kenneth Play's wisdom on tapping into a partner's desires is simple yet revolutionary. Whether you're buying this book for yourself or for a man in your life, prepare to transform your sexual experience by steering your focus back to what matters most: pleasure."

—**JORDYN TAYLOR**, Men's Health deputy editor and coauthor of *Men's Health Best. Sex. Ever.*

"Kenneth Play is the future of sex ed!"

—**BRYONY COLE**, CEO, Future of Sex (futureofsex.org)

"If you ever wished your partner knew exactly how to pleasure you, buy this book."

—**ERIKA LUST**, award-winning adult filmmaker

"Kenneth has an innate ability to simplify more complex sexual and scientific material in a manner that's accessible to everyone. That's why his work is so revolutionary—any and everyone can learn something from him."

—**ZACHARY ZANE**, sex columnist and coauthor of *Men's Health Best. Sex. Ever.*

"If you want to hack your sex life with science-backed techniques, Bruce Lee's philosophy, and Tim Ferriss' tactics, this is the book for you."

—**DESTIN GEREK**, author of #1 bestseller *The Evolved Masculine: Be the Man the World needs & the One She Craves*

"After experiencing more pleasure than they ever thought was possible at my retreats, women often ask, 'Who can teach my man how to pleasure me like this?' The answer is simple: Kenneth Play."

—**PAMELA MADSEN**, Founder, Back to the Body Retreats; author of *Shameless*

"A transformation from totally geek to totally chic, Kenneth's origin story will not only amaze you, but as an added bonus, this book will help you to become the kind of lover that makes your partner say, 'What the heck happened to you?'"

—**PETER SHANKMAN**, author of *Faster than Normal*, an Amazon multi-category #1 bestseller

"Kenneth teaches you how to expand, explore, and embrace what turns you and your partner on! He has changed my sex life for the better and can no doubt do the same to yours!"

—**WHITNEY MILLER**, relationship coach;
co-host of *True Sex & Wild Love* podcast

"When it comes to hacking pleasure in any fashion, there is one person you can always rely on for an answer—and that person is Kenneth Play. He's a one-stop shop of all sex information and has completely revolutionized the way many people understand their own body's capacity for pleasure. Kenneth knows his stuff. You don't want to miss this new book."

—**GIGI ENGLE**, certified sexologist; author of
*All the F*cking Mistakes: A Guide to Sex, Love, and Life*

"Kenneth Play is my go-to expert for explicit sex education. He provides you the skills and tools to master both connected sex and peak sexual experiences."

—**DR. MEGAN FLEMING**, world-renowned speaker
and clinician specializing in sex and relationships;
clinical psychologist for over fifteen years

"Kenneth's work is the perfect accessory to the work that I do as a sex coach. He is able to show you what is possible in the realms of sexuality and pleasure like no one has done before. He makes great sex attainable for anyone."

—**ALEXA MARTINEZ**, sex coach;
business mentor, Founder of Kaleidoscope

Beyond Satisfied

A Sex Hacker's Guide to
Endless Orgasms, Mind-Blowing
Connection, and Lasting Confidence

Kenneth Play

LIONCREST
PUBLISHING

BEYOND SATISFIED
A Sex Hacker's Guide to Endless Orgasms,
Mind-Blowing Connection, and Lasting Confidence

ISBN   978-1-5445-1635-6   *Hardcover*
       978-1-5445-1634-9   *Paperback*
       978-1-5445-1633-2   *Ebook*

Contents

Foreword

by James G. Pfaus, PhD

Professor of psychology and neuroscience,
Charles University, Prague, Czech Republic

In a letter to the noted writer and psychoanalyst Princess Marie Bonaparte in 1925, Sigmund Freud said, "The great question that has never been answered, and which I have not yet been able to answer, despite my thirty years of research into the feminine soul, is 'What does a woman want?'"

Freud's rhetorical question was as much an enigma to the princess, who spent a good portion of her adult life on a quest for an orgasm, even undergoing clitoral surgery to move her clitoris closer to her vagina in a failed attempt to cure her own inability to have them.

They both should have had this book!

Kenneth Play has crafted an eminently readable, engaging, and masterful course of sexual exploration for both men and women in a book that is as much about women's sexual discovery as it is about men's nuanced understanding of sexual technique, attitude, partnership, and—near and dear to my heart—complementary sexual anatomy and neurophysiology. Kenneth relates his personal experiences as a young, cis-gendered, heterosexual male overcoming low sexual self-esteem and his physical and spiritual growth as a bodybuilder and personal trainer who then discovered an underground sex-positive subculture. And Kenneth did what so many do not: he wisely threw away the typical sexual scripts that encumber heterosexual men into thinking that sex begins and ends with an erect penis, that bigger is better, that all women are the same but impossible to understand, and that porn is somehow real and "optimal." He discovered that, as he mastered his own sexual abilities and techniques in a manner much like martial arts training, he was more and more able to give women erotic sensory experiences that were transformational, perhaps as much for him as they were for the women. He realized that great sex doesn't come from a huge penis alone, but rather stems from the ebb and flow of erotic feelings between partners, reactions to reactions, and from discovering his partners' unique sexual landscapes, fertile ground for play and flow, and for the discovery of new abilities and sensations. In his ten thousand hours with over one thousand partners, Kenneth has become a sexual virtuoso.

As a sex researcher and behavioral neuroscientist, I have observed young rats at play—honing each separate movement that their brains will eventually string together as sexual behavior in a sophisticated dance of synchrony with sex partners. I have studied how female rats initiate and pace their sexual interactions with males, controlling the males to provide the kind of clitoral and vaginocervical stimulation they want when they want it. I have studied how male rats respect female desire and adjust their own sexual behaviors to suit the desires of the particular female they are with. In rats and other animal species this is natural. But in humans, culture has constrained our natural sexual desires and responses into proscribed "norms" that fit almost no one. We ask how many times a week we have sex, not how many times a week we *enjoy* it.

Kenneth seeks to make sex play an art that you can learn and practice and transform into any kind of experience you wish, from a simple song to a symphony. And he relates the science of sex—from genitals and autonomic function to nerves and brain and back again—in a way that is elegantly simple, accurate, and informative. This book will teach you about real sexual arousal and desire, and the exquisite forms of sexual pleasure and orgasm that you can give and take and experience to the fullest in every cubic millimeter of your erotic body and soul. This is your guide to a great sexual awakening.

Introduction

I'm one of the internet's most unlikely porn stars.

Throughout my teens, I never let any of my would-be sexual partners touch my underwear. On top of my low self-confidence, as a skinny-fat Asian immigrant kid, I was very worried about my equipment. I have an average-sized cock, but I was nervous it was too small. I heard constant jokes about Asian guys having small dicks, and *mine* isn't as big as the giant cocks I saw on porn. I was so terrified of rejection due to the size of my penis that I refused to let anyone reach for my cock. I lost my virginity at twenty, but I kept my underwear on until the very last minute.

Since then, all my teenage fears of being doomed to a life of sexual rejection and inadequacy have been reversed. How could my nerdy, hesitant, twenty-year-old self possibly have imagined that one day *GQ* would call *me* the World's Greatest Sex Hacker? That I would go from feeling debilitatingly insecure about sex to getting paid to tell people how to do it better? Through my own explicit sex ed videos,

I've taught millions of people specific sex hacks to pleasure their partners. I also co-founded an intentional sex-positive community in Brooklyn, New York, where we host all-night play parties and sex education events. My life is brimming with wonderful lovers, and as of this writing I'm about to get married to an awesome woman who loves me exactly as I am.

Throughout puberty and early adulthood, I assumed there was no way in hell my sexual fantasies could become my everyday normal. Now, a wild threesome is just, well, Tuesday.

I'm not telling you this just so I can boast. I'm telling you so I can show you how I surpassed my own dejected and distressed headspace, in case you're in a similar headspace when you decide to crack open this book. Even if you're just reading this on a whim, or looking for small pointers, my point is this: if I can rise to this level of confidence and sexual fulfillment, I know you can create the sex life you want, too.

So why *don't* you have the sex life you want?

Perhaps, like many men, you're hung up about your penis size, or your ability to stay hard enough for long enough. Attempting to please your partner might feel like putting on a blindfold and trying to break open a piñata with a stick. You might avoid asking her how you're doing because you don't want to hear the answer. You might be so caught up in whether you fit what women want that you haven't even asked yourself who you want to be sexually.

And no wonder: despite how much we want it and chase it, sex is so taboo in our culture that we don't actually talk about sex in practical, actionable terms. Men especially are expected to just know what to do when it comes to sex; culturally we look down on people who seek out sexual education, as if seeking knowledge indicates a lack of essential skills that are "supposed" to be inherent. No one wants to be seen reading *Sex for Dummies*—and yet in any other discipline, we value when people's education precedes their experience. You never want your surgeon to just "wing it"—so why would you do the same with sex?

The Sex Education You Never Had

Sex education *is* improving dramatically, but when I was in high school health class, we learned about the anatomy and function of our genitalia, we learned what diseases we could get, and we learned to put a condom on a banana. Nothing was said of pleasure. Hands-on experience was not encouraged.

Think about how fucked up it is to try to learn that way. If you want to learn to cook a delicious meal, go ahead and get your hands dirty in the kitchen. Imagine if you were told to bake a pie and were provided with an ingredient list, but you weren't given any instructions on how to actually make it. Now imagine if no one ever told you how to turn the oven on.

If that was the kind of education you got about cooking, you'd probably prepare a shitty meal. Sure, you can get by—you don't have to be a great cook to satiate hunger. But if you learn to cook well, you can create foods that excite all of the senses and make people sigh with pleasure.

Most of us have not been taught the skills to create pleasurable partnered sex. We didn't really learn how to cook, and we felt crestfallen when no one craved our food.

Even though many women can have multiple orgasms (more on that later), studies show that in heterosexual couples, men still report having significantly more orgasms than women.[1] Women in heterosexual couples also report having fewer orgasms than women in lesbian couples, or women masturbating alone. That means that on average, heterosexual women are experiencing less pleasure than everyone else.

Let's face it: we live in a society where most representations of sex—from movies, to TV, to porn—have evolved around male-centric views. In the typical media story line, the guy gets really horny, passionately grabs the woman, lays her down, and climbs on top of her. The woman's vagina is basically used as a masturbation sleeve. So much of our daily practice with sex, such as watching porn and jerking off, is in that vein. This limited and singular view of sex robs women of exceptional sexual experiences, because there aren't many models for how to give pleasure to women.

What if we did not see sex as an itch to scratch, but instead appreciated it as both the art and science of sharing pleasure?

If we can flip the script on sex, and prioritize women's sexual pleasure, we can begin to close the orgasm gap. By investing in yourself to become a better lover, you can become the partner that people crave.

How to Hack Your Sex Life

This isn't a pickup artist's guide on how to manipulate women into having sex. If you picked up this book solely with the intention of

---

1   D.A. Frederick, et al., "Differences in Orgasm Frequency among Gay, Lesbian, Bisexual and Heterosexual Men and Women in a US National Sample," *Archives of Sexual Behavior*, 2018, 47: 273–288.

getting a lot of women to sleep with you, I hope to convert you into caring more about their satisfaction. However, the pleasant by-product of being extraordinary in bed is that it's likely that a lot of people will want to sleep with you, even if that's not your goal.

This is a guide for how to be a partner and a lover who is worthy of admiration, love, and respect. That's why, before diving into the specific techniques that make for pleasurable sex, we'll look at the philosophy of sex hacking.

In Part One of this book, I'll share my own journey from insecure immigrant kid to professional sex hacker, and unpack the methods I used to tap into a learning mindset so that I could gain confidence and grow my skills. You'll learn to identify the myths that are holding you back in sex, and how to open your mind to new possibilities.

In Part Two, we'll take a deep dive into the elements of sex. You'll learn how to communicate with your partner and negotiate the sex you both want. We'll also take a detailed look at how pleasure works in your partner's body, in her nervous system, and in her brain. We'll talk about how to tap into your partner's orgasm potential. Then we'll look at how to build confidence by understanding who you are sexually and how to work with what you've got.

In Part Three of this book, we'll break down the most popular and pleasurable techniques you can use to discover what drives your partner wild, from fingering and oral to squirting and anal. Don't worry, we also cover P-in-V penetration, of course. We will look at some of the basic techniques of kink, which uses power dynamics, impact, and a variety of sensations to amplify your sexual experiences. And we'll flank these techniques with ways to create a mind-blowing experience from foreplay to aftercare.

Hands-On, Explicit Instruction

Before I became a sex educator, I had a prior career as a personal trainer. I love nerding out over biomechanics and the best ways to break down complex movements into simple steps. I've taken the same approach to sex, and I've learned that just like fitness, if we want to get better at sex, we have to practice.

As I got more involved with sex-positive communities and became an educator myself, I quickly learned how important it is to break down sexual skills into actions that are easy to replicate. But I faced a dilemma early on in my sex education career: censure laws prevent educators from showing explicit sexual content. I knew people needed to see real-life examples of what different sex techniques look like and how different partners respond to them—but the only place explicit content is allowed is in porn.

I had to make a choice: if I continued to follow censure laws to devise a traditional sex education business, I'd be able to make my content more widely available to people, but I wouldn't get the same results. By using explicit videos, I wouldn't be able to advertise in traditional ways, or participate in social media to promote my content. But I decided, fuck traditional business. I choose to teach with an unapologetically explicit style because I know it's an exceptional way to help you get a better sex life.

In this book, I'm going to get real with you. I'm going to get vulnerable about my own journey of raising my sexual self-confidence and building my sexual skills. I'll share the nitty-gritty details of the techniques I've found to please my partners.

The orgasm and pleasure gap is currently greatest for heterosexual women, and I see it as my job to help fellow straight men relate to female pleasure as best I can without having the equipment. I teach directly from my firsthand experience, and being heterosexual, my advice is angled towards heterosexual men. There are many excellent educators and experts who can speak to the domains that are outside my own lane, such as pleasure in the LGBTQ+ space. Scan the QR code below for a list of experts worth following.

Throughout this book you'll see QR codes like this one with resources that are outside the text. The two-dimensional, black-and-white format required for books creates limitations in illustrating some concepts and movements, but we've used QR codes to expand your learning opportunities.

Because of my fifteen years of personal training experience, I know how important it is to convey movements properly. These animations are made to be easy to understand and intuitive, and should help you visualize sex techniques the way you would a squat or any other physical movement. We have animated versions of many of the graphics in this book, and you'll find QR codes throughout the text that will take you to those animations on my website. You'll also find additional bonus material that we continually refresh to stay up to date on research and techniques that work. Try the one below if you want to get a feel for how this works.

Some recommended products mentioned throughout this book are made by companies who sponsor my work and generously offer discounts to my audience. One of my core values is authenticity, so I only recommend products that I personally use and can wholeheartedly stand by. The QR code below will take you to a resource page on my site that has all the recommended products and discounts in one spot, so you can easily find anything that piques your interest.

No doubt as you read this book, you'll be tempted to skip ahead to the technique you want to learn. I've created an entire process in this book to guide you to mastery in sex, and while it's natural to skip around, I recommend you read all the sections eventually. Topics like physiology and anatomy that may not seem interesting at first blush can elevate your sex life when you have the knowledge

you need. If you hit a stumbling block implementing these techniques with your partner, the answer is in the system: I've focused on the 20 percent of skills that create 80 percent of the results, so you know I'm not wasting your time.

I've distilled techniques from world-renowned sex educators to tantric masters in order to bring you the very best hacks to level up your sex life. This isn't an exhaustive list of every technique ever—but it *is* a collection of the best, most effective techniques that have worked for me with most partners.

You're probably familiar with the 80/20 rule popularized by lifestyle hacker Tim Ferriss. The idea behind the rule is to find the most essential skills or hacks that will give you the most bang for your buck. Focusing on those essential skills—the 20 percent—can produce 80 percent of the results. So it is with the sex hacks in this book: I'll teach you the essential techniques that can make your sex life 80 percent better—or more.

Your job is to put your knowledge into practice along the way.

PART I

From Compensation to Competence

1

Sexual Learning

L *et's talk about cocks.*

Men get force-fed a cultural script that says genital size and stamina are the most important factors for good sex. We obsess and worry over our cocks. How big is it? How hard does it get? How long does it last? Every movie portrays penis-in-vagina sex as the pinnacle of passion and intimacy. Men and women feature penis size in their jokes, insults, and gossip. And those big dicks in porn that magically stay hard forever and cum on command? They represent only the top seven percent of the population. Comparing the size of your own penis to a porn star's is like benchmarking your height against an NBA player.

Unfortunately, this is one of the sex myths (among many that I'll address later) that caused me crippling insecurity and brought emotional devastation for most of my teens and twenties. Because I didn't know that statistic growing up as an Asian immigrant kid. When I heard the stereotype that Asian men have small dicks and saw how Asian penis size was used as the butt of so many penis jokes, I assumed my cock must be really small compared to other people's. My penis is 5.6 inches long, which actually puts it squarely in the middle of average.[2] But my anxiety over my size caused me to avoid sex throughout my adolescence and early adulthood. I didn't want girls to reject me because of the size of my cock.

I dated a little bit in high school, but I didn't lose my virginity until I was twenty. Throughout my teens, if I made out with a girl and we started fooling around, I would touch her breasts and pet her body, but I wouldn't let her touch my penis. I kept reminding myself I was still in puberty, and I hoped that as I matured, my cock would grow.

I loved girls so much though (I still do!), that I started taking yoga to be around them. I became a lifeguard, and because there was no men's swimming team at my school, I got to be around the women's swim team. Back then, I was five foot nine, 125 pounds, and skinny as a string bean. And I was Asian. In my mind, I was the unfavorable nerd with the small dick. I didn't fit the cultural image of what an attractive man should look like, so I compensated by developing my emotional skills to help me connect to women. Try as I might, each time I got near the edge of connecting sexually with a woman, I found a way to cockblock myself. The prospect of rejection was so

---

2   Debby Herbenick, et al., "Erect Penile Length and Circumference Dimensions of 1,661 Sexually Active Men in the United States," *Journal of Sexual Medicine*, 2014, 11:93-101.

terrifying to me that I rejected myself before my partners even had the chance.

As a result, I experienced endless rejection—but it all came from me. But because I never let a potential partner reject me, I held onto the hope of being accepted someday.

The flaw in my thinking was that I assumed there was something inherently deficient in me that someone (and myself) would have to accept. I thought that someone would love me "despite" this perceived problem. What I didn't realize at that age was that there was nothing wrong with me in the first place. That someone could love me because of, not despite of, the things about me I thought were so wrong.

The journey to figuring this out was sometimes brutal, confusing, and hopeless. But on the way, there were so many lessons and gifts that I never would have found otherwise—and that I can share with you now. Because I thought I had to solve some huge problem that I couldn't fix, I explored sexuality with a level of depth and intensity I never would have otherwise summoned. I went to every place, inner and outer, that you can go to learn about sex: the complexities of academic sex research, the mysteries of tantra, the forbidden world of BDSM, and the lustful chaos of underground sex parties. This book is the result of that journey.

Growth Mindset

During my sophomore year of high school, I had an experience that profoundly shaped my attitude about what I am truly capable of. This experience was initially about only one dimension of my life, but I later learned that I could apply the same mindset to almost everything, including sex. The story began when I was at the pool, training for swimming, and I was talking to a teacher's aide about how I was planning to start lifting weights to get in shape and bulk up.

"Just focus on the books," she told me. "Asian people are not meant to be athletes. You're not going to grow bigger."

That pissed me off. *Fuck you,* I thought. *I'm going to work out like a motherfucker!* By that point, I'd already seen myself progress from being a terrible swimmer to a decent swimmer. I'd trained hard and I'd gotten faster, and I knew I could improve even more. At the core of her comment was a fixed mindset about what she thought was possible, but I knew better. That moment stoked the fire of my growth mindset towards my body.

In case you're not already familiar with growth mindset, it's a concept that was defined and popularized by psychologist Carol Dweck, whose studies at Stanford University showed that the expectations teachers held for their students influenced their students' outcomes.[3]

The concept behind growth mindset is simple: if you believe your ability in anything—from math tests to sexual performance—is fixed, you'll achieve lesser results than someone who believes they can improve. Before you can make a change, you have to believe change is possible.

When you believe you can improve, you accept the challenges that come along with growth. You invest in yourself by learning and practicing a skill until you get better at it. If you believe you'll always

---

3   Carol Dweck, *Mindset: The New Psychology of Success* (New York: Ballantine Books, 2007).

suck at something, you don't practice, you shut down in the face of obstacles, and you ultimately reinforce your own negative loop. But when you believe you can improve, you start to take an interest in stretching outside your comfort zone. That's when the process of learning becomes inherently pleasurable.

Stepping outside of my own story for a moment: I've gotten so many messages from men who believe they're broken because something about them is not changeable. Whether it's the size of their cock or how long they can stay hard, these men are focusing on the wrong thing. We all have fixed attributes about ourselves, but becoming a better lover has a lot more to do with your mindset and your connection to your partner than your equipment.

The truth is, to get better at sex, we don't need better equipment. We need practice. In an influential TED Talk, Eduardo Briceño talks about how the most pivotal step we have to take to get better at anything is to step outside our comfort zones.[4] Most of us hate stepping outside our comfort zones when it comes to aspects of ourselves that we feel insecure about, whether it's our sexual performance or our physical prowess. And yet, it's the only way to improve.

Back in high school, that teacher's aide may not have believed in my ability to get stronger and faster (because...I'm Asian?) but *I did.* First, I had to challenge the myth that Asian people cannot become athletes, and from there, I could adopt a growth mindset to my fitness. In sex, you have to challenge the sexual myths (covered in Chapter Two) that keep you locked in a fixed mindset, and then you can start to actually grow as a lover.

---

4   Eduardo Briceño, "How To Get Better at Things You Care About," *TEDx Manhattan Beach*, November 2016.

After that, I read every fitness book I could get my hands on. I'd sit in my lifeguard chair on rainy days and read the bodybuilding encyclopedia by Arnold Schwarzenegger. Between lifting weights, eating more, and taking supplements, I started to gain confidence. By senior year, I was a solid swimmer and a fit athlete. By eighteen, I'd graduated high school and became a personal trainer. I had figured out how to radically change my body by applying a growth mindset, rather than a fixed mindset, to my fitness and appearance. In the illustration below, you can see how much I was able to change my body. Little did I know at that time that I could apply this same mindset to sexuality.

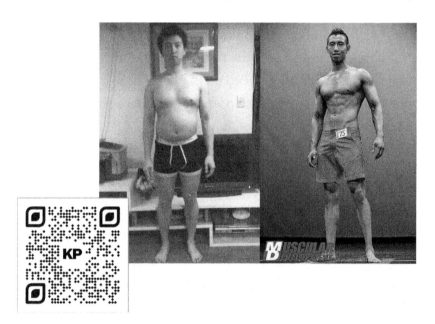

The 80/20 Rule in Fitness and in Sex

As I began to coach many different people with many different body types, I quickly learned there is no universal "right way" to train.

Each of my clients had different training needs because each of their bodies responded to exercises and nutrition differently.

Many of my clients came to me because they were stuck in their fitness routines, not seeing results, and feeling like their bodies had betrayed them; they had a fixed mindset about their bodies. (Later, when I became a sex coach, I found that many clients came to me with this same perspective about their bodies and their sexuality: they believed they were broken, and there was little they could do about it.) My job was to help my clients zero in on the practices that created the biggest benefits and the greatest transformation.

One day, Tim Ferriss called my gym asking to use our location as the setting for a photoshoot for his new book, *The 4-Hour Body*.[5] I was thrilled—I'd followed Tim's work since his first book, *The 4-Hour Work Week*, and I'd obsessively read everything he'd written on learning, productivity, and effectiveness. In short, I was a super fan boy.

When *The 4-Hour Body* came out, I wasn't just excited to see our gym in the background; I was also excited by the concepts he introduced in that book. Among them was the idea of the "minimum effective dose," or the single most effective action that moves the needle towards your goal. Alongside the minimum effective dose, Ferriss popularized the 80/20 rule, which states that 20 percent of your efforts produce 80 percent of your results. Combine these two together, and the solution to better fitness was simple: Focus on the most effective action to create the greatest strides in your fitness.

Years later, when I became a sex coach, I realized the same principles still apply to sex. In my quest to find the most effective

---

5   Tim Ferriss, *The 4-Hour Body: An Uncommon Guide to Rapid Fat-Loss, Incredible Sex, and Becoming Superhuman* (New York: Random House, 2010).

techniques to become a better lover, I had to figure out which 20 percent of sex skills I needed to acquire to produce 80 percent of the results. While most of the world can't even get their partner to orgasm reliably, that 20 percent of sex skills literally takes her beyond satisfaction. In order for you to be world-class anything, you have to be in the top 5 percent, and believe me, this 20 percent of skills totally brings you into that top 5 percent of results. These techniques are what I later distilled into my sex hacking approach.

How Meta Learning Made Me a Better Lover

I found another helpful concept in Tim Ferriss's book, *The 4-Hour Chef*, in which he talks about "meta learning," or learning how to learn better. Ferriss broke learning down into four stages, as you'll see below. I later realized anyone could use these four stages to become a better lover.

1. Deconstruction: When you begin learning something new, you first have to understand what the basic building blocks are. In sex, the building blocks include all the components you have to work with: the pressure and speed of a stroke, the connection you make with your lover, and the quality of your attention, among many other elements that we'll cover in the technical chapters of this book.

2. Selection: Pick the right elements to work on that will produce the most results—this comes back to the 80/20 rule. In sex, this means determining the techniques that are most likely to be pleasurable for your partner. I base all the

recommendations in this book on scientific evidence as well as my own experience of what has worked most often with over a thousand partners.

3. **Sequencing:** Figure out the best order and timing for learning the elements. If you wanted to learn Japanese, for example, you'd need to learn the most commonly used words first, because you want to be able to apply your new language skills immediately. The same goes for sex. If you don't know how to arouse your partner, you can't jump into learning how to do anal. If you want to learn to tie your partner up, you need to learn a single-column tie before you try complex binds and knots. And if you don't know how to communicate openly with your partner, you can't go straight to trying something that's new to both of you. Lucky for you, I've done this work for you already, and by walking through the book in order, you're getting the best sequencing built in to help you go from foreplay to orgasm to aftercare with the best skills at your fingertips.

4. **Stakes:** Outline the consequences for needing to learn, which will help motivate you to follow through. Of course, in sex the stakes are already inherently high—we're generally hardwired to bond and mate, and we're invested in feeling sexually confident and competent in bringing pleasure to our partners.

Tim Ferriss's four-step meta learning process has been invaluable to me in learning how to design my path to my own sexual mastery and that of others. But before I became a sex coach, I first applied these learning stages to physical fitness. I used meta learning to isolate the specific learning needs for each client and discovered how to break down the elements of fitness and sequence them to produce results—and I was able to create incredible results in my own physical fitness as well. This later became part of the foundation of my accelerated learning approach towards sexuality.

Self-Sabotage

Despite these improvements in other areas of my life, my cock was still the same size, and I still had crippling insecurity because of the myths I believed about penis size. And I was still sabotaging my sex life.

When I hit age twenty, I thought, *Shit, I can't go on like this forever.* It was clear my penis wasn't going to grow anymore. It was time to start working with what I had. I started flirting with a girl at the gym, and we hit it off. Somehow, despite my awkwardness, we ended up in bed together. I was going down on her when she moaned, "I want you to fuck me already."

Fuck, I thought. *This is it!* I was vibrating with anxiety, like a kid in an alley about to do a big weed deal. I'd built up so much anticipation around penetrative sex that I couldn't decide whether it would be mind-blowing or horrible.

In the end, it was...*meh*. Okay, but not great. I was so anxious, I could barely enjoy sex, even though it was happening. It turns out, if you don't know how to pay attention to the sensations and allow yourself to experience the pleasure, and you're caught up in thoughts, all the sex you could ever get in the world is just kinda...meh.

My low self-esteem continued to affect our relationship after that. I always felt like I wasn't good enough for her; the dating world was still so foreign to me and I lacked the social skills to create a good sexual connection. We had sex a few more times, but she didn't seem to enjoy fucking me. In my own insecurity, I kept defaulting to going down on her and putting myself in a sexual service position; I was very giving, but I still had a lot of anxious energy. The sexual rejection I experienced with her reinforced my own false belief that I wasn't worthy of her.

How Sex Parties Changed My Sex Life

In my twenties, I started to recognize I had a high novelty drive. Once I got past the infatuation period in a relationship, my desire would drop off. I never cheated on my partners, but I was conflicted. I still felt insecure about my own body, and at the same time I had an intense appetite for new sexual experiences. I was confused, and felt like a mess, and my sex life was continually disappointing.

Then, on a Match.com date, I met the first sex-positive person I'd ever had in my life. She was the first person with whom I could talk about sex in a celebratory way. With her, sex wasn't a shameful topic—it was an interesting one, worthy of serious discussion. She invited me to a sex party, and I instantly got nervous as hell. I remember walking home as a high schooler and fantasizing about sex parties and orgies, but I always shut myself down. *I could never go to a sex party*, I told myself. *I don't have a porn-star cock*. I agreed to go with my date to the party. I decided I might not be the most impressive guy in the room, but at least I wouldn't get kicked out.

Leading up to the party, I was so stressed out about being able to enjoy it that a friend gave me an Adderall. I took it in the morning on the day of the party, and when it kicked in, I felt amazing. When you deal with dyslexia, as I do, it's hard to pay attention to things, but I suddenly found myself blazing through all my work. *This is the shit*, I thought. I was excited for the party.

When I walked in the door, there were people walking around naked, casually socializing or milling around between couples who were engaging in kink scenes. I was simultaneously turned on and totally blown away to watch people express their sexuality so openly.

As I walked around the party with my date, I was surprised I wasn't getting hard, because I usually had no trouble getting an erection. I assumed I was just nervous. Partway into the night, my date proposed a threesome with another woman—it was my teenage fantasy come true. They were both so hot, and I was ecstatic to play with them, but even as we started to roll around together, my cock refused to get hard. It was like I'd skinny-dipped in an ice-cold pool. My worst nightmare come true at the worst moment possible.

I excused myself to go to the bathroom. I was just nervous, I told the girls. In the bathroom, I talked to my reflection in the mirror. "What's wrong? This is everything you ever wanted. Don't be nervous. Man up." I slapped my cock a few times, trying to get it to respond, but it just hung there. Defeated, I walked back to the girls and told them I was nervous and couldn't seem to get it up. It was only later that I learned one of the side effects of Adderall is an inability to get an erection. I was incredibly embarrassed, but my partners were incredibly sweet and loving about it, and we enjoyed the rest of the evening without the pressure to have intercourse.

As the night was winding down, I saw a beautiful woman standing by the door. She was naked, and her boobs were gorgeous. I love boobs; they're one of my favorite things on the planet. As I approached her, I drummed up the courage to say something. I wanted her to know how much I appreciated her beauty.

"This is my first time at a sex party, so I'm not sure if this is appropriate," I began, "but you have beautiful breasts. They're amazing."

"Oh, honey," she said, and broke into a smile. Before I could say anything more, she shimmied her shoulders, grabbed my head, and pressed my face between her bouncing boobs.

This moment, with my face cradled in a beautiful woman's breasts, shifted my sexual paradigm. In that instant, I realized all the fucking painful rejection I'd experienced from women had actually come from rejecting myself. I thought, *I'll never cockblock myself again.* It was a promise I've kept to this day.

I tapped into the growth mindset I'd adopted around physical fitness, and I started to nerd out about sex. After that first party, I dove headfirst into the sex-positive community, where I found a wealth of information about sex science and sexuality just by talking to people about their techniques and pleasures. When I saw someone doing something cool or exciting at a sex party, I would ask them: How did you do that? What did it feel like?

Turns out, people really like to tell you why they're good in bed. And sometimes, a conversation that started with, "Hi, I'm new to this community and still learning how to navigate—do you have any tips for newbies?" would end with the other person saying, "Oh, you're cute—let's play!" I felt a sense of belonging in the sex-positive community that I'd never felt anywhere else. When I stopped rejecting myself, I also stopped getting painful rejections from the outside world. After all, it's really hard to be a douchebag when you're half-naked.

I wish I'd had access to this kind of encouraging, positive sexual culture when I was in my teens and twenties. Throughout the formative years of my sex life, I'd had a shitty relationship with my dick, and my relationship with myself fucked up my sex life. It was through sex parties that I gained access to the kind of sex education that changed not only my life but my entire mindset about sex. This was the beginning of my journey towards mastery.

The One-Trick Pony

After that first sex party, I was hooked. Ironically, I gained self-confidence in the high-pressure, performative environment of sex parties. Like any athlete preparing for the big game, I wanted to be able to give my best, and I used the pressure to overcome my anxiety. I fingered partners in front of hundreds of people; I joined in on gang bangs with some of the most beautiful, big-dicked men on the planet. And I found my curiosity to learn different sexual techniques became an amazing tool for defusing male competition. Instead of comparing myself to someone who was performing really well, I would often go up to them and ask, "What's your tactic?"

So one night, when I saw girls lining up to play with a particular guy in the corner of the room, I was instantly curious to learn what he had to offer. This guy was not your typical Casanova; he was nerdy, with funny glasses, curly hair, and an unexpectedly high-pitched voice. But he lined his partners up, and within minutes he got each one to squirt, one right after the other.

My jaw dropped. Before that moment, squirting had seemed like an elusive, mythical sex act, but here he was, using some replicable process to create this miracle with every partner. This was my first time seeing evidence-based learning at a sex party. I waited for him to take a break so I could bug him about his technique.

I found him smoking a cigarette outside, and I told him how amazed I'd been at his performance. I asked him how he did it, and he said, "There's one secret to it; I'll teach you."

He showed me the angle to hold my hand, how much pressure to apply, and how fast to move. Suddenly, I had a new magic trick. I felt like I'd hacked sex. I wanted to try my new technique on every partner I played with.

I quickly realized that one technique would work really well for one partner, but it wouldn't work for another. There was no single technique that worked 100 percent of the time. I couldn't figure out why the same techniques didn't consistently work. It drove me crazy.

I'd become a one-trick pony, and I didn't know how to adapt. One partner gave me feedback that during sex my techniques were as mechanical as watching someone opening a can of beans.

When a technique I was trying didn't work for my partner, it sometimes left us both feeling bad. I would feel bad because I thought it meant I couldn't do it right, and she would feel bad because she would worry there was something wrong with her. Slowly, I began to realize I was putting too much pressure on the situation.

After accumulating all the different techniques, what I ultimately learned was how to calibrate and troubleshoot with each individual partner. I learned to vary my techniques, but I also learned that there was more to sex than technique. At this point, I knew there was some missing element in sex, beyond just the mechanics of it, but I was totally lost on what it was. On the next part of my journey, I started looking for this missing piece, and the search for it led me to some people and experiences I never could have imagined.

The Pool Boy Learns to Count Cards

After a few years working as a personal trainer by day and moonlighting at sex parties, I became less interested in helping people eat fewer carbs or lift more weight, and *way* more interested in helping them have more orgasms. I went to the first-ever Sex Geek Summer Camp, hosted by Reid Mihalko, and gained the confidence to leave the fitness industry and help build an intentional sex-positive community, Hacienda Villa, with my business partner Andrew Sparksfire and his wife, Beth. But back at Sex Geek Summer Camp, Reid taught me that sex was more than smut; helping people have better sex is, in Reid's eyes and now in mine, a legitimate pursuit worthy of attention. It was also at Sex Geek Summer Camp that I met Pamela Madsen, a legendary somatic sex educator and the founder of Back to the Body retreats. Women come to these retreats from all over the world to truly discover their orgasmic potential and to expand their conceptions of what is possible sexually through experiencing things they never have before.

I'm good at sucking up to people when I want to learn from them, and I sucked up to Pamela by becoming her pool boy. I suggested that she host her next retreat at a house Andrew and I were building in New Orleans, and I offered to be her pool boy during the retreat for free.

After that, Pamela became one of my dearest mentors. I worked for her for six years in an environment that I can only describe as a Navy SEAL training camp for female pleasure. I got thousands of hours of hands-on experience working with women at her retreats, who all experienced different desires and different struggles with their sexuality. During my encounters with all kinds of sexual situations, Pamela taught me about sex like a good teacher of martial arts might teach about fighting. While she taught me how to win each individual "fight," she wove in lessons about sexuality in general that would forever change the way I viewed pleasure. She gave me the missing piece I was searching for. She was the Morpheus on my journey through the Matrix.

Pamela taught me one of the most important lessons about sex: skill doesn't count for shit if your partner isn't aroused. I stopped focusing on technique and instead focused on the woman in front of me: I listened to her body and learned to cultivate enough sensitivity that I could feel what she felt. The subtle cues women gave off, from the slightest contraction of vaginal muscles to the changing rhythms of breath and textures of and volume of moans became as clear as directions on a GPS, guiding me to a destination.

I also learned to look at sex from my partner's perspective. Because our cultural sexual norms (based on porn and old-school sex education that disregards pleasure) are male-centric and focused on male performance, many women are unfortunately used to not having orgasms during sex. Some even have a built-in mistrust in sex; they don't believe their needs will be met by their partners.

To reverse those sexual scripts, I realized I needed to help my partners have early successes in experiencing pleasure. Some techniques, like G-spot or cervical stimulation, are pleasurable only after a partner is highly aroused, but the probability of these techniques creating pleasure early on is not high. I started to map out the

techniques that worked best early on—techniques I describe especially in the Foreplay and Fingering chapters—and I now think of
this kind of sexual sequencing like card counting in Vegas.

When a gambler counts cards in poker, they make bets based on
their calculations of what cards are left in the deck, and predictions
of what values are most likely to come up next. Similarly, I learned to
calculate the potential success of a technique based on how aroused
my partner was, and what signs and feedback she gave me, as well
as data from scientific studies and surveys on sex that showed what
most women tended to respond to.

The more pleasurable experiences I could create for my partner
early on, the more her pleasure would build, and her sexual confidence would build with it.

Some of my knowledge of what techniques to use came from
experience, and a large part of it came from science. As I got deeper
into my role as a sex coach, I began to nerd out with scientists and
scientific research. Dr. Zhana Vrangalova, a researcher who teaches
human sexuality at NYU, became my business partner, gave me
access to a treasure trove of intellectual resources about sex, taught
me how to think about sex in a more academic, evidence-based way,
and became one of my dearest friends. With her, and on my own,
I read data on female sexuality to back up the observations I was
seeing with my partners.

For example: only 18.4 percent of women orgasm from penetration alone, while 81.6 percent of women either require clitoral stimulation alongside penetration or prefer clitoral stimulation alone to
orgasm.[6] This kind of data informed my ability to card count and

6   Debby Herbenick, "Women's Experiences with Genital Touching,..."

bet that I could create a higher degree of pleasure for my partner by giving her clitoral stimulation at all stages of arousal.

But this is only one example of the way that sexual science changed my game. Not only did I read articles by people like Dr. Jim Pfaus, one of the most brilliant and cutting-edge sex researchers alive today, but I had the unique privilege of getting him to answer my personal questions with Dr. Zhana and learned unique and often surprising methods of applying their findings to sex. One time, when one of my clients just couldn't figure out how to have an orgasm with a partner, I actually called Dr. Zhana and she asked Dr. Pfaus my question about the issue while they were on a car ride together. I got a recorded version of his answers. Then I went back and applied it to the client, and I was able to help her resolve a lifetime of struggle and pain.

This kind of unique information totally changed my game. There is so much cutting-edge sex research hidden away in academic literature, and once I learned how sex researchers on the inside were thinking of it, I learned to leverage this information to optimize sexual experiences. At this point I became able to create sexual experiences with a level of precision I had never experienced before.

What Bruce Lee Can Teach Us about Sex

One of the core philosophies behind being a good martial artist is to see the world with fresh eyes. In every moment, the martial artist has to be willing to drop the assumption that he already knows

---

...Sexual Pleasure, and Orgasm: Results from a US Probability Sample of Women Ages 18 to 94," *Journal of Sex & Marital Therapy*, August 9, 2017.

what the hell is going on. Only then can he adapt to the actual circumstances in front of him. In the famous fight scene in *Way of the Dragon*, Bruce Lee is getting his ass kicked by Chuck Norris when he realizes he needs to change his strategy. He sees that the moves he used in the beginning of the fight aren't working and he adapts his fighting style. It's only by being flexible and responsive that he's able to win the fight.

Your partner's responses to the techniques you try give you a wealth of data on what feels good to her in the moment. But your partner's body isn't static. These data points or "parkinG-spots" will change from moment to moment and from day to day. Your partner's body changes depending on how aroused or relaxed she is, whether she's on her period or close to it, how much stress she's been experiencing, and dozens of other factors.

There is no one trick that works for every partner (even though there are a lot that work a lot of the time), or even for the same partner in every situation. Instead, there is only what works for your partner *right now*. By staying in the moment and paying attention to your partner's feedback, you can overcome your own assumptions about what your partner will find pleasurable. When you're willing to let go of those biases in yourself, you can observe your partner's responses more clearly and give her the stimulation she craves.

Bruce Lee spoke about skill development as happening in three stages (there's also a Western psychology model known as the four stages of competence that echoes the same idea). When we're first learning a skill, like fighting, we act instinctually. Our punches and kicks are reactionary, but not always coordinated or effective. So in the second stage, we begin to break the skill down. We learn the mechanics of an effective punch—how to stand, how to rotate the body, how to direct our force—but because we're getting so scientific about the movement, we can no longer relax or be expressive with it. In the third stage, we become familiar enough with the movement that we can actually shed everything we've learned and be in the moment again. Technique goes away, and it's just you and your opponent.

The same thing happens in sex. I had to go through my awkward mechanical-man phase to break down the techniques enough that I could become fluent with them. In the next stage of my life, I learned to engage with my partner in a sexual dance, each of us responding to the other. Sex to me transcended a set of skills; it became an art.

PornHub Gets Educational

Western scientific thought is great at explaining the world. Eastern philosophy is great at teaching us how to experience it. For great sex, we need both: we need to have the knowledge of what kinds of touch and techniques are most likely to be successful, and yet, at the same time, your partner's pussy doesn't need explaining. When it comes down to it, you don't need a lecture on how the pussy works as much as you need to understand how your partner feels and experiences her own pussy, and how the two of you feel and connect during sex.

As I developed my own methods of hacking great sex, I kept teachers like Dr. Zhana and Pamela Madsen in my head. Dr. Zhana represented the West, and all the data I could observe and collect about my partner's body and her responses; Pamela represented the East, and reminded me to tap into my experience, feelings, and intuition as I connected with my partners. Like Bruce Lee predicted, I went from approaching sex instinctively, to dissecting it down into its various mechanical elements like Tim Ferriss, to putting it back together again in flow and in response to what was happening moment by moment.

As I began to teach what I'd learned to people in the sex-positive community, I realized how valuable it was to have live-action instruction. In other disciplines, we share knowledge by demonstrating technique directly from teacher to student. You can log onto YouTube and find videos of world-class violinists instructing how to play violin; you can watch Bob Ross paint on TV for hours; you can watch any number of top chefs on cooking shows. And yet, when it came to sex, the only resources available were theatrical (usually male-centric) porn videos, in which the pleasurable moans are all fake.

One of my best friends, Beth Sparksfire, helped me shoot a video of the squirting technique I'd developed, and I quickly realized it's extremely challenging to shoot an instructional video on sex and capture authentic reactions to pleasure on camera. It was easy to make something look fantastic when making porn, because everyone was in performance mode—but to teach, we needed to dial in all the elements to make sure the instructions were clear and demonstrable. It was important to me to leave in mistakes so viewers could see what sex looks like in the real world.

When we posted the video of my squirting technique on PornHub, it became an instant hit. It now has over fifteen million views and counting—a testament to how much people want to learn about sex!

The Krebs Cycle of Sexual Creativity

When I learned about the Krebs Cycle of Creativity (from an episode of the Netflix series *Abstract*), all the pieces of my sexual development—and the pleasure hacking system I wanted to teach to others—clicked into place. The Krebs Cycle of Creativity comes in four stages—science, engineering, design, and art—and each of these stages relates to how we develop the art of great sex.

The cycle starts with science. The goal of science is to gather information and convert it into knowledge, which is key in our sexual education, as well. It's important to know, for example, that the majority of women require clitoral stimulation to orgasm.

In the second stage of the cycle—engineering—we convert that knowledge into utility. We learn the techniques that create the stimulation our partners like. In our previous example, we need to learn the actual techniques and varieties of clitoral stimulation in order to turn that information into something useful.

But the techniques alone don't create great sex—which is where the next step, design, comes in. Design converts utility into cultural behavior and context. In the case of sex, this is about sexual behavior expressed in the context of eroticism and arousal. We must take the techniques and learn to use them in a way that facilitates arousal of the entire person, mind, emotions, and body. It's about creating an experience.

The next step is art. Art takes cultural behavior and questions our perception of the world. In sex, we begin by reimagining sex based on what we now know to be true based on our experience. Sex becomes an art form where we have the opportunity to express ourselves honestly and continue to explore, never taking any moment or achievement as the final one but continuing on a perpetual process of discovery.

Now you know how to learn and how to think more accurately about sex—so let's take these principles and learn *how* to have great sex. The first step is to deconstruct the myths about sex that stand in your way.

Free Erotic Play

A famous sportswriter, Grantland Rice, once said, "It's not whether you win or lose; it's how you play the game." In the rest of the book, I will give you all the science and technique necessary to become a world-class lover. However, none of this will make a difference if you don't use it to enrich your sexual experience. Having a rich and fulfilling sexual experience doesn't only involve abstract learning and skill acquisition. The best part of sex arguably has to do with self-expression, freedom, and enjoying the process. The reason why Bruce Lee's teachings lived so far beyond his lifespan is that he didn't just teach how to punch and kick, but about the philosophy of how to express yourself through movement. He used martial arts as a vehicle to attain self-actualization.

After studying and practicing sex hacking for many years, I noticed that there is progression of stages on the way to peak sexual experience. You could call these stages many things, but I named them *feel, calibrate, connect,* and *play.* While you can enjoy yourself at every stage of this experience, I find that the further you progress through the stages, the more rewarding the experience is. Before I get into educating you on the science and techniques of sex, I want to explain what this process will look like as you learn.

The first stage is *feeling*. Learning to feel is learning to let go of all of the stress of the day, your history, your attachment to how things need to be in the future, and just completely immersing yourself in the present moment. You've seen this moment in a lot of superhero or martial arts movies, when in the midst of chaos, the hero just takes a pause, takes a breath, and centers their awareness before engaging further. The way you do this is by feeling your internal and external world through your senses, becoming immersed in your erotic experience, as well as your partner's, and paying attention to erotic cues like breath and sound. If you were a surfer, this would be a moment when you are sitting on your surfboard, trying to get a feel for the water, your own body, the weather, and the currents. This is the moment when you open your field of awareness to experience more of what there is to be felt.

Once you master feeling and noticing your own erotic experience, you can start to learn to calibrate. Because you can use all the feedback you are getting from your senses, you begin learning to navigate the experience. *Calibrating* means that you assign meaning to the cues that you are getting from your partner. You begin to understand what that person's movement, sounds, and emotional expression mean *for them*. You understand how they respond to specific types of touch. You are now decoding the language of their erotic cues. You could view this like developing a compass for your experience. You know when to touch softer or harder, depending on what noises or movements they make. As a surfer, this is where you find your balance and timing. You're learning how your movements and techniques interact with the water. You're getting the hang of surfing.

In the third stage, *connection*, you begin to feel seamlessly interwoven with your own and your partner's erotic experience. You can fully connect with her and stay present in the experience without detaching to analyze what is happening or what to do about it. At this stage, it feels like everything clicks into place. You're no longer observing your experience from the outside. You are completely connected with your lover. If you were a dancer, you could imagine that leading and following disappear, and you both begin to enjoy the experience as a whole entity, moving together without thought. If you're a surfer, you merge with the waves and the entire ocean so that your motions feel like you are effortlessly moving along with the currents of water as they shift, grow, crest, and dissolve.

In the last stage, you enter a state of spontaneous *play*. You really get to be free and express yourself. You're busting out your signature moves, inventing tricks in the moment, and letting your creativity guide you wherever it feels right. There's no recipe for this stage, because it's about letting go of the rules and allowing complete spontaneity to arise. We all have different bodies, temperaments, outlooks, ideals, and preferences. In this stage, you can express those preferences, or try on new flavors of expression you never have. It's free, erotic play.

My intention for this book is not only to tell you how to have sex perfectly. You could learn everything there is to know about sex and do all the technical elements perfectly and be relatively unfulfilled doing it. Just like you could have a six-pack and be miserable in your own body, or be rich and hate your life. What makes all of this worth it is enjoyment in the process of learning and of the experience itself. Being in flow, playing, and connecting is what makes it all worth it.

Keep in mind you will likely go through all four stages within each sexual encounter. Even if you're experienced with your lover, and something goes awry, it never hurts to go back to stage one and focus on feeling deeply. If you were a martial artist, and a fight started to go wrong, you might take a moment just to center yourself and really feel before reengaging. However, the more you do this, the faster you will progress through the stages and get back to the stage of play.

Arguably, this free erotic play is really the best part of the entire sexual experience. It's a place where we can bring all parts of ourselves out to be seen and known, utilize our creative capacities, have deep intimacy with ourselves and others, and create some of the deepest bonds human beings are capable of experiencing. I hope that by learning all I have to teach, you'll learn to freely play in your erotic life. If you ever wonder why my name is Kenneth Play, now you know. I think play is the best part of life.

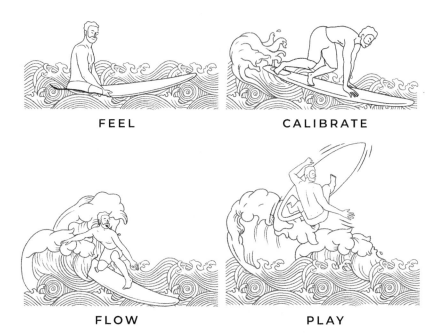

FEEL   CALIBRATE

FLOW   PLAY

2

The Myths that Hijack Our Sex Lives
And What to Do About Them

If you pass by Franklin Barbecue in Austin, Texas, on any given day, you'll see a long line of people stretching out the front door, wrapping around the corner, and ending a block later down the street. Customers wait four hours in the Texas heat to get a taste of this world-famous barbecue. Why? Because the food is just *that good*.

If you want a lot of sex in your life, you have to raise your craveability.

Of course, what we crave is entirely individual and subjective. I've had incredible, Michelin-star meals, and I've also salivated over a Popeye's chicken sandwich (which drives me crazy—some pleasures we just hate to love).

Just as there are dozens of ways to make eggs, there are dozens of styles your partner may love, or hate, or hate to love. You could make the fluffiest, most delicious French omelet for your partner, but if it's not to her taste, you won't have her moaning in pleasure. If your partner doesn't like the way you've prepared her eggs, it would be useless to blame the egg. Your job is to work with the egg, and learn to cook it the way your partner likes.

The point is, if you're trying to level up your sex game, you can't just focus on the sensations, positions, and techniques *you* like. You have to learn to cook with a wide variety of techniques so you can make the dishes your partner likes.

We're all born hungry, but not everyone knows how to cook. In fact, it's easy to fuck up cooking an egg. Let's say you wanted to hard-boil an egg, but you had to take a random guess at how many minutes to boil it for. You'd easily end up with an under- or overdone egg. But if you know it takes six minutes to boil an egg, suddenly the task is simple. The line between success and failure is a simple piece of information. Many of the sex techniques in this book are equally simple—and creating mind-blowing sex is a matter of mastering technique and learning what your partner likes.

If a particular sex technique isn't working for your partner, it's useless to blame the technique. Instead, you can learn to read your partner's signs, learn her likes and dislikes, and create sensual experiences for her to try. Over time, you will learn to create dishes for her that are irresistible.

As you learned in the last chapter, it took a long time for me to learn this lesson. And one of the reasons is that there are dozens of myths we inherit about sex—cultural scripts we get from porn and regressive sex education programs—that try to convince us that there are certain norms we're all supposed to follow when it comes to sex. We're taught to make eggs all the same way, even though not everyone likes the same kinds of eggs.

Like it or not, we buy into a variety of myths about our sex lives and our bodies—*my cock is too small, my vagina is too big*—that erode our self-esteem and confidence. Often these myths take hold because they play off of our deep insecurities and entrenched cultural norms.

Myth #1: Bigger Is Better

So many of us worry about the size of our genitals, as if there's one size that fits all when it comes to providing sexual pleasure. But imagine if we brought that same mentality to shoe shopping: it would be ridiculous to buy the wrong size shoe because "bigger is better." The best shoe is the one that fits.

What matters is not size alone, but genital compatibility between two partners. Everyone has a sweet spot, as the range of sizes and shapes available in sex toys clearly indicates. We're all looking for just the right-sized shoe. Contrary to cultural belief, not all women prefer big dicks: a study found that while most women prefer an above-average-sized cock for a one-night stand, they don't want a huge cock for a consistent partner.[7] (After all, a big cock takes a lot of warm-up.)

The question of size gets trickier when we consider the additional psychological component of what we find sexy. A woman

---

7   Nicole Prause, et al., "Women's Preferences for Penis Size: A New Research Method Using Selection among 3D Models," *PLoS One*, 2015, 10(9).

with a small vagina may experience physical pain from a well-endowed partner, for example, but if she enjoys pain during sex, a big cock might still work for her. When our psychological turn-ons *don't* match up with our physical attributes, we have to decide what's more important to us.

The cultural norms that dictate what's sexy also change over time. In the Roman era, a smaller penis was more desirable; people who had big penises were considered oversexed and stupid. Just like penis size doesn't determine brainpower, it also doesn't determine how much pleasure you're able to give to a partner during sex. But if you hang onto your internal biases and low genital self-esteem, I guarantee you'll have a shitty sex life.

The truth is, every person's body will appeal to and feel pleasurable to some people, but not to everyone. We each have our own biological equipment to work with. Some women like to be pounded by a gigantic, porn-star-sized cock. But those women are a small minority, and even for them, penetration with a big cock isn't the only available form of pleasure. One of my partners is a super-size queen who likes her cocks in the top two percentile. Yet I'm one of her favorite lovers, because I know how to lean into my own strengths to give her pleasure. If I spent the entire time we were having sex worrying whether my penis was enough for her, the sex would be terrible—as I'd discovered from previous experience.

Men's and women's physiological traits are distributed along a bell curve, where most people are in the middle, and there are some outliers on either end. Giant cocks and micropenises are not all that common. About 70 percent of men have a penis that's between 4.7 and 6.3 inches in length, and between 4.3 and 5.5 in

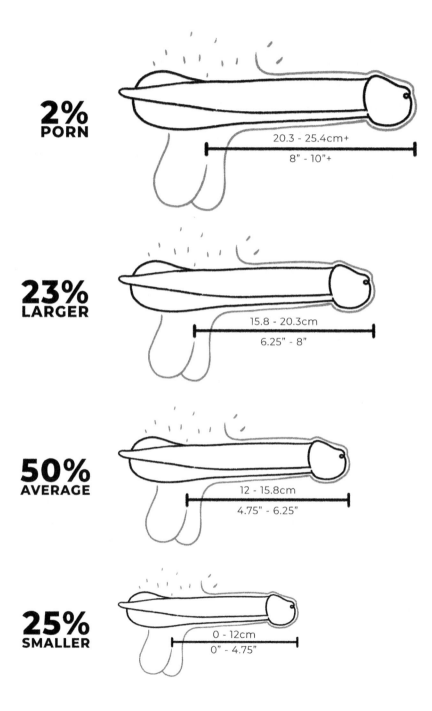

2%
PORN

20.3 - 25.4cm+
8" - 10"+

23%
LARGER

15.8 - 20.3cm
6.25" - 8"

50%
AVERAGE

12 - 15.8cm
4.75" - 6.25"

25%
SMALLER

0 - 12cm
0" - 4.75"

circumference.[8] The previous diagram illustrates the exact percentages of penis sizes among the population, so you can get a realistic idea about where you fit in. Because most of us are somewhere in the middle of that bell curve, it's likely that we have genital compatibility with most other people, who are also in the middle of the bell curve for vagina size. (There are even more statistics on penis and vagina size in Chapter Thirteen.)

Essentially, most of us who worry about the size of our genitals worry for nothing. Even men who are far above average can become convinced that their cocks are not big enough, because watching porn distorts our view so much. I've seen so many men who have perfectly good penises destroy their lives over their pain and insecurities. This needless worrying wreaks havoc on our sex lives, when there's actually no physical issue at all.

The takeaway: Genital compatibility matters far more than the objective measurements of your cock. Even if you're not perfectly compatible with your partner, there are still a million ways to have pleasurable sex with your partner, and your penis is just one tool.

Myth #2: Every Penis Should Function like a Jackhammer

There is a billion-dollar industry based on increasing penis size, making erections last longer, and extending performance. The size of that industry is a testament to how many men worry about

8   Debby Herbenick, et al., "Erect Penile Length and Circumference Dimensions of 1,661 Sexually Active Men in the United States," *Journal of Sexual Medicine*, 2014, 11:93–101.

getting an erection quickly, maintaining it under pressure, and being able to hammer away for hours.

This expectation is fed in part by the athletic performances of porn stars who seem to be able to keep their cocks hard on screen on command. The reality is that porn stars often have to stop filming to step away from the set and maintain their erection, as well as taking dick pills beforehand to stay hard. Through the magic of editing, the viewer is none the wiser. Many men hold themselves to standards that are not only unrealistic, but entirely mythical.

The idea that a man's erection should never falter is not very different from the damaging misconception that men should never cry. We're told to get our shit together, man up, and never let our emotions come into play in our performance. In reality, what happens in our world affects our sex drive. Penises aren't power tools; if a guy loses his job, he might not be in the mood for sex, and his body's response will reflect that.

If we're not willing to be vulnerable with our partners, we can't be intimate with our partners. Sex without vulnerability is just a performance. A sex life built around performance becomes like a never-ending first date, the Amazon Prime for orgasm. I spent a lot of my own sex life in that mindset—it takes one to know one. In the quest to impress our partners, we lose our connection with ourselves.

The takeaway: Sex isn't always perfect. Sometimes it's awkward, weird, uncomfortable, and messy—in short, it's *real*. Instead of focusing on your equipment, focus on being mindful in the moment with your partner. Ask yourself: what's arousing in this moment right now? Pay attention to your senses. Look at your partner's beautiful lips and the curves of her body. Soon enough, you'll be out of the anxiety loop and on to great sex.

Myth #3: We Should Be
Fucking All Night Long

Innumerable pop songs, movies, and stand-up acts lead us to believe that people are having nonstop penetration all night long. But a study in the *Journal of Sexual Medicine* looked at the average length of time most couples tend to have penetrative sex. The number of minutes people typically spend fucking? Three to ten.[9]

In reality, by the time we've spent fifteen or twenty minutes pumping in and out, most people get kind of bored. Or tired. While we may have a misconception that we're supposed to last forever, science (and biology) says otherwise. Penetration isn't the pinnacle of sex. It's one tool of many.

All-night sexual experiences happen by enjoying each other fully and playing with a wide variety of techniques and possibilities. When you sit down for a meal at a Michelin-star restaurant, you're not there just to satiate your hunger. The goal isn't nutrient fulfillment; if it was, you could sit in your apartment and drink Soylent. The point is to be immersed in the experience, to enjoy the atmosphere, and to be satisfied by every bite.

Peak sexual experiences involve physical, emotional, and psychological artistry. When you recognize that penetrative sex is just one of the many ways you can bring your partner pleasure, you open up a wealth of new possibilities for giving your partner the best sex she's ever had.

9   Eric W. Corty and Jenay M. Guardiani, "Canadian and American Sex Therapists' Perceptions of Normal and Abnormal Ejaculatory Latencies: How Long Should Intercourse Last?" *Journal of Sexual Medicine*, May 1, 2005, 5(5): 1251–56.

The takeaway: Great sex comes from matching the experience to both partners' desires in the moment. When you each want to stuff your faces with a fast-food meal, a quickie will be the best match to your hunger; when you're desiring an elaborate nine-course meal, you'll want to fill the experience with variety and spice.

Myth #4: Penis-in-Vagina Is the Only "Real" Sex

To be honest, this myth is likely a holdover from a Judeo-Christian stigma around sex. While penis-in-vagina sex is certainly instinctual—it's the way we procreate, after all—it's not the only kind of sex humans have, and it's certainly not the only kind of sex we come across in the animal kingdom. Animals do all sorts of weird shit: they perform oral sex, anal sex, and genital rubbing in addition to reproductive sex.

For hetero couples, the major problem with holding the idea that penis-in-vagina sex is the only *real* sex is that it's not the most pleasurable form of sex for a lot of women (sex acts with a greater degree of clitoral stimulation rank higher). Think of the performance anxiety that men feel from overemphasizing PIV sex: if that's the only kind of sex that matters to you, of course you'll worry about your cock size and your ability to hold an erection, among all the other performance pressures that can leave men feeling like their bodies are broken.

This is not to say that PIV sex isn't a pleasurable part of sex—it absolutely is, and we have a whole chapter dedicated to it—but the point is that if it's the only kind of sexual expression you're leaning on, you're leaving out a lot of opportunities for incredibly enjoyable sex (with less performance anxiety).

When you look at the studies around the orgasm gap, nearly every study found that in lesbian sex between two women, the orgasm "gap" is hardly a gap at all—women have far more orgasms when they're having sex with each other, which should tell you how important non-PIV activities are in pleasurable sex.

Not only is PIV sex not the only thing, but when it's *your* only thing, it usually doesn't lead to pleasure or orgasm, and is boring AF. Most women would choose all the other stuff over someone whose only trick is PIV. Not only is PIV not the *only* thing, but it's not even the *best* thing most times. Other skills are arguably much more important.

The takeaway: There is a wide variety of sexual expression to tap into that can offer your partner more mind-blowing sex than you imagined.

Myth #5: Sex Is Only Instinctual

In addition to misconceptions about genital size, another common myth that holds many people back in their sexual lives is the belief that sex is only instinctual. Sexual connection should just "click" with a partner, and the sex should be perfect without either party having to talk or work through anything. This myth is fueled by poor sex education programs, which take for granted that teens can just figure out the pleasure part of sex on their own. When religion and cultural institutions interfere with our sex lives, we fight back with the argument that sex is natural—but then we leave people literally stumbling around in the dark trying to navigate their sexual connections with no social or cultural support.

Our current paradigm is torn between two poles. On one side we have abstinence-only sex education, in which purity is valued and a great sex life will somehow magically work itself out when you settle down into a monogamous marriage. On the other side, we have porn sites that deliver high shock value to drive clicks and sales, and incidentally provide many people with a skewed, ad hoc sex education.

I'm not against monogamy or porn or profit. But it's important to understand how these cultural stories create devastating sexual myths that ruin lives and deprive people of a comprehensive sex education.

It's important to look at these cultural influences and figure out, on an individual level, how do we each manage our own sex lives? In the book *Why Good Sex Matters*, Dr. Nan Wise argues that sexual pleasure is at the core of our mental health and wellness.[10] In the same way that we learn different workout techniques to increase our fitness, or we learn to cook better to feed ourselves well, it's worth investing our energy in learning how to have great sex.

If we assume that great sex is "natural," we won't think of it as something that needs investment and refinement. While there are parts of it that are certainly instinctual, just like eating, we can elevate it to an experience that is much beyond simply satisfying base desires in an adequate fashion. Most people would think of eating raw chicken for their entire life as a relatively sad way to fill their instinctual appetite for food. Yet in sex, we expect not to have to

---

10   Nan Wise, *Why Good Sex Matters: Understanding the Neuroscience of Pleasure for a Smarter, Happier, and More Purpose-Filled Life* (New York: Houghton Mifflin Harcourt, 2020).

apply the same learning and artfulness that we do to cooking, thinking that we should "just know" how to do it. Sexuality deserves at *least* the same amount of attention as food.

The takeaway: Like Bruce Lee taught us, we first have to break down the elements of movement and technique before we can put them back together again with mastery. Open yourself up to learning more about sex, and you'll get even more sophisticated in your techniques and your taste for pleasure.

> **PRO TIP**
>
> What myths hold you back in your sex life? Write a list. For each one, consider the inverse. What is the truth that can accelerate your sex life?

Performance Anxiety

For many men, the fear of being a sexual disappointment, and therefore being sexually rejected, is one of the most innate and primary fears they have. The fear of not being big enough, hard enough, lasting long enough, or being good enough in any other way is a source of great anxiety.

When you think about all these myths and the pressure they create, it's really no wonder that so many men are dealing with low genital self-esteem and performance anxiety. It can feel really crippling to worry about sexual rejection. This worry can cause problems in functioning like psychological erectile dysfunction and premature ejaculation, which in turn can evoke yet more anxiety and dread. This feedback loop can crystalize over time, and it's hard to know how to break out of the cycle.

The feedback loop leads to what psychologists call "learned helplessness," which is when animals and humans get the sense that there is no way out of a situation, and they no longer try to alter their environment to stop a painful stimulus from reoccurring. In the worst case, this leads to incel culture and potentially causes massive harm because of the rage that is stoked in these groups.

A lot of this unnecessary pain and the needless harm it causes is due to lack of legit sex education and sex-positive culture and community. You don't need to have a porn-star cock, look like Channing Tatum, or drive a Ferrari to have a good sex life, which is what mainstream culture preaches. You need competency and empathy. That's why I wrote this book.

If you're an average guy struggling with worries and concerns about your sex life, believe me, I get it. Like I mentioned earlier in this book, I lived with this crippling, immobilizing fear for most of my sex life. I used to be someone who wouldn't even let a girl touch or see my cock for fear that they would actually laugh. Now, I can perform on porn sets, and fuck right next to mainstream porn stars at gangbangs.

Luckily, like we mentioned above, the pressures we often feel around sex come from standards that are artificial. It's like keeping up with the Joneses in the age of Instagram and Pornhub; we're emulating things that were fake to begin with. But sometimes, just knowing that is not enough to reduce anxiety, especially if this anxiety has been with you for a long time. Let's face it: when you're trying to have a good date with a lover and your penis isn't hard, you're not going to feel great about it no matter what statistics I throw at you, or how common it may be. Sometimes, you just want to perform.

Before I get into how to tackle performance anxiety, I want to convey how essential it is that you start with a growth mindset about it. Georges St. Pierre, UFC champion, says that confidence is a choice; it's something you can work on and build up, even if bad things happen to you. As you develop the skills I mention below, you will start to collect more positive experiences and competency to develop lasting confidence.

We can learn a lot from elite athletes when it comes to confidence and performance anxiety. Because athletic performance has been studied extensively, we can take proven lessons and methods from the science and apply them to sexual performance. When an athlete experiences performance anxiety, they often experience a failure to perform because of the perceived pressure, also called "choking." This is a very similar situation to what happens in sexual performance when we experience anxiety.

Bruce Lee says that obsessive ego-consciousness takes you out of the moment. That's the reason anxiety is the silent boner-killer. Because there's a limited bandwidth on attention, paying attention to worrying about your hard-on takes away from your ability to pay attention to your partner's bodacious tatas.

Just like in sports, the key is to reduce the perceived pressure and focus back on the game. In bed, the same applies. We want to reduce perceived pressure, and focus back onto the erotic. Here's my play-by-play guide to overcoming choking in the bedroom.

The first step might sound counterintuitive. When you're experiencing choking, and tell yourself you shouldn't be choking, it only perpetuates the anxiety loop and increases the self-imposed pressure. The hack here is to do a Jedi mind trick with yourself. Tell yourself that your dick doesn't need to be hard right now, and that it's OK if your dick isn't hard and you're anxious. What you resist persists, and the more you resist these two things, the worse they'll get. Instead, feel into the anxiety and allow the experience to exist exactly as it is, without trying to change it. By allowing and accepting the moment, you allow it to pass.

Next, use your breath to actively relax. Focus on lengthening the breath, breathing in and out for longer periods. Breath work is the foundation of the self-regulation skills used in martial arts, sports, yogic practices, and more. In addition, relax your face, shoulders, solar plexus, abdomen, and pelvic floor.

It may take time to be able to access, feel, and control internal structures like your solar plexus and pelvic floor. The first step is to *try* to feel them: direct your attention to where your solar plexus is at the top of your abdomen, for example, and focus on any sensations you can feel there. These structures are typically under involuntary control, but sex hacking is about gaining voluntary control and mastery. Learning to feel and relax these inner structures is one of the most powerful things you can do to change your experience of sex from the inside out. This is the key to feeling deeper feelings inside yourself.

I learned the power of relaxation from Chelsey Fasano, who taught me that when we relax, our natural bodily genius takes the reins. She taught me that the body knows what to do if we give it the space to feel and function naturally. When we stop imposing on and trying to control our bodies, and let the body guide us, it can naturally self-regulate and is capable of more pleasure than we ever imagined. She says that it is also through letting go of unnecessary tension that we see what the body is capable of in terms of performance, and how it can guide us with a unique form of intuitive genius. Relaxation is a skill and depends on paying attention to our breath and body, slowly coaxing them to let go over time.

The final step is to focus on something other than your dick getting hard. Thinking about how you wish your dick was hard is about as effective as trying to force yourself to feel sleepy when you're experiencing insomnia. Instead, refocus on an area where you do have control.

Allow yourself to get in touch with what is occurring that is erotic to you. Direct your attention back to what feels good about the moment. Engage your five senses, and actively notice what kinds of smells, sights, touches, sounds, and tastes are enjoyable. Luckily, there are a lot of these to focus on in sex (if the sex is good). Notice things like the softness of her skin, what kind of noises she's making, the shape of her body, curve of her hips, beauty of her eyes, the smell and taste of her vulva. Eventually, this sensory experience will take on a life of its own, and you will be immersed in your sense of eroticism, all thoughts and feelings of anxiety far away. And then voilà, you'll notice that your dick gets hard as easily as when you are at home alone, consumed by your favorite porn.

The second most common anxiety that men feel is about lasting long enough. Unfortunately, this is not my personal area of expertise because it has not been a personal challenge of mine. However, in my quest to attain all the knowledge about sex I can, I have had the fortune to learn from one of the best in the industry, Destin Gerek, who runs a course called "Sexual Self-Mastery" for men. He teaches all the tools you'll need to experience ejaculatory choice (a.k.a. come when you decide to), experience full-body orgasms, nonejaculatory energetic orgasms, and even male multiple orgasms. When I did his program, I witnessed a group of men who struggled with premature ejaculation all of their lives break through this problem, learn to achieve ejaculatory choice, and completely rebuild their confidence. Some even learn how to have male multiple orgasms! Scan the following QR code to check out Destin's course.

For some of you, your sexual performance issues may stem from biological roots in addition to or rather than psychological. There's tons of great biohacking treatments and options available—everything from optimizing testosterone levels to ED drugs to fitness and nutrition protocols—and I have had tremendous success with them personally. Unfortunately, it's too much to cover here, but this is a topic I will continue to write about on my blog, so follow me at kennethplay.com if you want to learn more.

These skills might take time to acquire, but practice makes perfect. When you're feeling stressed during sex, practice the three techniques described in this section. Accept yourself and the moment as they occur, focus on your breath and relax your body, and pay attention to what feels good through the five senses. Learning is a process, but you can trust that by engaging with these three practices, change will slowly begin to occur, and eventually, those nagging insecurities won't be keeping you from enjoying a very enjoyable experience.

A Recipe for Pleasure

In the end, orgasms require more than just the push of a button. I had the privilege of taking a workshop with sex educator Betty

Martin, who taught me that sexual pleasure is derived from a combination of three important ingredients:

- Tactile data
- Mindfulness
- Erotic context

All our sensory input—from touch to sight, smell, sound, and taste—contributes to our pleasure in the moment. When we think of the sensations we like during sex, we usually focus on genital stimulation, but tactile data can come from anywhere, turning your partner's whole body into an erogenous zone. We'll discuss how all this sensory data activates the brain—and lights up our sense of pleasure—in far more depth in Chapter Five.

Of course, tactile data doesn't matter if you or your partner aren't in the moment to pay attention to it. If your partner is caught up in the stress of her workday or the length of her to-do list, it's much harder to connect with the pleasurable sensations in the moment. In Chapter Four we'll take a deeper dive into mindfulness, both for your partner and for yourself.

And finally, erotic context is where psychological arousal happens—a necessary step before physical arousal can come online. Erotic context can be as simple as a flirtatious text or as elaborate as a script to perform and an outfitted dungeon to play in. But when done well, erotic context allows you to tap into your authentic sexual identity to turn on your partner, as we'll discuss in Chapter Seven.

Focusing on these three elements allows you to create innumerable creative sexual expressions, and in Part Two I'll show you how.

PART II

The Elements of Sex

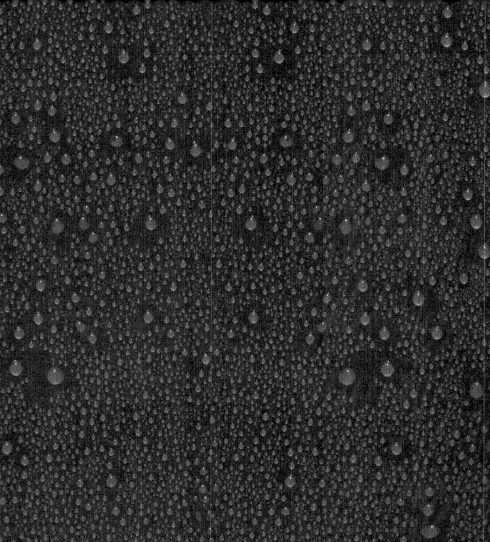

3

Consent, Communication, and Negotiation

S exual consent is one of the hot-button issues of our time. It is also a huge and incredibly complex topic. How exactly should we communicate our consent or lack thereof? How should we make sure that our partner is consenting? Do nonverbal signs of consent count? How much alcohol does someone need to drink before we consider them unable to consent? What type of power dynamic between you and your partner makes the less powerful unable to consent? These are not easy questions to answer, and some of them may have more than one right answer.

I grew up in Hong Kong, where the general perception is that the first time you will ever have sex is on your marital bed; anything else would be crossing all sorts of boundaries. But I went through adolescence in America, where watching *American Pie* as a horny teenager was not just arousing and funny, but an experience of total culture shock. So much more was allowed among young people here than I had ever dreamed of!

At twenty, I was still a virgin wondering whether I should lean in for a kiss on a date. After a few sexually mediocre relationships, I started going to swinger parties in my late twenties where heterosexual couples openly shared each other with other couples. Witnessing public sex was totally mind-blowing, and consent for even the wildest sex acts was negotiated with few to no words.

When I became part of the NYC sex-positive community a few years later, I entered a world that wasn't so couple-centric, and all sexual orientations and genders were celebrated. It felt more like home than all the other ones. Consent there was discussed a lot more, and often had to be negotiated verbally.

Seeing sex from such different cultural and subcultural vantage points has made me aware of just how complicated consent really is. Every community has its own set of assumptions and rules for how sex should happen (or not happen), and each of us brings our individual preconceptions and past experiences. For example, some kink play parties in New York have no rules against alcohol or substance use. Others ban all substance use. Many of my female friends and partners appreciate the "ask-before-you-touch" model of negotiating consent that many poly play parties operate on. Others complain how much they hate that model and prefer to negotiate consent nonverbally most of the time. There is no one-size-fits-all.

To make matters even more complicated, norms within each culture shift over time. Over the course of nearly a decade in the

NYC sex-positive community, I've seen the culture around consent change a lot. For instance, in the early days of the Hacienda parties, it wasn't weird at all for friends (of whatever gender) to greet each other with a kiss on the cheek and a squeeze of the butt. Today we wouldn't dream of even hugging someone at a play party without asking first. The #MeToo movement brought the topic to the forefront and forced us all to examine our thoughts and experiences with it.

This part of the book was by far the most difficult to write. First, because consent is complex, and I'm not an expert on this topic. Many people today attempt to simplify things and portray consent as pretty black or white, but I'm not convinced that's the best way to accomplish our common goal of having great sex that leaves everyone feeling good about it.

Dr. Zhana argues that both our internal "wantedness" of sex in any given situation, and our externally communicated signals of that wantedness, exist on a spectrum.[11] By "wantedness," we mean how much you personally want the sex. On one end of the spectrum is the "green" zone of 100 percent wantedness and a clearly communicated "yes." On the other end is the "red" zone of 100 percent unwantedness and a clearly communicated "no." In between is a huge "gray" zone of internal ambivalence (being unsure if you want the sex, having reasons for *both* wanting and not wanting it) and external ambiguity (sending unclear or mixed signals of consent to our partners).

I refer you to Dr. Zhana's work if you'd like to delve into this deeper, but I'll say this much: the gray zone is real, and it's not always easy to know what to do when you're in it, or to even realize

---

11   DrZhana.com

that you are in it. Like what happens when you're both slightly intoxicated from having a few drinks at a bar? Or when you say "yes" to the spouse you love, even though you have zero desire for sex at the moment?

I've found myself in that gray zone more than once. I've made mistakes when it comes to navigating consent, I've made decisions I've regretted, and I've acted in ways that hurt my partners. That's the other reason this was the hardest chapter to write. I'm not going to paint myself as someone who's never failed the purity test, preaching to you from a high horse. I'm far from it. I'm human, and humans make mistakes. And I think that almost anyone who's had a lot of sexual experiences with a lot of different people will be in the same boat. But I have spent a lot of time learning from my own and other people's consent mistakes, continually growing, and continually upgrading my consent practices. I'm a work in progress, same as everyone else.

What follows in this chapter is not a rulebook on how to execute flawless negotiation—because the rules differ from partner to partner, and from one encounter to another. Instead, I want to give you the tools to understand what you and your partner want from your sexual encounters, and how to have open conversations to decide what you'll do together. Because there's no better sex than the kind where both people get what they want.

Why Consent Is Awkward—and Arousing

Before we get into how exactly to establish consent, let's talk about why some people resist having conversations about consent with their partners.

The first reason: talking directly about sex can be awkward. Especially if you're not used to talking very much about sex with your partner. Many people worry they'll kill the mood if they speak explicitly about what they're interested in (or not) before having sex. They assume planning what they want to do in advance could suck the magic and spontaneity out of sex.

But in reality, when you talk about desires and set boundaries and limits with your partner, you greatly amplify your sexual experience in the long run. Negotiation is an opportunity to get more vulnerable with your partner and develop trust in your connection. The more you know about what you want, and what your partner wants, the more creatively you can play with what feels good.

PRO TIP

While talking about sex explicitly can feel awkward at first, it's a small price to pay for earning the respect and trust of your partner. With practice, these conversations become more comfortable—and sexy! You both get to imagine all the delightful things you'd like to do to each other and have done to you. And the only way to get more comfortable with this is to start doing it! Practice makes perfect.

Now, to be totally honest, even if you are pretty good at these conversations, sometimes they're just awkward and not super erotic. But even if negotiation sometimes kills the mood in the short term, it enhances it in the long run. Safety is sexy. And there are deeply rooted biological reasons why this is the case.

Each time we have sex, our brains and our bodies assess how safe it is to get vulnerable. In order to become aroused, each partner has to be in a relaxed state. In a physiological sense, we have to switch on the parasympathetic nervous system that controls our ability to rest and digest. From an evolutionary standpoint, to get fully engaged in sex, we have to first make sure we're safe to do so—that we won't have, say, a saber-toothed tiger coming after us. Even with saber-toothed tigers now extinct, we still have to honor those evolutionary needs and create an environment where our bodies know it's safe to let go and stop scanning for danger. And this isn't just true for women; too much adrenaline (the neurochemical that is produced during fight-or-flight) kills your boner, as Aaron Spitz, MD notes in *The Penis Book*.[12]

One of the primary things that dictates safety (especially for women, who are often smaller than their partners) is the partner we've chosen, and whether that partner is safe. It's important to create a safe space for our partners to share their feelings, to encourage them to be vulnerable, and to let them know we'll respect their changing desires—especially with a new lover. Once we feel safe, we can turn off our hypervigilance and tune in to our pleasure.

The point of negotiation around sex is partly to decide what we plan to do and not do with our partners. But more than that, negotiation is an opportunity to establish trust with our partner. When we demonstrate that their well-being is our number one priority, we create a safer space for them to be vulnerable and ultimately to let go into a mind-blowing experience.

12   Aaron Spitz, *The Penis Book: A Doctor's Complete Guide to the Penis—from Size to Function and Everything in Between* (Pennsylvania: Rodale Books, 2018).

Unpacking Consent and Fear of Rejection

The second reason that many people don't want to go through negotiating sexual activities is because they fear that checking in with their partner increases the chances of being rejected and losing out on the chance for sex. They think that bypassing the initial conversation will create a situation where the person is more likely to say yes to sex, because they won't have the time to think through things and check in with their feelings.

Sometimes people think it is better this way for both parties; that all the taboos we have around sex often make it very difficult for people to enthusiastically acknowledge our desires for it, and that being caught up in the moment and losing track of worries and hesitations is the way to go. But many people do this for purely selfish reasons: to get what they want in the moment, even if that means getting their partners to bypass some of their boundaries. If that's the game our ego is playing, this is straight-up fucked up and inexcusable.

And in the long run, this strategy actually backfires: it leads to less sex and worse sex. While going straight in for the kill without giving her time to think about what she really wants might work to get her to bypass her concerns in the moment, it leads to hesitation and ambivalence in the long run, not someone who is truly and completely on board with what she's doing. The more we talk to our partners about our desires and boundaries, and the more we check in to understand and respect our partners', the more we're likely to create an environment where both of us are highly enthusiastic and excited about what's happening and what's about to happen. Ignoring those nagging voices and feelings that aren't on board isn't the way to make them go away.

Plus, the more we communicate upfront with our partner, the more we can mitigate risk in our sexual experiences, because we decide in advance how we're going to engage with our partner. The less we communicate, the riskier sex becomes. When we get wrapped up in the prospect of having sex *right now*, we can lose sight of the well-being of our partner. And when we do that, we increase the likelihood that they will regret what they did. You might have more sex initially, but you're also likely to encounter a lot of avoidable consent accidents. In the worst case, this leads to a lot of trouble for both of you. But even if it's not super painful, it's just not optimal; it doesn't illustrate that you are a caring, trustworthy, considerate partner who reads and respects her emotional and erotic cues. And this is what women are looking for in a lover.

At the end of the day, checking in and talking about things is just a way better ethical strategy. And it makes you a better person; you choose the well-being of your partner over your own self-interest, and this is essential to not just being a good lover, but a good human being. You want to avoid buyer's remorse. Don't be a used-car salesman, selling a lemon. Be the guy that's chosen for his integrity. Choose to be someone that a woman would choose when she considers all the pros and cons, not the sleazy pickup artist that can only get laid by playing a game of subtle manipulation. What you do in these circumstances is about who you want to be, what you will feel about yourself when you look in the mirror, and the kind of integrity you can offer the woman who freely chooses you of her own volition. Be the guy who treats women the way you want the daughter you might have someday to be treated.

Ground Rules for Consent

Now that we've covered some of the "why," let's get into the "how." In my opinion, a good starting point to establish what is consensual is to check that your partner's consent is both informed (they know exactly what they're signing up for) and enthusiastic (they're not only willing, but excited to engage).

Here are some of the ground rules I use to negotiate consent. Remember, this is not an exhaustive list, but some of the most essential things to practice.

Prioritize Your Partner's Well-Being

A good basic rule to go by is to look out for our partner's best interest above your own self-interest at all times—or at least as much as you look out for your own. This means that at any point in the interaction, you should be willing to put her needs first, above your own desires. This means not holding her responsible for your orgasm or accusing her of "giving you blue balls" if she doesn't make you cum. It means being willing to stop whenever she is uncomfortable, or slow down to a pace that feels right to her. It takes self-control and relinquishing the sense that she somehow owes you a sexual experience of some variety. But it is well worth it to demonstrate to your partner you know how to care for her.

In their book *Mate*, Tucker Max and Dr. Geoffrey Miller explain how women are evolutionarily hardwired to look for men who are "tender defenders." Throughout evolutionary history, men who were more cooperative, kind, and agreeable were more likely to survive and create offspring, because in the evolutionary past, conflict and hardship were frequent and often dangerous parts of life. Being able to handle tough situations and remaining kind and caring of a female partner was crucial to survival. Women learned to pick mates who were able to defend them not only from the surrounding environment, but from their partners' own more aggressive, selfish impulses. Putting her first and being a gentleman is a deeply attractive trait, especially in the medium and long term. This kind of behavior symbolizes that you are an attractive prospect for short-term sex and longer-term companionship.[13]

More importantly, this is the ethical way to act. I hope that as a culture, we are moving away from the pickup artist mentality of short-term gains regardless of the damage done, and towards embracing this more gentlemanly approach to women and sex.

Consent Can Be Withdrawn at Any Time

When I set out into new sexual territory with a partner, we first agree on what we each want to do. As we get started, I literally ask, "Can I count on you to tell me if you change your mind?"

This simple question helps to put the responsibility on my partner to speak up if something I'm doing doesn't work for them. If they tell me to stop, I stop immediately, and there are no consequences for withdrawal. I want to encourage my partner to talk about what feels good and what doesn't, so I don't defend my actions or shame my partner for speaking up; we simply move on to something that we know is pleasurable for both of us, or we stop altogether.

---

13   Tucker Max and Geoffrey Miller, *Mate: Become the Man Women Want* (New York: Little, Brown and Company, 2015).

Signals Need to Be Clear and Unambiguous

We rely on a wide range of verbal and nonverbal signals to express our desires during sex. Verbal communication tends to be the clearest—no means no, and yes means yes—but we also use movements and sounds to express our pleasure and displeasure. Nonverbal signals come up organically, and they also tend to be more ambiguous. It's important for both partners to be aware of whether their communication is landing. If not, we need to continue to escalate communication (verbal or nonverbal) until it is not ambiguous.

For example, if a guy kisses his partner and touches her body, and she kisses and touches him back, in the moment he may conclude sex is a go. Let's say he progresses to putting his hands down her pants. Her guard may come up as she assesses whether she feels ready for sex, and she might send a mixed signal: she may continue to kiss him, but move her hips away from his hand. He may interpret the signal correctly and pull his hand back, or he may interpret the signal incorrectly, thinking she's teasing, and continue to try. She can ramp up her signal by taking his hand and moving it away. He may still misinterpret the signal and think she wants sex but just needs more warming up. When he moves in again towards her vagina, she gives a clear signal by saying, "No, I don't want you to touch my pussy."

Ideally, the exchange wouldn't have to go that far. The advancing partner can exercise more caution and pause to check in at the first ambiguous signal. He can check his understanding by asking, "Did you move your hips away because you're not ready?" He can reassure her that there's no pressure to go further or faster than she wants. The receiving partner can also give clearer feedback about what she wants and doesn't want by telling her partner directly.

PRO TIP

If you are ever in doubt or anything is ambiguous, make sure that you check in verbally. If your partner is unsure or ambiguous verbally, back off until they are sure. Make sure they know that you would rather kill the mood or have an awkward pause than to be unsure if they truly want what is happening to be happening. This is where you really don't want to roll the dice, hoping for the best.

The key on both sides is to be self-aware enough to have a clear understanding of what we want, and to be sensitive to shifts in our partner's behavior. Sometimes, even with the best of intentions, communication can be tricky, and there is much complexity to navigating the nuances of it. The next section will explain in more detail how to think about and navigate these kinds of communications.

The Gray Zone

Dr. Zhana has written extensively on consent, especially on the "gray zone." Her website, DrZhana.com, contains a wealth of resources to explore. At a basic level, she describes our decisions around consent as reliant on two factors:

- Internal wantedness: whether the sex is wanted or unwanted

- External communication: whether the signals sent are communicating a yes or a no

Neither of these factors is a binary. We can be 100 percent sure we want a particular action, or we can be 100 percent sure we don't—but much of the time, our desires fall into a vast gray area of ambivalence in between. These are the times when we're not sure if we want the sex or not, or when we're conflicted about it because we have both reasons to want it and reasons not to want it at the same time. We may want to try something new, but we're not sure whether we'll like it in reality. We may like a particular action sometimes, when the conditions are just right, but not always. We may be really attracted to the person, but they happen to be our best friend's partner. The list goes on. There are myriad factors that can make us unsure or ambivalent about how much we want the sex. Think about the last three times you had sex: were you 100 percent up for it all three times?

Similarly, our externally communicated signs of consent are not always a clear yes or a clear no. Through both verbal and nonverbal signals, we can certainly give a "hell yes" or a "hell no." But we can also send signals that are ambiguous, conflicting, and hard to read. There is a huge middle area between yes and no, and much of sexual communication between humans falls into this ambiguous "gray zone."

To make matters more complex, our yeses and nos don't always line up super clearly with our levels of wantedness and unwantedness. Sometimes we say "yes" when we mean "maybe," or say "no" when we really want something.

On top of our internal ambiguity, all sorts of power dynamics (money, status, age, experience, etc.) can also come into play and make it more difficult to express what we truly want, or to be able to read our partner's signals. Yet, our verbal and nonverbal signals are all our partners have to go on. And our partners' signals are all we have to go on. No one is a mind reader.

Because of all this complexity, navigating these situations is tough. I asked Dr. Zhana to break this down even further, and this is what she had to say:

A big part of consent is checking in with our own desires in the moment, as well as figuring out under what circumstances we'd like to say yes and when we'd like to say no. For example, there's no hard-and-fast rule that says that you aren't allowed to say yes when you are a maybe. But by doing that you're making a riskier decision: consenting to sex when you're internally a maybe is more likely to go poorly than sex that you enthusiastically want. Are you OK taking this increased risk? Some of us are, others are not. You need to figure out which one you are.

Similarly, you need to decide how much risk you're willing to take when reading your partners' signals. If your partner is sending ambiguous signals, you could choose to interpret that "maybe" as a "yes" and go ahead with the sexual activity. This may turn out great for them, but there's also a pretty big chance it will turn out poorly, that they'll walk away from that encounter feeling hurt, confused, used, violated. Are you really OK taking that chance?

Some of us are greater risk-takers, others are more risk-averse. There is no one right way for everyone, but there is a right and wrong way for each of us individually. Which is why it's so important to check in with yourself as well as your partner, and figure out what each of you is and isn't comfortable with. And the less you know your partner and what works for them, the more you should be erring on the side of caution.

Reading nonverbal cues can be even more tricky than communicating in words. The next section will help you learn some techniques for nonverbal communication, both giving and receiving.

Reading Your Partner's Nonverbal Signals

If you were trying to communicate with someone at a party but the music is too loud, you'd quickly come up with simple sign language to make your thoughts known. Similarly, you can develop a vocabulary of nonverbal communication with your partner to understand their experience and desires in the moment. The reason why sign language works or why your friend might know what you're talking about in the loud bar is because the meaning behind the signals is clear. Sign language is composed of a preexisting set of meanings. But in sex, the same sign can mean totally different things for different people or in different moments. This is why, if they're not made clear in advance, some signals can be ambiguous and hard to read. If you're fucking a partner from behind, for example, and she reaches back to grab your hand, she could be signaling *stop*, or *that feels good, don't stop*. The solution is simple: when the signal is unclear, stop and ask—and the next time she reaches back, you'll know what she means.

Pay attention to your partner and watch what her natural signals are when she's experiencing pleasure. Signals can be counterintuitive. Some women get close to orgasm and go completely silent and still for a full minute. If you're not aware your partner responds that way, you might think she's not enjoying the sensation—and you'd shake it up just at the point where she most wanted you to keep going. Everyone responds differently, and the more you observe about your partner's responses, and ask her to help you understand what they mean, the more you'll start to learn her language and ride the waves of her pleasure.

PRO TIP

I often direct my partners to give me nonverbal cues during sex. For example, if I'm about to spank someone, I tell her to wiggle her butt if she likes it and move her hips away from me if it's too hard. Our communication in the moment becomes very clear, and we can dial in the intensity of the spanking without stopping to talk about it.

One of the things that can help you to understand a partner is something I got from Midori, a great kink and sex educator. She talks about how useful it is to ask them in advance, "What do you look like, sound like, and speak like when you're really having a good time?" This way, you can calibrate based on their particular signs and signals.

The other great hack to conquer this problem is to ask multiple-choice questions with only two answers, not open-ended questions. If you ask someone what a nonverbal signal means without giving choices, they might go into their head, trying to figure out the right words. It's better to simply ask things like "Good or bad?",

"Keep going or slow down?", or "More pressure or less pressure?" Then the person can pick a choice and stay in the moment, rather than having to search for the right words.

What Kink Can Teach Us about Communication

Some of the most effective protocols for negotiating and communicating around sex come from the kink community. Because kinksters engage in sexual activities that are inherently higher risk, they have a clearer communication protocol to match higher-risk play. For instance, engaging in what kinksters call "impact play" often involves inflicting pain as well as playing with dominance and submission. Knowing which kind of pain is the "good kind" that a partner wants, and which is the "bad kind" that they don't want, involves a whole host of negotiation skills and prenegotiated signs and specific words that help both parties communicate effectively in these high-stakes scenarios.

People in the kink community are able to negotiate complex sex scenes because they first develop a clear picture of their desires and boundaries in their own heads. As a result, they can describe what they want and don't want in detail, and their signals are clear and unambiguous. They continually ask themselves:

- What do I enjoy receiving, and what do I enjoy doing to my partner?
- What do I want to try?
- What do I not enjoy for myself, but am willing to receive or do for my partner?
- What are my hard limits?

Not only do they start out with some idea about this, but they continually develop and refine the answers to these questions with each accumulated experience, letting their partners know along the way how their thoughts and feelings have evolved.

The Traffic Light System

Kinksters have a basic "traffic light" system for dealing with in-the-moment feedback. If someone says "green," it means the activity is wanted and going smoothly. If they say "yellow," it means slow down, caution, sensation is starting to near a limit or needs recalibration. If they say "red," it means stop right then and there, immediately. The top (the doer) can say "check" or "traffic light" or any other prenegotiated word to elicit this specific type of feedback from the bottom (the receiver). This gives both parties a clearly thought-out, easy way to know that their play will always be safe, even when trying risky things. It also simplifies communication so both parties can stay in the moment.

The Five-Second Rule

It can be hard to speak up in some situations. We're social animals and we like to be cooperative. We may experience something we don't enjoy and hesitate as we evaluate whether to say something. The longer we wait, the less and less likely we are to speak up—and the same goes for our partners. To mitigate this tendency to wait, I set up a five-second rule with my partners: each of us agrees to let the other know within five seconds if something isn't working. The idea isn't to put a cap on when each partner can speak up; instead, it encourages each of us to be as upfront as possible about what's pleasurable and what's not.

Kink Protocols for Further Reading

There are many more negotiation protocols that kinksters have come up with and many of them are posted on the internet, in my course, and in books. If you want more tips and tricks like this, there are a wealth of kink resources to explore. Scan the QR code below for a list of places to get started.

Check out SSC (safe, sane, and consensual), as well as RACK (risk-aware consensual kink). These camps view healthy negotiation and rule-making around sex and kink slightly differently, though both have similar basic principles. In different sex-positive communities, there are slightly different protocols, ranging from "no until yes" to "yes until no" and lots of variation in between. It's important to figure out what approach works best for you and your partner. I recommend researching consent protocols so that you know the variety of what is out there. After that, you can check in with new partners about what approach they prefer, and if they are not sure, err on the side of caution. This is an area where education should precede experience, and you can recommend that your partners boost their education on this topic.

Now we'll look at some of the options for how you can negotiate specific activities and combinations of activities.

Desire Checklist

When you begin to negotiate sex with a partner, the first step is for each of you to get clear about what you want to give, what you want to receive, and what your limits are.

The kink community has great resources for negotiating play, which you can also find in my Sex Hacker Pro course. On *The Pervocracy*, a kinky, feminist sex blog, you can find a kink negotiation worksheet to help you and your partner understand what you want from sex, what you'd each like to do, and what you don't want to do, and what protections you want to put in place to minimize risk.[14] The questionnaire isn't just for kink; it also contains considerations for any kind of sex:

- I want to play because _____.
- When I play, I want to feel _____.
- One thing I would most like to experience today is _____.
- Do I want to act out a certain role or scenario?
- Do I want to use toys? If so, which ones?
- My safe word is _____ and my caution word is _____.
- We will avoid STI transmission and/or pregnancy by _____.
- Is there anything else my partner should know about me, my needs or desires?

Another way for you and your partner to communicate your desires is with a yes/no/maybe checklist. You can find dozens of

14 "Kink Negotiation Worksheet," *The Pervocracy* (blog), 2012.

examples of kink checklists online.[15] From anal sex to whipping, you can go down the checklist and note whether you've had an experience with each act and how willing you are to engage in it, either for a single session or at some point in the future.

Each person's desires set the range of activities that are possible. From there, you begin to think about communication preference and style.

Communication Styles and Preferences

Sometimes one of the most dreaded questions on a date is "What do you want to eat" or "What do you want to do tonight?" If you're Pinky and the Brain, the answer to this latter question is always "The same thing we do every night, Pinky. Try to take over the world!" For everyone else, the answer is much more complicated.

Below are three of the main communication styles to help navigate sexual choices with your partner. There's no one style that is better than the others; it's a matter of what you and your partner are comfortable with and enjoy.

Let's See What's on the Menu

Just like you would walk into a restaurant and survey the options to see if there's something there you want, one option for sexual negotiation is to create a list of sexual possibilities, and have your partner choose from the list. There are a few ways of going about this.

---

15 "Yes or No or Maybe," *That Other Paper*, 2008.

If you're in a longer-term relationship and have the time to do a deep dive, you can really spend time exploring all of the things you love, are curious about, and want to try with your partner. You can take the time to review all the possibilities—even doing some research or creating imaginary scenarios with a lover—and develop a really extensive menu for yourself and your lover.

I recommend Justin Lehmiller's *Tell Me What You Want* for learning about some of the most popular fantasies in America.[16] And my colleague Lola Jean has created an actual set of menus on her website that provide an example of how you can do this.[17] If you come up with examples that you and your lover are curious about, this is a great time to attend some classes together and be copilots on your sexual adventure. This process of imagining new possibilities together and exploring them is erotic and fun in and of itself. From there, once you've created your menus, separately and together, it's about choosing what you'd like to try that evening. This is a rather in-depth way of going about this style of play and can be a great way of figuring out new things to try with a long-term partner.

If you'd like to try a simpler version of this, you can simply offer your partner a set of options from which they can choose an experience. For instance, if you are on a first date or just meeting someone, you could create an actual paper menu of a few sexual possibilities. When you are eating dessert, you could ask them if they'd like to see what's on the menu after dessert, and then excuse yourself from the table while they read the erotic menu you present them. This

---

16   Justin J. Lehmiller, *Tell Me What You Want: The Science of Sexual Desire and How It Can Help You Improve Your Sex Life* (Massachusetts: Da Capo Lifelong Books, 2018).

17   Lola Jean, LolaJean.com/sex-menu.

should be small enough to not be overwhelming, but include some creative options that can be mixed and matched in.

For instance, you could create three multiple-choice options: spanking or blindfolds; lingerie or latex; rimming or anal penetration. Then they choose one from each column. This is just one example of a menu. What you put on the menu should be representative of what you know they like, or what you think they might like if you don't know them well yet.

The more options you have to present on a menu, the higher the likelihood that when a new partner walks by your restaurant, so to speak, that she'll choose to come inside. Knowing more makes you more versatile and adaptable; you can tailor your approach to a new partner or to your current partner's mood that night. You have new things to try with a long-term partner or something novel with which to wow a new date.

If you're still fucking the same way you did in high school, you're basically offering the same burger and fries to everyone, every night. Women complain in private about the "basic bro package": the guy makes out with them for a few minutes, squeezes or sucks on a boob for another few, and does a few minutes of obligatory pussy eating before sticking his dick in. I have seen more than a few women make vomit faces when it comes to this type of experience. Moral of the story: don't be boring. Develop a variety of techniques (and spend time on actual foreplay).

Once you develop your menu, either solo or with a partner, this option is a great way to let both parties have some degree of control, without getting bogged down in an endless cycle of indecision or ending up repeating the same sexual routine all the time. Plus, it's fun!

Chef's Choice

When you order a chef's special at a restaurant, the chef whips up something of their choosing. The chef still intends to delight his guests, but he does it through his own sense of taste rather than through the specific preferences of his guests. Similarly, if your partner orders the chef's special, you get to pick what happens. The receiver can still opt in or out, just as the diner can choose to eat or not eat the dish the chef sets in front of them.

This style of communication is for people who strongly prefer that others take the lead. They love to be taken out to dinner at restaurants they don't know yet, surprised with gifts and experiences they didn't expect. They thrive in an environment where their partner figures out what they want and need. Some people in this group make decisions all day at work and just want to switch roles when they get home. Or they are the kind of person who pretty much never wants to make a choice; they would prefer letting someone else take the lead, even if they could theoretically do things better or even get more of what they wanted if they took the reins. For this person, or this couple, bliss lies in letting one person run the show.

If you're trying this style and playing with someone new, it's still good to check in about hard limits, just like the chef would check in about allergies at a restaurant. I also strongly recommend setting up the traffic light system in advance that we mentioned above, and checking in throughout, while paying special attention to her erotic cues. You can cook a steak and still ask her how much salt she wants on it. You really need to be great at reading erotic cues and calibrating to her if you are going to take on this much power in the dynamic. Otherwise, this could quickly turn into a not-so-fun experience for both of you.

This isn't about you selfishly ordering her to do whatever you want; imagine this style more as a chef who wants to provide an even more delicious experience than the guest could imagine on their own, and surprise them so that they don't have to even lift a finger to make a decision.

Make It the Way I Like It

In this scenario, the receiver tells you exactly what they want to happen from moment to moment. Imagine you are giving someone a massage, and they give you explicit instructions: "higher, lower, right there, more pressure" and you just follow along. Basically, you just do what you're told. The key is to be egoless and enthusiastic while doing so.

This is a fun way to switch roles and power dynamics once in a while if you are used to being in charge. Or maybe you don't like making decisions at all and just love being told what to do all the time. This doesn't make you weak. In fact, a majority of the customers of dominatrixes are high-powered men who just need to switch off their brain after being in control all day. This sexual style is super common among men who work in industries like finance, and want their woman to handle things when they get home from running the world. So, if this is what you secretly want, there is no reason why this can't be your permanent sexual preference—you'd be in good company with many other men.

Even if this isn't something you want to do every day, it can be a really nice way of offering your lover a chance to take the reins. There is a cultural stereotype that women who are bossy are not likable and hot; many women fear that being too controlling in bed will be the end of their partner's attraction to them. It's great to let her know that this is not the case, and give her the opportunity to get exactly what she wants, exactly how she wants it, at least once in a while.

Touch for You, Touch for Her

Throughout sex, as we shift between the roles of giver and receiver, we also shift between being mindful of our own pleasure and being attentive to our partner. Betty Martin, the sex educator we referenced earlier in this chapter, created the Wheel of Consent to help us be more conscious of when we're switching roles and why.[18]

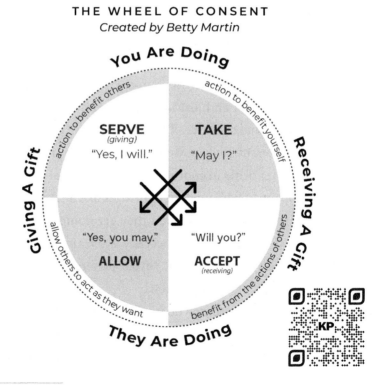

THE WHEEL OF CONSENT
Created by Betty Martin

---

18   Betty Martin, "The Wheel of Consent," bettymartin.org.

Martin's wheel can be broken down along two poles: whether we're giving or receiving, and whether we're doing an action or having an action done to us. On Martin's chart, these two axes create four basic possibilities: you can touch someone because you want your touch to bring them pleasure (making you the giver), in which case you're paying attention to your partner. Or you can touch someone because you want to feel her body (making you the receiver), and your attention would be on how her body feels to your hand. Your partner could ride you for your pleasure (as the giver) or for her own (as the receiver).

This is a general overview of Betty Martin's system, and you can read more on her website.[19] But the essential idea is that we don't spend enough time checking in with what we want or being clear about it with our partners. To practice checking in with desire and communicating it, Betty Martin and her collaborator Harry Faddis created the "Three-Minute Game." Scan the QR code below to check out the instructional videos on their site.

Three-Minute Game

The rules of the game are simple. Each partner asks two questions:

- How would you like me to touch you for three minutes?
- How would you like to touch me for three minutes?

---

19   Betty Martin, bettymartin.org.

The partner answering the questions has an opportunity to request what they want. For example, in answer to the first question, you might tell your partner, "Please scratch my back." To the second question, you might say, "May I give you a massage?"

Through this game, both partners get to practice identifying what they want and using language around taking and allowing. While it may seem easy at first, this game can be confronting because it requires you to be honest and clear that you're touching your partner for your own pleasure.

The difference is in being clear about your intentions. For example, if you give your partner a massage because it's how they want to be touched, then your intention should be completely on them, not on how you'd like to touch them. Often when we touch our partner, we're doing it partly for them and partly for ourselves. This game requires us to separate the two and take ownership over our desires.

This game is the most powerful when we catch ourselves not admitting what we actually want because we're afraid it might be rejected. For instance, when it's your turn to say what you want, you may really want to squeeze your partner's boobs. Instead, you say you want to give her a shoulder massage. Even when we're being given full permission to ask for exactly what we want, just for ourselves, we often default to something that feels more acceptable. This is one of the primary ways that our sex lives become less than awesome—we begin rejecting ourselves before another person has the chance to.

Women tend to do this sort of thing much more than men, because in our society (and in our porn), we focus primarily on the guy touching his partner for his own pleasure. I've experienced incredible sex (and plenty of it) by flipping the script and focusing on touching my partner for *her* pleasure. When we focus on making our partners feel good, we make sex more pleasurable for them as well as for ourselves. So ultimately, it's for our pleasure through hers.

We'll talk about the implications these questions have on consent and negotiation in Chapter Five. But the more you understand when you are touching your partner for her pleasure or for yours, the more clearly you'll be able to focus your attention on the dance between giving and receiving, on observing your partner's pleasure and enjoying your own.

I hope that this section gives you a good general overview of what consent is and can look like in real life, as well as fun ideas to try, and how to make it as sexy as possible. But this is definitely the tip of the iceberg when it comes to consent education. I encourage you to keep learning and continue to evolve in regard to your consent practices.

4

Quality Attention for You and for Her

I *magine you're watching a beautiful film,* but it's in French—chances are, unless you speak French, you'll lose track of the plot and start playing with your phone instead of paying attention to the movie. No single element of the movie is responsible for pulling you in; it's the combined effect of the soundtrack, stunning visuals, and engaging narrative that suck you in.

Sex can be similarly all-encompassing. When you calibrate the tactile data, spin a compelling erotic narrative, and help your partner stay tuned into the moment, you can create captivating, irresistible sexual experiences for your partner.

There are a million reasons our attention gets pried away from the moment during sex. While you're between your partner's legs, trying to figure out how she likes her eggs, so to speak, there may be a wild range of thoughts flying through her mind: *Do I look fat right now? Is my body sexy or ridiculous in this position? I feel gassy—oh no, what if I fart? Does my pussy smell weird? What if I take forever to cum? What if I make a mess on these expensive sheets I just bought? Did I remember to put laundry detergent on the grocery list?*

(This isn't a hypothetical—I was once playing with a partner who loved her expensive white sheets, and as we played, she started her period. She wasn't able to relax, and I could see the tension on her face. I looked up at her and asked, "What's going on—are you worried about your sheets?" She nodded, and we got a towel.)

With all the killjoys we bring to partnered sex, it can be easy to fall into an anxiety spiral. And of course, the more you encourage your partner to get out of her head, the deeper she gets sucked in as she tries to think about not thinking. Instead, coax your partner to hold her attention on the pleasure in the moment.

Paying attention to the present is the most effective tool we have discovered to break habit loops. If we're caught up in a bad habit, the only way to hack it and start a new habit is through the power of attention. You could have the sexiest partner, the perfect erotic context, and the right techniques—but if you're not paying attention to your own pleasure, you're fucked (or rather, the opposite of fucked). Mindfulness is a vastly undervalued tool in the pursuit of great sex.

Receiving Is a Trainable Skill

I used to run a big kink event in a sex-positive nightclub in New York City. For many attendees, it was their first time being in a sexually charged social experience. Attendees are there to experience pleasure, but it can be hard to focus in a room full of people milling around and watching. When I found a new attendee who wanted to play with me, I would often start with a little game. The object of the game is simple: I ask my partner to be 100 percent selfish for two minutes.

I have my partner choose the sensation she wants to try, which could be anything from being spanked to sitting on a Sybian machine (the world's most powerful rideable vibrator). To most people, two minutes of that sensation sounds like a reasonable, even small, amount of time. When I can tell that the person is starting to feel good with the sensation, I say, "Okay, now focus. I'm going to count to thirty, and as I count up, I want you to feel more and more of the sensation and focus on the sound of my voice."

I steadily begin to count. By coaching the person to listen to the sound of my voice, we've snapped her brain into focus. Sometimes by the time I get to twenty, she has had an orgasm.

You don't need a dungeon or a Sybian machine to give your partner mind-blowing orgasms. Often, you simply need to help your partner focus on her own pleasure and direct her attention entirely on herself. Even in an average bedroom, there are many things that could be distracting your partner from her pleasure. She might worry, for example, about a cell phone notification on a phone nearby, or notice the broken light fixture that you've been promising to fix for weeks. Meanwhile, waves of pleasure are rolling through, and your job is to help her catch a wave and ride it. Help her focus and lose herself in whatever is hot about the experience.

When you develop a deeper understanding of what arouses your partner, you can help her focus on those sensations and fantasies at the pivotal moment to push her over the edge and into orgasm.

Different women have different baseline levels of focus, so this process won't look the same for everyone. Some could have sex in the middle of a circus and remain totally immersed in pleasure, and for others the slightest thing can be a huge distraction. It's ultimately everyone's personal responsibility to develop the capacity to focus on the things that are important to them. At some level, this is an inside job. But you can support your partner in getting there, by working with them to reduce distractions, increase pleasure, and direct attention towards the things that feel good.

Help Your Partner Be Selfish

When we masturbate, we're usually not thinking about our own hang-ups, our grocery list, or any of that shit. Your lover isn't self-conscious about her pussy when she's by herself; she's at one with her vibrator. She reads the erotica she likes, or watches porn that turns her on, or she thinks of that last hot encounter she had fucking somebody. She sets her vibrator on the right setting, in exactly the right spot, and she lets herself feel it. When she's consumed by her own pleasure, she doesn't pay attention to much else— except to make sure she doesn't press that annoying button on her vibrator that does patterns (fuck that button).

Your job as a giver is to re-create the same conditions and make it even better. Often in partnered sex, it's hard for the receiver to stay mindful of her own pleasure because she's distracted by her to-do list, worried about what her partner thinks, or mired in her own insecurities.

Take one of the most common worries, for example: *What if I take too long to cum?* If your partner is focused on trying to get excited, she may wind up frustrated instead. As Dr. Jennifer Gunsaullus writes in *From Madness to Mindfulness*, increasing pleasure is sometimes not about stepping on the accelerator, but about letting off the brakes.[20]

Chasing an orgasm is like chasing a fairy: the closer you try to get to it, the farther it flits away. If a partner I'm with tells me she's frustrated at having a hard time orgasming, one of the ways I hack this is to flip the script. At the start of sex, I tell her she's not allowed to cum. All of a sudden, when she feels close, she realizes the waves of sensation are building—and she has a new experience of choosing whether to fight the sensation or not. This reversal helps her experience her pleasure more fully, and focus on the sensations in her body—because in order to *not* cum (or at least playact at resisting), she has to pay attention to what it feels like to cum. Ironically, she's no longer focused on how she's not cuming, because denying her an orgasm takes away the pressure to cum. When we release our expectations and stop chasing a particular sensation, we can experience the sensation more fully.

Your partner may have anxiety about something that has a simple fix. If she's worried she might pee during sex, encourage her to take a break and pee. If she's worried about squirting and making a mess, get towels or a puppy pad. If she's self-conscious about her pussy being smelly or dirty, she may be more comfortable after a quick shower (or a long one, where you shower together). If I sense a partner has low genital self-esteem, I tell her I love the way she smells and tastes, so she can let go of wondering what I think.

---

20 Jennifer Gunsaullus, *From Madness to Mindfulness: Reinventing Sex for Women* (Jersey City: Cleis Press, 2019).

If you can draw her out about her concern, you may find there's a simple solution that will help her relax. Being relaxed is the only way to get aroused—and whether your partner is scanning for a lurking saber-toothed tiger or the potential that she might be shamed by her partner, she won't be able to relax until she feels it's safe. By showing care for her concerns, you can help build the intense connection that comes from being authentic and present in the moment with each other.

Hard Skills Are Sexy, but Soft Skills Matter More

It's easier to touch someone physically than it is to get close psychologically. The "hard skills" of sex, like specific fingering or oral techniques, are straightforward enough to learn. But how do you learn to connect with your partner's mental and emotional state during sex?

The quality of our attention is contagious. When you're at dinner with a group of friends and someone pulls out their phone, everyone else is more likely to check their phones. It's embarrassing—lonely, even—to be the person left sitting at the table looking at everyone. The same goes for staying present with your partner. If she's ready to give you her attention, but you're not in the moment with her, she might feel like she's out on a limb. Be willing to be the one on the edge of vulnerability. Be present even if your partner is checked out. Your presence can invite your partner to be in the moment with you.

Checking our phones during dinner or an awkward social interaction serves an important function: to distract and dissociate. There are a lot of reasons people dissociate during sex, particularly if they've had trauma associated with sexual experiences or if they experience negative emotions with sex.

The problem with dissociation, however, is that blocking ourselves from fully feeling a sexual experience means we block feelings of pleasure, too. Have you ever wondered why when some people orgasm it's like they've seen God, but other people never seem to have that reaction? While there are many factors to the intensity of an orgasm, including genetic components, some of it has to do with our access to feeling. To learn to feel more, we have to learn to feel it *all*: sensations and emotions.

Sex is more than a physical experience; it's an emotional one—which is why it's not uncommon for people to cry after an orgasm. Make it clear to your partner that all of her emotions are welcome. Hold space for whatever might come up for your partner. If your partner is experiencing deep emotions, take note of what comes up in your own body. Are you feeling anxious or fearful, or tense? See if you can relax those emotions in yourself.

Don't try to fix or change the emotions that are coming up for you or your partner. Observe the emotions that are coming up with as little judgment as possible, like watching a cloud pass across the sky.

When we allow ourselves to fully feel emotions that come up, without trying to shove them down, our systems are able to naturally move through those emotions and relax. This is where mind-blowing connection begins: with your ability to be with your partner whether she's feeling sadness or ecstasy.

Often when we've done deep emotional processing, like from a good cry, we don't have a lot of cognitive energy left. Keep things simple for your partner. Ask if she'd like to cuddle or have a glass of water or a snack. When you offer a few simple options, you give her easy choices to say yes or no, and she doesn't have to think too hard about a decision. A good cry releases cortisol (the stress hormone) and endorphins, and can create almost as much relaxation and bliss as a good orgasm. Let your partner take time to enjoy the feeling of release (even better, skip to Chapter Fifteen on aftercare for tips on how to continue treating your lover).

It's not always so simple to flip from distraction to mindfulness in a single moment. It can take time to unwire rumination habits or establish enough intimacy to be vulnerable about one's fears. It's possible your partner may even have physical or emotional trauma that keeps them from being fully in the moment during sex. Or, your partner may experience inhibition simply from being in "performance mode." These larger factors can't be reversed in an instant. If you notice your partner is having trouble paying attention to her own pleasure, it's important to take a step back to help her pay attention to herself, rather than to focus on the sex techniques you're trying to use. The better you get at being mindful of yourself, the more you'll be able to help your partner attend to her own pleasure.

Mindfulness is a trainable skill, and there are many resources on how to pay closer attention to sensations: check out *Coming to Our Senses* by John Kabat-Zinn,[21] *Better Sex through Mindfulness* by Lori A. Brotto,[22] and the book we mentioned earlier—*From Madness to Mindfulness* by Jennifer Gunsaullus.[23] With practice, you and your

21   John Kabat-Zinn, *Coming to Our Senses: Healing Ourselves and the World through Mindfulness*, (New York: Hachette Books, 2006).

22   Lori A. Brotto, *Better Sex through Mindfulness: How Women Can Cultivate Desire* (Vancouver: Greystone Books, 2018).

23   Jennifer Gunsaullus, *From Madness to Mindfulness: Reinventing Sex for Women*, (Jersey City: Cleis Press, 2019).

partner can each make the choice in each moment to stay connected to sensations in your bodies.

> **PRO TIP**
>
> One hack you can use to shift your partner's attention to her own body and her own sensations is to start with massage and slow, sensual touch at the beginning of sex. Tell her to pay attention to your touch and focus on where your fingertip goes as you trace the lines of her body. Simply by paying attention to your touch and anticipating the movements of your finger, your partner will have a higher degree of focus on the sensations she's feeling.

Calibrating Touch for Your Partner

In partnered sex, it's magical when what feels good to one person also feels good to the other—but it's more common for each person to have their own preferences. Like we talked about with the Wheel of Consent, it's important to be clear about when we're touching our partner for our own pleasure or for theirs, and to make time for each partner to fully relax into receiving mode.

When you're learning the kind of touch your partner likes, it can be difficult to discern pleasurable signs from negative signs. As you immerse yourself fully in the role of giver and pay attention to your partner's unique signs, you'll develop a shared vocabulary: when your partner twitches one way, you learn that it means *stop*, and when she twitches a different way, you learn that it means *more please*.

But beyond running a constant mental translation, you can learn to be in the moment with your partner and watch how your own body and your own responses mirror hers in a process called *attunement*. We all have mirror neurons in our brains that fire when we see another person act or emote; we end up feeling their action or emotion in our own bodies to a degree. This wiring in our brains makes us each a resonating chamber of what is happening around us.

Some people have a high degree of activation in their mirror neurons and access to empathy, and others don't. But wherever you're starting out from, you can learn to tune into your partner's feelings in the same way you can learn to hear more variation in pitch when you're learning music. Many ancient traditions of sexual learning, from taoism to tantra, are aimed at developing and refining the body's ability to pick up on more nuances in their partners and in themselves. As you learn to be mindful during sex, you can become more and more sensitive to how your own body's reactions mirror your partner's and learn to feel what she's feeling.

Attunement with your partner is an East-meets-West process. You have to be fully present in the moment in order to feel what your partner is feeling, and you also have to check your understanding to make sure your hypotheses are correct. You may hear your partner gasp a particular way and think it's a gasp of pleasurable surprise—only to find out it was a gasp in pain. Truly connecting with your partner requires tapping into your intuition as well as your detective skills.

Initially, you will be picking up intuitive data from a new lover, making some conjectures about what's going on, and then checking to see if you are correct. This part might be a little more awkward but is worth it to develop an understanding of their unique erotic cues. Think of it like moving to a new neighborhood: initially, you have to get directions (like higher, lower, faster, slower) to get anywhere, but eventually, as you learn the streets, you can walk from place to place intuitively, just enjoying the sunshine.

Each partner has her own map of what is pleasurable for her—so don't use your old girlfriend's map to get around your new girlfriend's neighborhood! Once you get to know what means what, you can stop checking in so often, because you will know that person's cues.

Ultimately, attunement is an underrated superpower. When it's done right, your lovers may feel like you almost know their body better than they do. This kind of trust is built on the fact that you know and care about how they feel on an intuitive level that goes beyond words.

Pleasure Sweet Spot

If you happen to have an iPhone, you've seen how your device responds to different kinds of touch. If you press on an app icon on the home screen, the app opens. But if you press *hard* on the app icon, you activate a 3D touch menu that helps you quickly navigate to the app's key functions without opening the app. Most people don't know their phone screen is pressure sensitive until they press down hard enough on their iPhone screen to trigger 3D touch. (As of this writing, this iPhone function is being eliminated because so few people used it. It was a largely misunderstood feature—not unlike the G-spot.)

Your pleasure depends not just on where you're touched, but on *how* you're touched. Similarly, your lover could have touched your whole body, but if you weren't touched in the right way, with the right amount of pressure to register the pleasure in your brain, you might never have activated the "3D touch" of your sexual experience.

Each person has a different threshold at which their brain perks up to a given sensation in their body. This sensory threshold is the amount of stimulation it takes for a sensation to register in the brain. Each person has a range of sensation they respond to, from the minimum stimulation it takes to register a sensation to the maximum amount of stimulation they can take before it becomes painful. The pleasure sweet spot is usually somewhere between these extremes, and it varies depending on where they are in the arousal cycle.

For some women, the cervix is a sensitive spot, and light, gentle touch gives the most pleasure—while for others, the cervix is less sensitive, and the pressure of being pounded by a big cock or dildo is what drives their brain wild. Some women experience pleasure from each of these types of sensation at different times, depending on how aroused they are.

Welcome to the Play Lab

How do you learn to help your partner relax, while also learning how to help them ramp up towards orgasm? Like the captain of a boat, you have to lick your finger and hold it up to feel the wind. You can learn to read the weather with your fingers and develop a sense for your partner's subtle shifts. (I actually mean this literally—it can be easier to learn the arousal and orgasm cycles of a new partner by fingering them. You get a sense of exactly what spots of her body turn her on the most, and how those changes in her body feel to you. More on that in Chapter Nine.)

When you focus solely on giving pleasure to your partner, you can stay more alert to the changes happening in her body and her mental state. You can watch her body and her face, and you can feel how her body is responding to your hands.

When I'm playing with a new partner, I make a point to intentionally explore rather than to perform. I call these sessions "play labs": practice spaces where I focus on learning my partner and what techniques work for them. Because these play labs are focused on practice, they allow space for different expectations than we often bring to sex. It becomes a place to make mistakes, experiment, and establish feedback and communication with my partner.

While you can still learn about your partner during "regular" sex, play labs help you set aside a specific time to learn rather than perform. Play labs help you and your partner take some of the expectations of sex off the table; rather than focusing on orgasms or doing everything smoothly and exactly right, you can take the time to learn your partner's body and get lots of feedback.

As you learn from the ideas and techniques in this book, don't feel pressured to bring them straight into performative sex. Start with a play lab and ask your partner to give you lots of feedback as you learn what feels good to them. Focus on your partner's pleasure and your own sense of play, and in no time, you'll create the dishes your partner loves.

5

Pleasure Mapping

When I was learning to be a personal trainer, I studied anatomy diagrams in medical journals to understand what the body looks like and how it moves. It wasn't until I became a personal trainer and started to work with real-life people that I realized everyone's body is unique; none of them exactly matched the diagrams I'd been studying. Some people have shorter arms, some have longer legs, some are built like powerlifters and some are built like marathon runners. As a personal trainer, I learned to look at each individual in front of me and adapt what I'd learned to what I saw in their bodies, their movements, and their responses.

I brought the same philosophy to the principles of pleasure. You can study diagrams of female anatomy, but every vulva looks slightly different: they vary in color, shape, and size. Every G-spot is in a slightly different place and responds to different amounts of pressure. That's why it's so important to take your knowledge into practice as you read this book. Your knowledge will help you explore, but it's in your experience that you gain mastery.

We're taking a close look at female anatomy in this chapter, but what's most important is to take a close look at *her*. The descriptions that follow will give you an intellectual understanding of your partner's genitalia, but the next step is to close this book and turn your knowledge into experience—go check out your partner (with the lights on!). Set up a play lab to gain a hands-on, practical understanding of her body and what she likes.

If you're used to fumbling around in the dark (literally), it may seem awkward to take a good look at her vulva. I like to take my time and make it sexy. I note whether my partner feels comfortable or uncomfortable when I'm looking at her, which can often clue me into whether she has high or low genital self-esteem.

I've had more than one partner cry while I was exploring her pussy, because it was the first time anyone looked at her vulva with adoration. I shower my partners with compliments as I touch and explore, and it not only boosts their genital self-esteem—it's also fucking hot.

A GPS for Your Partner's Pleasure

It's important to take the time to look at your partner's pussy and understand her anatomy so you can better navigate her pleasure. I think of understanding my partner's body in the same way I think of getting to know my own body when I want to get more efficient at the gym. I don't need to know the names and insertion points of every muscle in my body to work out, but I do need to know my basic range of motion. I need to understand how my muscles behave under tension, and what my power output is.

Similarly, you don't need an encyclopedic knowledge of your partner's genitalia to please her. But you do need to know how she responds to different kinds of touch and pressure, so you can learn how to combine different sensations to create the most pleasurable effects possible. The sections that follow detail the most common pleasure points for most women, and as you explore these spots on your partner, you can create a mental map of what feels pleasurable to her and what doesn't, and where her most sensitive spots are.

In the same way your penis can be flaccid or erect, your partner's tissues can change depending on how aroused she is, where she is in her hormonal cycle, how relaxed she is, and many other factors. When a woman is fully aroused, she lubricates, her clitoris becomes engorged, the urethral sponge fills with blood, the vaginal opening relaxes, the vagina lengthens and expands in a process called "tenting," and the uterus balloons upwards towards the abdomen.

It may take several sessions to dial in the exact techniques that work for your partner, but the more you practice consciously mapping your partner's body, the more easily you'll be able to dial in the reliable techniques that work for her, and experiment with new possibilities. Eventually, you won't have to consciously map your partner's body; you'll start to do it intuitively.

It's important to warm your partner up with foreplay techniques before you touch and play with her genitals, and we'll talk about warm-up techniques in depth in Chapter Eight. But in many cases, as I'll note throughout this book, it's important for your knowledge to precede your experience, so you know what to expect when

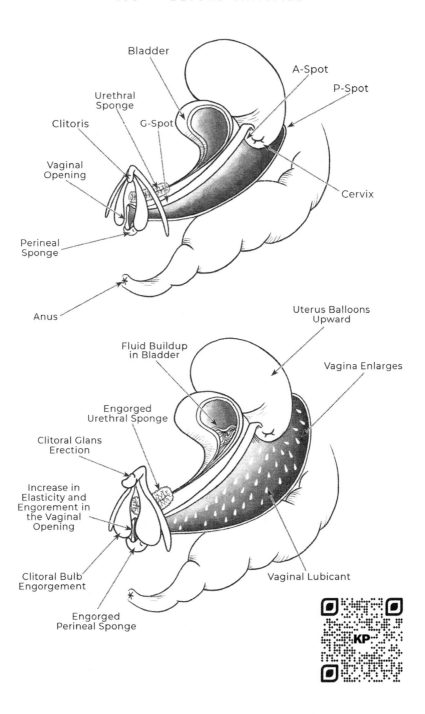

Bladder

A-Spot

P-Spot

Urethral
Sponge

Clitoris   G-Spot

Vaginal
Opening

Cervix

Perineal
Sponge

Anus

Uterus Balloons
Upward

Fluid Buildup
in Bladder

Vagina Enlarges

Engorged
Urethral Sponge

Clitoral Glans
Erection

Increase in
Elasticity and
Engorement in
the Vaginal
Opening

Clitoral Bulb
Engorgement

Vaginal Lubicant

Engorged
Perineal Sponge

you're with your partner. When you go to put the following information into practice, don't be clinical about it. You can turn your observations into a sexy massage. As you explore, tell your partner what you see and how beautiful she is.

Ready to dive in? Let's take a look at the different structures that compose and surround the female genitals, one by one.

Cliteracy

The clit isn't just a pea in a pod, or a little man in a boat—it's the head of a much larger internal structure that moves as your partner reaches different levels of arousal or gets stimulated in different ways. Many sex educators compare the clit to a penis, because according to current research, both organs have the same biological origins: we all started out with clits, and in men, those same tissues form the penis.

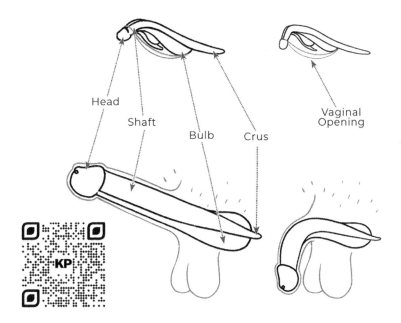

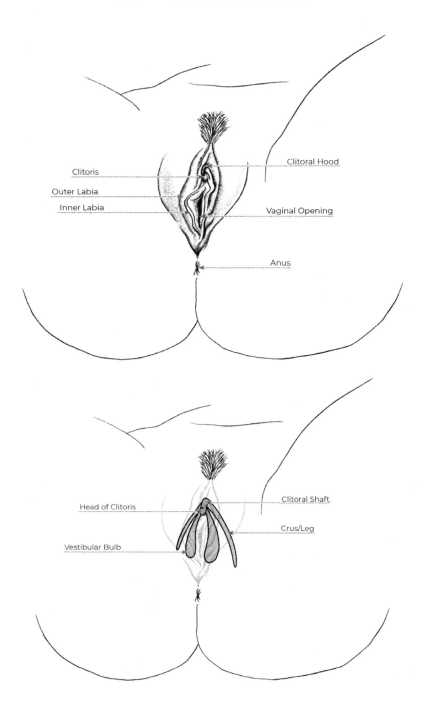

The exposed gland of the clit is similar to the head of a penis, while the hood of the clit is similar to foreskin. But the clit doesn't stop there: the visible head of the clit is one part of a larger organ that splits into two bulbs that wrap around the sides of the vagina.

The internal clitoris is stimulated through the vagina, and penetration with fingers, penis, and toys can all create pleasurable sensation for the clitoris. The head of the clit is the most sensitive part for most women, and it's the combination of internal and external sensations that brings most women to orgasm. Yet consider how heterosexual sex is represented in movies and in porn: much of the time, the guy pounds away in the woman's vagina, and no one is touching her clit. That would be similar to trying to get a guy off without ever touching the head of his penis. What if each time your partner wanted to have sex, she strapped on a dildo and only fucked you in the ass? Most men want their penis to be stimulated in order to cum. So it is with clits. Like a penis, the clitoris gets engorged when your partner becomes aroused, and you can feel a clear difference between when the clit is flaccid and soft versus swollen and engorged.

Clits come in different sizes, and so do clitoral hoods. Depending on how big a person's clitoral hood is, more or less of the glans will be exposed. For some women, the clitoral hood may give so much coverage that the head of the clit isn't exposed, even when they're fully aroused.

The amount of coverage the hood gives can influence how sensitive your partner's clit is. With a large hood, for example, the clit tends to get less friction, because it's covered up most of the time. When less of the clit is exposed, there's a high likelihood for it to be more sensitive.

UNAROUSED   **AROUSED**

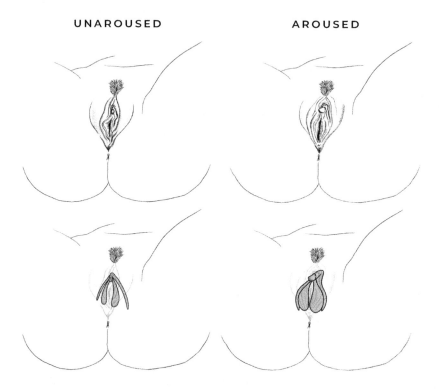

Your partner's sensitivity is also connected to how she masturbates. Some people like the clit touched directly, and some people like sensation over the hood. Think of the clitoral hood like foreskin. When you're a kid, you might never roll your foreskin back all the way if you're uncircumcised. But when you begin to masturbate and roll your foreskin back, it's super sensitive to touch at first. Sometimes touch even feels irritating in the beginning, until your body adjusts to the new sensations. Similarly, your partner may need different levels of pressure and friction depending on what she's used to and how sensitive she is.

You can ask your partner to show you how she touches her clit. One way is to ask her to masturbate while you watch. But you can also get a sensory experience of her technique by asking her to demonstrate on your hand. Place your thumb between your index and middle fingers, and then curl your hand into a fist. Your thumb can become a model of a clit, and the crease between your index and middle fingers becomes the hood. Ask your partner to rub your hand in the way she likes to be touched, and you'll be able to get a tactile sense of how she does it.

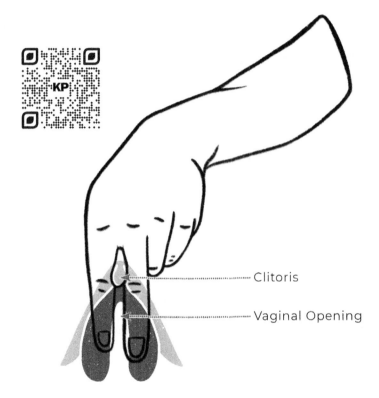

Clitoris

Vaginal Opening

Another feature that can affect a clit's sensitivity, especially during penetration, is the distance between the clit and the vaginal opening. Some studies have shown that the shorter the distance between the clit and the vagina, the easier it is for a woman to have an orgasm from penetration.[24] The idea is that as the penis thrusts back and forth, it tugs on the clitoris, which can provide enough stimulation to create orgasm. Another study noted that some women who had a longer distance between their clitoris and vaginal opening had a harder time orgasming because they didn't get the same stimulation.[25] This study illustrates how the clitoris is indirectly stimulated during vaginal penetration, which may or may not be enough for your partner—if your partner's clit isn't getting enough stimulation, rub it!

The important takeaway is that even in vaginal penetration, the clit plays a major role in your partner's pleasure. When your partner sits on top of you, for example, and grinds away in ecstasy, you may be tempted to think it's your penis providing the most pleasure when in fact it's a combo of your penis stimulating the G-spot (the internal anatomy of the clitoris) and the head of her clit rubbing on your pubic bone.

The Vulva and Vaginal Opening

Just like most of the dicks in porn tend to be a certain size, the vulvas in porn tend to look similar to one another. In reality, vulvas come in all different shapes and sizes. Outer labia can be big and puffy, small and thin, or any number of variations in between. Inner labia come in different lengths and sizes, too.

---

24 Susan H. Oakley, et al., "Clitoral Size and Location in Relation to Sexual Function Using Pelvic MRI," *Journal of Sexual Medicine*, April 2014, 11(4): 1014–1022.

25 K. Wallen and E.A. Lloyd, "Clitoral Variability Compared with Penile Variability Supports Nonadaptation of Female Orgasm," *Evolution and Development*, 2008, 10(1): 1–2.

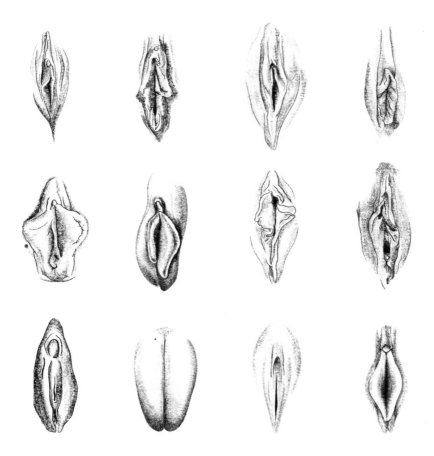

Depending on how big the labia are, they might cover other features, like the head of the clit, or the urethral and vaginal openings. Or, the labia might be small, and these features may be more exposed. Take a look at your partner's vulva, and as you stroke these different parts, take note of how sensitive each spot is. The inner lips can be sensitive, similar to the skin on your ball sack. Sucking on the labia won't necessarily get your partner off, but just like many men love having their balls sucked and licked, this feeling can be absolutely delicious, erotic, and sexy.

Just below the bottom of the clitoris, before the vaginal opening, you'll see a little pinhole; that's the pee hole. Take note of whether your partner likes sensation in that spot. In my experience, two women out of a thousand can orgasm from licking the pee hole; it's not common, but it's a possible spot of pleasure.

Once your partner is appropriately warmed up, feel her vaginal opening. How stretchy is it? Does she have vaginal pain? To gauge this, you can place your finger at her vaginal opening and press down towards her anus, which is the direction that will be easiest to stretch. The vaginal opening can be quite sensitive, so it's important to know what level of stretch feels good to her.

Some women experience pain when the vagina is stretched, especially if they have vaginismus or are near menopause. The vaginal walls often stretch more as your partner gets more aroused. Continue to map how sensations change for your partner as you feel her tissues engorge.

The G-Spot

Because the bottom of the vaginal opening has the most stretch, it's easiest to insert your finger or fingers into your partner's vagina while pressing against the bottom edge. Turn your hand palm-up and press the back of your index or middle finger against the bottom of her vaginal opening, pressing down towards the anus as before, and then slide your finger into her vagina. You can slide two fingers in by stacking your index finger tightly on top of your middle finger, and then press the back of your middle finger against the bottom of her vaginal opening and slide both fingers in together. This technique is illustrated in Chapter Ten, in the section titled "Internal

Touch." My online course also has detailed demonstration videos to show you what this technique (as well as all the other techniques described in this book) looks like in real life.

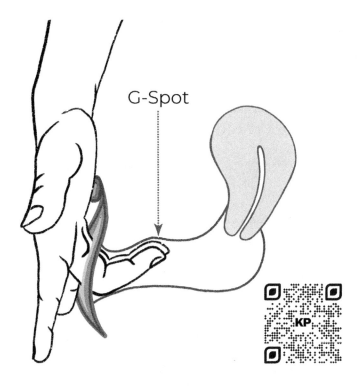

To find your partner's G-spot (the G stands for Gräfenberg), start by feeling the front wall of her vagina, reaching towards her belly button. According to research by OMGYes, 58 percent of women report that their G-spot is on the front wall of the vagina or slightly to the left or right of the front wall.[26]

---

26 Debbie Herbenick, et al., "Women's Experiences with Genital Touching, Sexual Pleasure, and Orgasm: Results from a US Probability Sample of Women Ages 18 to 94," *Journal of Sex and Marital Therapy*, 44:2, 201–212.

The rest report that it is on the sides, bottom, or moves around. How deep this spot is inside the vagina also depends on the person. Some people's G-spot is as little as half an inch in from the vaginal opening; others are most sensitive three inches in. Typically, the "right spot" is about two inches in for most women.

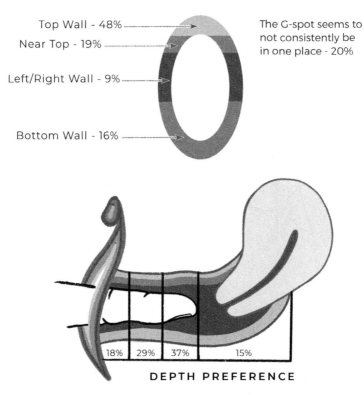

VAGINAL CROSS SECTION

Top Wall - 48%
Near Top - 19%
Left/Right Wall - 9%
Bottom Wall - 16%

The G-spot seems to not consistently be in one place - 20%

18% 29% 37% 15%

DEPTH PREFERENCE

Your partner will also feel different sensations on the front wall of her vagina depending on how aroused and engorged she is. This is because the clitoral body swells as she becomes aroused, and the clitoral body will feel more sensitive and pleasurable as it becomes engorged. The other structure that drastically changes as arousal increases is the urethral sponge. This spongy erectile tissue becomes more pleasurable to the touch as it swells during arousal and protects the urethra from direct stimulation, which can be irritating. You can actually feel this spongy tissue swelling up and even notice the contours of it as you become more aware of what you are touching. Ask her what spot feels best to her, and how much pressure she likes—some women like really firm pressure on this area.

When you stroke your partner's G-spot, you're stimulating the internal structures of the clitoris, which can get sensation through the vaginal wall. Because you're stimulating the tissues on the other side of the wall, including the clitoral body and urethral sponge, *pressure* tends to feel more satisfying to most women than *friction*. This also has to do with the nerves that are in this area—more on this in the section labeled "Wiring Pleasures Together." Don't focus on moving your fingers in and out, which tends to create friction but not pressure. Instead, curl your fingers forward towards her belly button to provide more pressure on the G-spot, and if she likes it, you can flex your fingers in a "come hither" motion.

PRESSURE VS. FRICTION

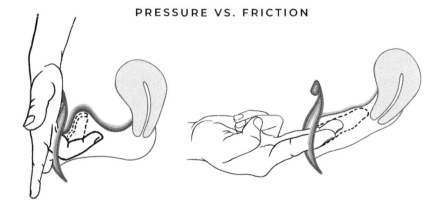

The Cervix

Not only can the vagina stretch more as your partner gets more and more turned on, but the vagina can also get longer. Feel for how long her vagina is, and how deep her cervix is. The depth may change based on how aroused your partner is, or where she is in her hormonal cycle.

As the illustration below depicts, when women are closer to ovulation, and are more fertile, the cervix ascends higher into the vagina, softens, and opens. At this time, slipperier vaginal secretions come from it in greater volume.

During phases of the cycle where she is less fertile, the cervix descends lower into the vagina, closes, and gets firmer, and will be much drier to the touch. These kinds of changes can make a big difference in how a woman experiences cervical stimulation. The cervix can feel much more or much less sensitive at different points in her arousal cycle, and the kinds of positions that she might like will change. This even mystifies some women, who cannot understand why doggy style feels so good one week and hurts like hell another week. These fascinating changes that happen throughout the cycle are the answer.

Regardless of what point she is at in her cycle, be careful not to poke the cervix or put too much pressure on it right away. Some women love to be pounded on their cervix, and others are very sensitive and may not like any cervical stimulation at all. This is an area that not only varies a lot in one woman throughout the month, but between women in general.

Because this anatomical area is so deep and so incredibly sensitive, many women require a lot of trust with their partners in order to fully enjoy cervical sensations. You would be surprised at how much the sensation of the cervix can change for women based on whether or not they trust their partner, and whether or not they have a sense of control around what kinds of stimulation they receive.

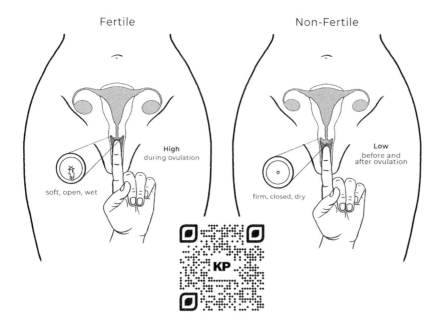

As for how to reach this sensitive spot: if your partner's cervix is farther back than your fingers can reach, you can have her hold the backs of her knees and pull her legs up. This little "crunch" in her abdomen can shorten the distance to the cervix and make it more accessible.

The shape of the cervix is like a donut at the end of the vagina, and you can feel all the way around it. Make circles to see where your partner likes sensation. If your partner likes cervical stimulation, you can gently use your finger to trace the donut and stroke across the center hole.

Always trim your nails, as no one likes these tender tissues scratched on accident. It's easiest to explore your partner's cervix when she's fully aroused and these deep internal sensations are most likely to be pleasurable for her.

Many women have had the experience of receiving cervical stimulation too early, when it felt painful—those experiences could make your partner reticent to try cervical stimulation in the future. If your partner has cervical pain during intercourse, there's a product to help relieve the sensations of going too deep while simultaneously lifting the anxiety of having to hold back from pounding too hard. The OhNut is a series of stackable stretchy rings that you can wear around the base of your penis to help customize penetration depth.

For most women, cervical stimulation only feels good after they've become highly aroused—possibly after a few orgasms. You wouldn't know this from watching porn, where cervical stimulation typically looks like a guy with a giant cock jackhammering away with his partner after only a brief introduction. Take time to warm your partner up, and pay attention to how cervical stimulation feels to her at different stages of arousal.

The A-Spot (Anterior Fornix)

You can trace your fingers around the cervix to the front, towards your partner's belly button, and there you'll find the anterior fornix, or the A-spot. This is the deepest spot on the front wall of your partner's vagina.

Depending on her anatomy, your fingers may not be long enough to reach all the way up to the A-spot. For example, my middle finger is just over three inches long. To reach this deep-spot, I have my partner curl into a ball, to essentially get her clit as close to her belly button as possible, and that helps shorten the distance to the A-spot and allows me to reach deeper.

A-Spot

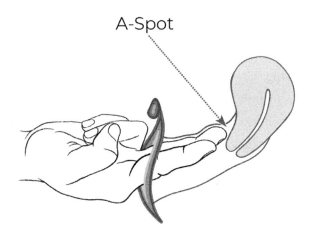

In studies, researchers found that pressure on the A-spot can often stimulate the vagus nerve, which is a nerve that stimulates the parasympathetic rest-and-digest nervous system.[27] This deeP-spot may not feel great to your partner right away, but after a few warm-up orgasms (yes, that's a thing!), stimulation to the A-spot may become more pleasurable.

The A-spot is part of what can make sex with a medium to large penis so pleasurable for women, because the head of a long penis can pound away at this spot. The sensation from this spot typically feels visceral—it's a radiating sensation from deep inside. For some women, stimulation of the vagus nerve can create a crampy

27   Chua Chee Ann, "A Proposal for a Radical New Sex Therapy Technique for the Management of Vasocongestive and Orgasmic Dysfunction in Women: The AFE Zone Stimulation Technique," *Sexual and Relationship Therapy*, 1997, 12:4, 357–370.

sensation, and for others it is something that initially feels strange but which can become intensely pleasurable with practice and the right stimulation and context. Be sure to get feedback on what your partner is feeling before you go to town. Use a circular motion, like you're trying to massage a knot out of a muscle.

To sum up: the three methods of stimulating the A-spot include deep pounding; slow, deep lovemaking; or circular motions with a penis, toy, or hand. Some women like a little pressure here, and some women like a lot; ask for feedback about what feels good to your partner so you can calibrate the level of sensation she likes.

The P-Spot (Posterior Fornix)

With your fingers inside your partner's vagina, carefully turn your hand palm-down and trace your fingers around the cervix to feel the back wall of the vagina. This spot behind the cervix is the posterior fornix, or P-spot.

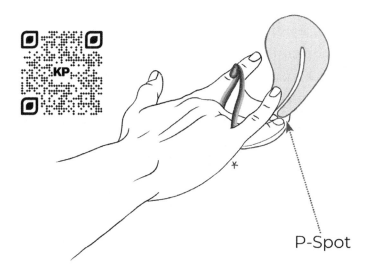

P-Spot

You can roll your finger back and forth across this spot, tracing a half-moon shape from side to side or hip to hip. Press down towards her anus, and see how much pressure she likes. Here's an additional tip: if your partner likes a lot of pressure and stimulation on the P-spot, chances are good (though not guaranteed) she may also like anal sex. The P-spot stimulates the same tissues that anal sex does, but on the other side of the wall between the anus and vagina.

For some women, sensation to one of these deeper spots may not be pleasurable on its own. Stimulation to the cervix, A-spot, and P-spot isn't "a thing" for everyone, especially if the sensation is unfamiliar. But as the saying goes, neurons that fire together wire together. By combining stimulation to one of these deeper spots with a sensation you already know your partner likes, such as rubbing her clit, you can create new combinations of sensations. With experience, the brain may recognize the new sensations and realize with pleasure, "Oh, this could be 'a thing.'" Your partner needs time to associate these sensations with pleasure, mentally and emotionally as well as physically.

Pelvic Floor Muscles

Inside the bowl of the pelvis are three layers of muscles—similar to hammocks in shape—that are responsible for movement in the lower inner organs, including the genitalia. These muscles can pull in and push out—in men, these are the muscles that you can flex to make your cock jump.

In women, these muscles are partly responsible for clitoral erection, and they also run alongside the vaginal canal, making it possible for your partner to squeeze, pull in (like to hold back pee), and push out (like to eject a tampon). We flex them to hold back pee, and we can also bear down with these muscles (your partner is likely familiar with what it feels like to use these muscles to push a tampon out). They contract during orgasm. Women can train these muscles to flex and squeeze, making it possible to give a hands-free hand job to their partner. They can also gain conscious control over these muscles in order to increase pleasure for themselves.

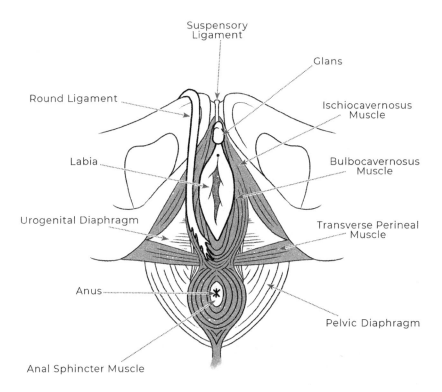

You can do a little exercise to experiment with turning these involuntary impulses into voluntary actions. Insert your finger into your partner's vagina, and ask her to squeeze your finger as if she's trying to suck it in. Then ask her to bear down on your finger as if she's trying to push it out. Repeat the motions until she has conscious control over the action of these muscles.

Then, begin to massage her G-spot. If she flexes her pelvic floor muscles to clamp down and pull in, it likely won't feel good; most women will get the uncomfortable sensation of trying to hold in their pee. But ask her to bear down as you vigorously massage her G-spot, and her muscles will apply more pressure against your fingers, creating a more intense sensation that feels good to most women. When she's first learning how to consciously control these muscles, the exercise may distract her from orgasm. After she's more familiar with the technique, manipulating these muscles can be a fun element to play around with, and potentially a new way to orgasm.

Your partner can play with the timing of flexing these muscles during penetrative sex, too. If she pushes out while you're pulling out, the action might just push your dick out; but if you collaborate and your partner pushes out as you're thrusting in, you can increase the pressure—and the pleasure—on the G-spot. If she gets to ninja-level coordination, she might be able to time her flexes with every thrust. Sometimes your partner may find pleasure in paying attention to the actions of these muscles; at other times it may be best to relax and lose herself in the moment.

Even during oral sex, your partner can use her pelvic floor muscles to squeeze around the clitoris and create different sensations for herself as you lick. Working the pelvic floor muscles can also be a mindfulness hack that helps her tap into the specific sensations in her clit. You can use your fingers to pinch the labia and clitoral hood, and if you hold steady, your partner can flex her pelvic floor muscles and slide her clit back and forth between your fingers, giving herself a hand job.

If you and your partner have never tried to gain conscious control of these muscles it might be awkward at first to experiment with these techniques, just like it was probably awkward the first time you ever tried to pedal a bike. But with practice, activating these muscles can become fluid and subconscious.

I learned from Dr. Barry Komisaruk, coauthor of *The Science of Orgasm*, that much of the pleasure that comes from sexual stimulation and orgasm is related to the strength of muscle contractions.[28] With stronger pelvic floor muscles, the involuntary contractions that accompany orgasm would be much stronger, resulting in a more pleasurable orgasm. This is one reason that exercises that tone the pelvic floor muscles have such a great effect on female pleasure.

Pleasure Balance

You're already familiar with the mental state and the environment you need to get an erection. Your partner has her own set of conditions that she needs to get hard (literally, as you've seen already from this chapter).

The state of arousal is governed by the nervous system and the balance between the *sympathetic* and *parasympathetic* systems. These two systems control our automatic body functions like heart rate, breathing, and digestion. The sympathetic system turns on our fight-or-flight response and motivates us to react to stressors, while the parasympathetic system calms us down and gets us into

28 Barry Komisaruk, Carlos Beyer-Flores, and Beverly Whipple, *The Science of Orgasm*, (Baltimore: Johns Hopkins University Press, 2006).

rest-and-digest mode. During sex, our bodies need a balance of activation in both of these systems, which work together to create the arc of sexual pleasure.

Relaxation and arousal are controlled by the parasympathetic system. A shift into the rest-and-digest system creates changes in your partner's body as she warms up: she is able to turn off the part of her brain that is related to task orientation and survival needs and focus on the sensations in her body. As we discussed earlier, she's able to shift her attention away from potential dangers and onto the opportunity for pleasure and connection. She can relax so that arousal can start to build.

The intense experience of orgasm happens when the body kicks over into the sympathetic system. When we're near orgasm, we go back to fight-or-flight sympathetic mode as we get near the edge and lose control. Some people's bodies switch easily from the parasympathetic to sympathetic system, and they can quickly go from arousal to orgasm. Other people have a harder time switching from one mode to the other. It's useful to know what level of intensity your partner needs to shift gears.

I learned about the complexity of how this whole thing works on a much deeper level from my conversations with neuroscientist Dr. Jim Pfaus. His understanding of sexual arousal is vast and extremely complex, but one simple takeaway I learned is this: while the beginning of sex and the moment of orgasm are largely governed by either sympathetic or parasympathetic systems, the arc of sexual arousal between the two ends is composed of an interplay between the two systems.

To put it in simple terms, you need to be both relaxed and excited at the same time—two things that don't normally happen simultaneously. It is the unique interplay of deep relaxation and intense activation that makes sex so uniquely pleasurable and so different from our everyday experience. When one of these systems is out of balance, the arc of arousal doesn't work. If we are either overly tense and focused, or too relaxed, things tend to come to a halt. It is the mutual engagement of both of these systems that is the recipe for success in sex.

These two systems function largely on an automatic setting. While you don't need to understand the details, it's important to be able to read where your partner is. Is she worked up about something that's stressing her out? Then she probably won't be able to shift quickly to the relaxed state she needs to get aroused. If you sense that she is thinking more about how to navigate a threat than how to enjoy her current experience, the most helpful thing to do is likely to think about how you can help her to release some of the tension. When she's already on the edge of her seat, excess excitement is the last thing she needs.

On the other hand, if she's bored, you might need a way to help her become more engaged and excited. To kick the system into sympathetic gear, there are lots of novel ways to heighten intensity. Many of them are things people commonly do without being aware of the biological reasons that they work. Look at some of the classic turn-ons that bring people to orgasm: Fucking in a public place where you could get caught. Spanking. Choking. All of these heighten the fight-or-flight response. For some people, these scenarios create the extra intensity they need to cum. Not everyone needs high intensity to trigger the sympathetic system. For some people, gentle, slow lovemaking sets just the right conditions for orgasm. Others like the excitement of "riskier" play, possibly because they have a harder time accessing the sympathetic system to tip over into orgasm. To the nervous system, a spank or a hand on the throat creates an emotional emergency—and it's the threat itself that cues the system to switch into sympathetic mode. Done appropriately, it's possible to "threaten" your partner with the good time she craves and kick her over the edge into orgasm.

Other partners' systems have completely different needs, and for most women, consistency is key. There's nothing more annoying than when the technique is perfect, everything is feeling amazing, she's riding the edge about to tip into orgasm...and her partner chooses that moment to try something brand new that kills the vibe. Suddenly the flow is broken, the intensity screeches to a halt, and her sexual buildup drops back to baseline.

The trigger that sends your partner into orgasm could be a spanking sequence or a simple dirty word whispered into her ear at exactly the right moment. By watching how her body (and her mind) responds to each sensation, you can begin to mentally map when she's relaxed and aroused, and when her body is ramping up to orgasm. As you build up your sexual skillset with the techniques in this book, you'll learn how to pick up the erotic cues that tell you when to apply what technique to help her make the switch.

The Brakes and Accelerator of Pleasure

There's another important pair of systems that work to control sex, but instead of working together, like the sympathetic and parasympathetic systems do, these two systems work against one another.

The first system is the sexual excitation system, which is responsible for "turning on the ons," as Dr. Emily Nagoski describes in her book *Come as You Are.* The excitation system is like a car's accelerator, pressing on the gas when we encounter sex-related stimuli.

The second system is the sexual inhibition system, which is responsible for "turning off the offs." Like the brakes on a car, our inhibition system slows or stops progress towards sex when we perceive a threat—for example, a cultural script in our heads about sex being "dirty," or an actual dirty pile of laundry on the floor that keeps us from relaxing in a clean, safe space.

The sexual inhibition system blunts the action of the sexual excitation system, just as hitting the brakes in your car will stop or seriously slow down the car, even if you have your foot pressed to the floor on the accelerator. Scientists and sex educators refer to this as the dual control model.

As Dr. Nagoski puts it, "Sexual arousal is the dual process of turning on the ons and turning off the offs."[29]

In *Come as You Are,* Dr. Nagoski discusses the science of Drs. Erik Jansenn and John Bancroft at the Kinsey Institute, as well as my friend and colleague Dr. Pfaus, and their findings about the dual control model. I've had the privilege to teach an online class on this topic with Dr. Pfaus himself and with Chelsey Fasano, my Head of Research and Development.

In it, we went into detail trying to explain the neurochemistry and neuroanatomy of these systems. But more importantly, we wanted to give people a way to recognize the feeling of inhibition and excitation in their own bodies, and the tools to work with these feelings. We wanted to help people understand that sexual arousal

---

29   Emily Nagoski, *Come as You Are: The Surprising New Science that Will Transform Your Sex Life* (New York: Simon and Schuster, 2015).

isn't just about ramping up excitement, it's also about decreasing inhibition. Scan the following QR code to access this class for free!

We learn what kinds of sex-related things qualify as sex-related and what qualifies as a threat through life experience, so each person's turn-ons and turn-offs will vary. While one person might be turned off by emotional issues, another one might be more sensitive to the details of the physical space she's in. For the first, feeling disconnected from her partner might make it impossible for her to get into the mood, whereas for the second, a pile of dirty laundry in the corner will make it hard to focus on sex.

All inhibition is not necessarily bad. If someone is uncertain whether they want to engage in sexual activity, having high inhibition is a good thing.

Turn-ons vary, too. While one person might be turned on by a sensual massage, candlelit rooms, and a fancy restaurant date, another might be more turned on by the idea of having sex with a stranger in the bathroom of that fancy restaurant with no foreplay. As these examples illustrate, what constitutes a turn-on or turn-off varies wildly.

We also each vary in our natural set point. Both inhibition and excitation systems vary among the population. Some people have sky-high inhibition, and everything needs to be just right for them to get in the mood. These people are like pandas; they only mate in perfect conditions. Some people have sky-high excitation, and are pretty much constantly turned on. These people are like a wildcat in heat; one whiff of pussy is all they need to pounce. However, what is true for every single person is that if you're too

inhibited by turn-offs, you probably won't be able to get turned on. In other words, taking your foot off the brakes will always be important in order for the accelerator to work.

It seems so obvious once you know it, but before I figured this out, I was a bit lost when it came to this arena. I was doing somatic sex education sessions with Pamela Madsen at Back to the Body retreats, and after hundreds of sessions, I still couldn't understand for the life of me why some women would get so easily sexually excited, and others were seemingly impossible to arouse.

Even though the women in the second camp desperately wanted to experience their own arousal, and I was doing everything right in terms of technique, nothing seemed to work. Reading Dr. Nagoski's book lead to an earth-shattering paradigm shift. I realized that without teaching these women how to let go of the brakes, I could not give them pleasure, regardless of what technique I used or how desperately they wanted to feel something.

Before I understood this, all I was doing was tapping on the accelerator. I thought that if I pressed the accelerator hard enough, the brakes were going to let go. But I found that sometimes, the harder you push, the harder the brakes work, too.

In the retreat, I help people let off the brakes in multiple ways. First, I help them tune into their own thoughts. Once they are more aware of their thinking, I try to help guide them away from thoughts that would cause inhibition, like "don't be slutty," "I look fat," or "I'm too noisy." There are a few ways to quiet these kinds of thoughts.

The first is to simply acknowledge them and refocus on something pleasurable. The second is to view them as an invitation. If they are afraid of being too slutty, I invite them to be more of a slut.

Then, I focus on physical relaxation, while coaching them to pay attention to the way my hand feels on their skin. I reassure them that there is nothing they can do wrong.

In real life, this might be more complicated. Relationship context, a shared life and responsibilities, and potential past trauma all add their own flavors of complexity. The dynamic in a couple or of the person with themselves can become quite entrenched and in these cases, sex therapy is really useful. My colleagues Dr. Zhana and Chelsey Fasano put together this handy resource guide, which you can access by scanning the QR code that follows, for all types of therapy, including sex therapy. In the guide you'll find advice on how to find the right therapist, if this is something you think will help you or your relationship.

What I learned from all of this is that you can't barge into sex like a bull in a china shop with someone who's in a highly inhibited state. I learned to read the signs of lowering inhibition, to feel for an invitation from the person's nervous system, to wait until they invite me in.

As I was doing this, I started getting feedback like "I don't know what it is about your presence, but I just want to let go and trust you." When you learn to read and respond to someone's nervous system through their body, and let them come to you rather than rushing them, you earn the trust of their body. The trick is that when you feel resistance, you back off and give them space. You don't rush or hurry. You're willing to let go of your own needs, so they can sense that you're not a threat.

You have to be willing to not have sex if that's actually what she wants. That's what actual safety means. It's kind of like petting an anxious pussycat. You can't rush in to pet the cat if it's not ready, or you'll just get scratched up and hinder development of trust. You have to allow the cat to come to you, and engage and play with it at its own pace. It's not about pushing, it's about offering a respectful yet playful invitation.

How do you know when someone is feeling inhibited? Well, you have to be able to feel your own body first. Through your own body, you'll be able to feel theirs, and when things are going well, it will feel playful and welcoming. Pay attention to things like how tense she is, what her microexpressions are, what the tenor of her sounds are, and her body language.

The more uninhibited she is, the more her body will relax, her facial muscles will soften, her sounds will be deeper and more breathy, and her body language will be open rather than closed. Rather than clenching her fists, her hands will relax. Rather than crossing her arms, she'll let them open. Her legs will spread naturally. She will look at you instead of look away. Think of the cat who spontaneously turns over to let you pet its belly—that's the kind of gesture that will naturally happen when your partner is relaxed and has developed trust. If you get confused, it's always better to ask than to assume. When you meet her where she is at, her body will learn to trust you to read her cues, and relaxation will come more and more easily.

The Neuroanatomy of Pleasure

You may have met—or at least you've heard of—people who are able to orgasm from brushing their teeth, or having their backs scratched, or getting a foot massage. These kinds of orgasms are rare, but they do happen. If you've ever wondered how someone could be driven to climax by something so mundane, the answer lies in how those pleasures register in the brain.

There are four major nerves that connect the genitals to the brain and control most of our sexual pleasure. The first is the pudendal nerve, which in women connects to the clitoris. Then there's the pelvic nerve, which connects to the vagina and the cervix. The vagus nerve runs down to the cervix, and the hypogastric nerve goes to both the cervix and the uterus. These four nerves are like superhighways that carry information up to the brain, and as they run through the body, they pick up additional signals from the muscles and organs they pass along the way.

I laid all of this out for you in a diagram that follows. This diagram might seem super complicated, but the reason I wanted to put so much detail into this is so you could see how similar male and female genital neuroanatomy is. We all have the same parts, just organized in different ways. When you understand that your partner's clitoris is innervated by the exact same nerve that runs from the head of your penis, and that her G-spot is innervated in a similar way to your prostate, you can really begin to understand how your touch might feel to her.

You can begin to see how each technique works to stimulate different nerves and therefore provide different kinds of experiences. Once you get the neuroanatomy, it's like Neo seeing the Matrix for the first time. You suddenly see the whole world of sex differently, and your entire perspective changes.

If you're curious, you can see images of this brain stimulation in a study done by Drs. Nan Wise and Barry Komisaruk on sexual

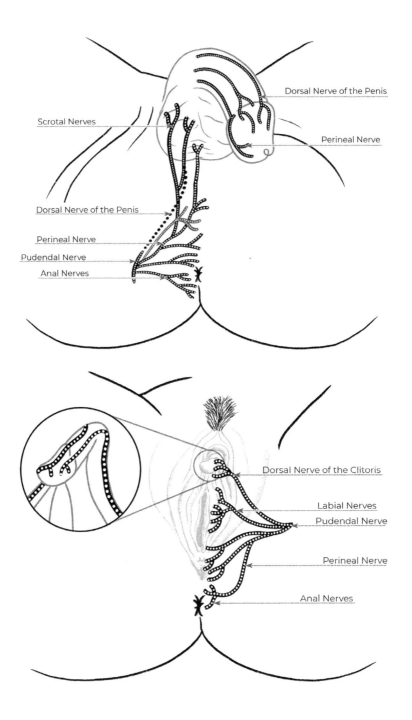

Dorsal Nerve of the Penis

Scrotal Nerves

Perineal Nerve

Dorsal Nerve of the Penis

Perineal Nerve

Pudendal Nerve

Anal Nerves

Dorsal Nerve of the Clitoris

Labial Nerves

Pudendal Nerve

Perineal Nerve

Anal Nerves

stimulation in the brain.[30] These researchers used brain scans to map activity in response to stimulation of the cervix, vagina, nipple, and clitoris. These pleasures light up regions in both hemispheres of the brain, and several of the areas overlap. The more nerves you stimulate, the larger an area of activation in the brain. The more awesome people you bring to the party, the better the party!

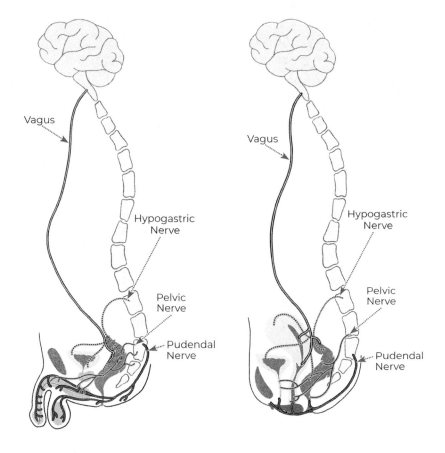

30   Barry Komisaruk, Nan Wise, et al., "Women's Clitoris, Vagina and Cervix Mapped on the Sensory Cortex: fMRI Evidence," *Journal of Sexual Medicine*, October 2011, 8(10): 2822–30.

PRO TIP

You can create pleasure across many different areas of the body, and when you build up enough pleasure, orgasm occurs (nipplegasm, anyone?). It's possible for women to have orgasms from visual stimuli and anal stimuli, because orgasms actually happen in the brain. The important factor is to increase pleasure until there's enough to trigger an orgasm; where the pleasure comes from is less important (to the body, at least—obviously your partner knows what she likes!).

Each of these separate nerves has its own distinct quality. Some of these nerves, like the pelvic nerve, carry stimulation directly from the vagina up the spinal cord to deliver detailed, localized sensations to the brain. Others, like the vagus nerve, take a meandering path from the cervix through the body on their way up to the brain. These nerves pick up stimuli from other parts of the body along their path, and they're called visceral nerves. Stimulation to visceral nerves tends to register as more full-body, radiating sensation in the brain.

We're getting nerdy here, but it's important to understand that stimulation of these different nerves creates different qualities of sensation. Somatic nerves respond to localized information: location, friction, speed, angle. Visceral nerves respond primarily to massage-like pressure. Because the nerves running to the cervix are visceral, stimulation to the cervix tends to create deep, radiating, whole-body sensations. Stimulation on the clit tends to create localized, textural sensations because the nerves that innervate it go directly through the spine. Your partner can feel exactly where she's being touched.

Nerves in men's genitalia work similarly. The head of the penis, for example, responds to nuanced touches and textures, like from a tongue and lips, while the shaft of the penis responds more to pressure and intensity. The prostate is even less localized and more oriented to pressure.

Additionally, because visceral nerve impulses travel through the body slightly slower and provide a more subtle, radiating sensation, it requires a different type of awareness to perceive them. While the somatic nerves that innervate the clitoris often seem to be amplified by muscular tension or intense mental fantasies, the awareness required to feel into visceral sensation is quite different. It requires a deep relaxation of both body and mind, and likely a redirection of the mind away from fantasy and onto the subtleties of sensory experience, in order to fully experience these sensations. This is often not a psychosomatic stance that is familiar, and takes some practice to figure out. Essentially, in order to enjoy deep sensation, you must cultivate the ability to be deeply emotionally and mentally receptive, not just physically.

Different people enjoy different qualities of sensation for different reasons. Some prefer the intensity and rush that comes with the more localized, somatic nerve sensation. Others can't get enough of the slow, radiating visceral nerve sensation. When you find out what your partner enjoys, you can tailor the experience to their preferences. When you use a tool like the nJoy Pure wand on your partner, the pressure it provides to deeper areas of the vagina likely stimulates more visceral nerve activity. In contrast, tiny vibrators such as the pen-like Zumio can be used on the clitoris like a laser pointer to focus on somatic nerve stimulation.

You might be wondering why I decided to go to such length to explain the neuroanatomy of pleasure here and to compare and contrast male and female nerve pathways. It's because I had one of my most earth-shattering epiphanies about women's pleasure once I started studying neurology. I realized that the default sex is female! We all started out having a clit and labia in the womb, and then, if you are a man, the clit actually grew into a penis while the labia descended and fused together to make a scrotum. More importantly, these shared anatomical structures share the same nerve pathways, even once they differentiate through the process of androgenization. So, for instance, the clit and the head of the penis are innervated by the same nerve pathway, and you can assume they feel relatively similarly when touched. When you think about things from this vantage point, you can see why the myth of vaginal orgasms being superior is ludicrous. This is like telling men that they are better off if they can orgasm only through anal sex and touching the shaft of their penis, but not the head. This would actually be the comparable neurological situation in men.

Thinking about things in this way begins to shed light on how many of our cultural narratives about sex are rooted in mythological bullshit, not hard science. When you stop thinking about women as elusive unicorns and start comparing their parts to yours, you begin to realize that women are not so mysterious after all. Developing the ability to relate to her experience and put yourself in her shoes is key to standing out from the crowd. Flex your empathy muscles— they're the sexiest muscles you can flex.

In *An Astronaut's Guide to Life on Earth,* Colonel Chris Hadfield described how he was able to control all the functions on his spaceship with a very small interface: a keyboard, a mouse, and a small screen.[31] With just these tools, he could manipulate all the parts and functions of his craft. I think of the vulva and the vagina in a similar way. They're the interface for your partner's entire sexual experience, and by engaging these parts with diverse sensory experiences, you can engage with your partner's entire body.

When you pay attention not just to which *spot* you're stimulating on your partner, but map it to which *nerve* you're stimulating, you can start to curate a sexual experience that's like something out of Doctor Strange: surgical and mystical at the same time (at least, that's how I like my sex). Layer visceral and somatic stimulation together, and you can create a full-body experience of deep, radiating pleasure that also feels like it's hit just the right spot. As French sexologist Gérard Leleu so eloquently says, we can give our lover the best possible experience by "playing the whole keyboard of orgasms."[32] This brings your experience from "row, row, row your boat" to a full symphony of orgasmic possibility.

The Pleasure Loop Game

In the next chapter, we've laid out all these pleasurable spots so you can get a sense of your partner's anatomy, but I don't recommend exploring them right away or all at once. I've learned from

31 Chris Hadfield, *An Astronaut's Guide to Life on Earth: What Space Taught Me about Ingenuity, Determination, and Being Prepared for Anything* (New York: Back Bay Books, 2015).

32 Gérard Leleu, *Le Traité des Orgasmes* (Leduc: Paris, 2007).

experience that trying to map out all the internal spots in one shot can feel too clinical. It's not a turn-on.

Let your partner get super warmed up, through masturbation or the techniques described in Chapter Eight. The more aroused she is, the more likely these spots are to light up with pleasure. Start by learning what sensations she already knows bring her pleasure, and continue to give her pleasure with those surefire methods as you explore new areas.

One way to stay sexy instead of clinical while trying out new sensations is to play what I call the Pleasure Loop Game. The rules of the game are simple. The giver chooses one spot to explore, and the receiver can give feedback on what they like when it comes to:

- Location (higher, lower, left, right)
- Angle (direction of touch)
- Speed (faster, slower)
- Pressure (more pressure, less pressure)

When you isolate the feedback options, you make it easy for the receiver to direct the giver to what she likes best.

You can start the Pleasure Loop Game in a nonsexual context. Try it with back scratching. Everyone knows how to direct their partner to scratch an itch at just the right location, angle, speed, and pressure—and think about how, when you're receiving instructions on how to scratch your partner's back, it's easy to set your ego aside and focus on scratching exactly the way she needs. When you get comfortable with giving and receiving feedback, you can apply the same skills to sex.

Use the Pleasure Loop Game to encourage your partner to give you signs when you're on the right track. When a hunter is tracking game in the forest, they get a boost of motivation with every foot-print, broken branch, or bit of snagged fur they see. These signs give the hunter a hit of dopamine because he realizes he's on track. Positive signals keep us motivated, and when there are no signals, we tend to get frustrated. Think of the experience of ordering an Uber and then staring at the map as you watch the car approach. If the car doesn't move, we lose our shit—but as it approaches, we feel anticipation. Similarly, when we're figuring out how to give plea-sure to our partner, positive signs show us we're on the right track and fill us with excitement.

It's important that neither partner fakes their pleasure here. Faking it doesn't just give false signals—it also trains the giver to do the wrong things. Encourage your partner to make whatever noises feel natural when something feels good, and not to worry about what she sounds like. Whatever noises she makes will moti-vate you—and give you a hit of dopamine—when you realize you're helping her feel good.

Of course, not everyone moans; some people go totally silent when they're focusing on their pleasure and feeling really good. You can use nonverbal signals with your partner—a squeeze of the hand or noticing the way she moves her body—to see that what you're doing is working. Whatever the cue is, tell her how rewarding it feels to see it.

You can play the Pleasure Loop Game to pinpoint specific tech-niques that feel good for your partner. For example, you can play this game with your partner's clit to dial in exactly where and how she likes to be touched. If you picture the head of the clit like a clock face, you can begin at twelve o'clock and have her give feedback on pres-sure and speed. Then try three o'clock, six o'clock, and nine o'clock to see which location she likes best. Some women are three o'clock girls, others love high noon. The great thing is that once you get going, and dial in the right pressure and speed, her feedback might shift from "right there, right there," to "don't stop, don't stop"—and possibly all the way over to orgasm. The key here is to allow for open exploration without attachment to an end result. Knowing what works for your partner requires balance: if you give up on your technique too early, you might miss something great; if you're too stubborn, you might get stuck on something that's not working.

You can use the Pleasure Loop Game to calibrate the way you touch your partner's G-spot, cervix, A-Spot, and P-spot. It's like looking for possible spots to park your car: with this game, you can find the reliable spots that bring your partner pleasure, and how much speed and pressure to use. When you've mapped out her favorite sensations, you know where you can "park your car" to keep the pleasure going throughout the experience.

Once you take the time to uncover your partner's full range of sensation and sensual experience, you can build on your knowledge and discover amazing new experiences together. Imagine what other pleasures could be possible in the sexual realm—and what value you could demonstrate as a partner who creates delicious experiences unique to your lover's tastes.

6

Orgasm Potential

One of my friends was a gorgeous woman who saw herself as highly sexual, but she'd been having a hard time orgasming in partnered sex—for ten years. She'd been dealing with her frustration around orgasm for so long that she'd started to think she was broken. She knew me as a sex educator, and we decided to do a session together to work with her hurdle. I took on the role of a teacher to coach her through relaxing and attending to her pleasure.

I started by setting the frame: our goal was to get her into parasympathetic arousal so she could relax, and I was going to tell her what to do every step of the way. She didn't need to remember to do anything, or make any effort. I told her to drop any expectation that she needed to cum, and just go with the flow of whatever happened, and I would support her the whole way.

I started by massaging her body until I could feel her relax. I built up arousal by teasing her slowly, waiting to touch her until she was aching to be touched. Specifically, I wanted to disrupt the script attached to her anxiety. Typically, in the lead-up to sex, she would get anxious, thinking, *Why is this not feeling good?* She was familiar with the anticipation, but she wasn't in touch with the *wanting* of sex.

Slowly, as I saw her wanting to be touched, I began to introduce new sensations. When she told me something felt good, I reminded her not to try to have an orgasm. I told her I had nothing to prove—I had no ego about whether she was able to cum or not. Her only job, I reiterated, was to be in the experience of the moment.

She was kinky, so I tied her up a little to help restrict her movement, and I put a blindfold on her. I wanted to take away all the things she had a natural tendency to focus on, so she could focus fully on the sensation.

When she got closer, I was careful not to react; when someone is having a hard time cuming, they tend to get anxious as they get close because they want to try to make it happen. This performance anxiety puts the brakes on arousal, which causes a decrease in arousal and pleasure, and then more anxiety. To get her to stop focusing on performing and orgasming, which would bring up this negative feedback loop, I kept the emphasis off of her orgasm, so she could enjoy arousal at its own pace. I stayed chill, and teased her a little more, and suddenly, she said, "Oh my god, I'm cuming." Her orgasm was totally involuntary and took her by surprise. Sometimes, having an orgasm has less to do with ramping up the intensity and more about taking the foot off the brakes.

"You're not done," I said, "that was just a warm-up." I wanted to change her mind about orgasms being an elusive rarity for her. I kept going, and going, and going—I wanted to make sure she had so many orgasms that she'd realize it wasn't a problem.

In total, she had ten or so orgasms in that session. And a bonus one in the shower afterward.

There are many, many women like her who think they're incapable of having one orgasm, let alone several in a row. But in one study, 47 percent of women reported having had multiple orgasms in their lives.[33] From my sample size of over a thousand partners, I've come to the conclusion that most women can have them. There is some small percentage of women that cannot have an orgasm for medical reasons. But, for the vast majority of women, it is a learnable skill. Just because it hasn't been learned, or the skill is a little rusty, doesn't mean that it is impossible.

The Mythical Orgasm Hierarchy

In my quest to figure out how to make each of my partners squirt, I was elevating one particular kind of orgasm, one particular experience, above the others. But squirting isn't the "ultimate" orgasm—in fact, for some people it's more like a party trick. What matters is not the objective outcome of my partner ejaculating all over the sheets; it's her subjective experience of pleasure.

Dr. Pfaus and his research team wrote an article on female orgasmic variety, focused especially on the clitoral versus vaginal orgasm debate.[34] (I highly recommend reading the study, which

---

33 Debby Herbenick, "Women's Experiences with Genital Touching, Sexual Pleasure, and Orgasm: Results from a US Probability Sample of Women Ages 18 to 94," *Journal of Sex & Marital Therapy*, August 9, 2017.

34 James G. Pfaus, Gonzalo R. Quintana, Conall Mac Cionnaith, and...

is entertaining as fuck and littered with *Star Wars* references.) In it, Pfaus describes a cultural perception of hierarchy we place on different kinds of orgasms, which date back to the Victorian era. Sigmund Freud theorized that women had different kinds of orgasms based on different stages of development. He considered external orgasms, involving stimulation of the head of the clit and the vulva, to be "infantile," while internal orgasms involving the vagina were more "mature."

As Pfaus points out, this idea is bogus. Women (and all people) experience pleasure from a variety of different sensations and areas of their bodies. Not only can these different sensations create different types and intensities of orgasm, but what our partners find pleasurable can change over time as they are introduced to new experiences.

In this way, our sense of pleasure in sex is a lot like our sense of pleasure for food. You could get full from eating a bowl of rice alone, just like you can orgasm from just one specific kind of sensation. But how boring would it be to eat only rice all the time? To experience more pleasure with our food, we layer the rice bowl with perfectly seared steak; crisp, crunchy vegetables; and tangy, peppery spices. A remarkable meal can give us a new reference point for how good food can taste. Our tastes change, and that allows us to explore different foods—and sexual pleasures—for the rest of our lives.

At the same time, we shouldn't judge people who just want to eat rice! It is perfectly valid to enjoy and be satisfied by only one

---

...Mayte Parada, "The Whole Versus the Sum of Some of the Parts: Toward Resolving the Apparent Controversy of Clitoral Versus Vaginal Orgasms," *Socioaffective Neuroscience and Psychology*, October 25, 2016.

thing. To help straight men understand this, I got some advice from Dr. Laurie Mintz, the author of *Becoming Cliterate*.[35] Think of it this way: most straight men will live a perfectly happy, fulfilling sex life while orgasming from penile stimulation alone, without the desire or pressure to explore their prostate sensation or prostate orgasm. In the same way, the most reliable stimulation for most women is from external clitoral stimulation. There's no reason to ever make women feel like there is something wrong with them, or they are missing out if internal sensations are not their favorite! If everyone believed this, we would make huge strides towards orgasm equality between the sexes. The primary goal, for everyone, is to find one preferred and reliable way to have dependable, satisfying orgasms.

Pleasure Wiring

While there are general similarities in our nervous systems, the nerve endings that branch out from the bigger superhighways are laid out slightly differently in each person.[36] The ends of these branches can also vary in density. In *Becoming Cliterate*, Dr. Mintz talks about how some women have up to fourteen times more neural density in their clitoris than others.[37] This explains much of the differences in preference for types of touch women have.

Certain areas, like the clitoris and the head of the penis, are sensitive on nearly everyone, but within these sensitive areas, we

35   Laurie Mintz, *Becoming Cliterate: Why Orgasm Equality Matters—And How to Get It* (New York: HarperOne, 2017).
36   Naomi Woolf, *Vagina* (New York: Ecco, 2013).
37   Laurie Mintz, *Becoming Cliterate: Why Orgasm Equality Matters—And How to Get It* (New York: HarperOne, 2017).

each have particular preferences on the most pleasurable kind of touch. Much of this is based on differences in nerve ending location and density.

I get frustrated by sex experts who claim that there's one magic spot on the clitoris that's the most sensitive for everyone. I know from experience that's bullshit. Within each one of our bodies, the layout of our nerves differs slightly. No two people's genitals are the same; they're different in their outward appearance and their internal wiring—which means each person has their own preferences and responses to the same kinds of touch.

Some women want touch directly on the head of their clit; some women want to be stroked over the hood; some women prefer sensation a little to the left, and others like it a little to the right. We each have different sensitivities based on our unique neural layouts. The goal of a great lover, then, is not just to try different techniques, but to pay attention to how our partners are responding to each sensation, so that we can create the "dishes" they love.

The Range of Orgasmic Experiences

It's very clear when a man has an orgasm: there's a clear visual sign and a mess to clean up afterward. Not so with women—there are a lot of different types of orgasms, and different ways they come about. An orgasm is part physical experience, part subjective pleasure. From scans, we know the brain lights up like fireworks and spits out a cocktail of happy chemicals. Different parts of the body, including various parts of the pelvic floor, involuntarily contract.

For some people the experience is about as dramatic as a sneeze, and for others it's intoxicatingly good. The range of just how good it can be is trainable: just like learning to orgasm can be trained, learning to orgasm more intensely can be trained.

My conversations with renowned neuroscientist Dr. Barry Komisaruk have given me some mind-expanding insight into this topic.[38] He explained to me how sensations work in the body in a way I had never really understood before. Based on his many years of research and experience, Dr. Komisaruk has come to the conclusion that there are areas of the body that we simply do not have practice feeling. We use our legs and arms all day in order to move around, and so we develop the capacity to feel those parts of our body with enough detail to precisely move them for all of the nuanced tasks we have to do each day. Because we don't spend a ton of time on tasks that involve feeling the insides of our bodies, we often don't spend much energy learning to feel these parts of us. However, it is possible to develop this awareness, says Dr. Komisaruk. These feelings are worth developing, as they provide some of the most moving experiences of our lives. It is here that we feel the deepest emotions of our lives, that we register our greatest joys and deepest sorrows. When we say we are "moved" by something, it is here in the visceral core of ourselves that we are moving, and by which we are moved. Surrendering to being moved by our depths, in life and in sex, is worth pursuing.

Letting Your Body Guide You

In civilized modern society, we've developed ways to inhibit our base instincts in order to function collectively. This allows us to

---

38 Barry Komisaruk, "Visceral-Somatic Integration in Behavior, Cognition, and 'Psychosomatic' Disease," *Advances in the Study of Behavior*, 1982.

work together and keeps us from, say, causing havoc in a line to get on the subway. But we haven't equally developed the skills to shut this inhibition off so we can experience the full expressions of our animal body.

We have calloused over this part of ourselves—we are taught not to feel our emotions, or the sensations that go along with them, like gut-wrenching crying or achiness in the heart. Whether you're in a belly laugh or crunched in the fetal position, there is a physical expression that goes along with our emotions. Feeling the visceral senses involves feeling these gut-level emotions and sensations. As Dr. Komisaruk points out, the motion of emotion is about allowing your body to move the sensations you feel throughout it. For instance, when you feel sad, you can bottle it inside, or you can allow your diaphragm to contract rhythmically, your face to contort, your body to heave, and your throat to produce moans and sobs. If you allow your body to express these sensations, all of the muscles and tissues will spontaneously relax after you have allowed them to move.

If you continually tighten the body's impulse to move and express, you will develop a body that is perpetually contracted around a series of sensations you are trying not to feel or show. The tricky thing is, this is the same body you will encounter when sexual pleasure wants to course through you as well. If you've spent most of your days tensing up, trying to avoid feeling and expressing the sensations inside you, this same psychosomatic attitude will be perpetuated in sex. You won't be able to let your body open up and fully feel what is available to be felt, sexually. The moral of this story is, if you want to be able to access these deeper sexual core sensations, you have to be willing to open your emotional channels as well. It's not just about opening up to your partner; it's about opening up to yourself.

Babies are amazing teachers when it comes to this. If you look at the range of emotions that flash across an infant's face in a matter of minutes, you see how fluidly they respond to the world and themselves. If you watch them breathe, you will notice their entire body moves with each breath. They are completely allowing life, their own and that which surrounds them, to be fully experienced in the body. My dear friend and head of research and development, Chelsey Fasano, has explained to me how it's possible to keep some of this childlike fluidity and expressiveness in adulthood.[39]

According to Chelsey, it's not about being as totally unguarded as a baby 24/7—that would not be functional. We wouldn't be able to go to work, perform in high-pressure scenarios, or put our own feelings aside for the sake of another person. She says what's important is to develop the capacity to move back and forth between different levels of openness, like how the aperture of a camera lens opens and shuts to let in different amounts of light.

The problem is, we practice having a small aperture so consistently that we get stuck, and we forget how to open back up. The solution is to practice letting in more sensation and more experience, so we can become more flexible in feeling and expressing all parts of ourselves to the degree that feels best in the moment.

But how, exactly, do we do this? Chelsey explains the process like this: the first step is to begin paying attention to the sensations you feel in the first place. These could be radiating sensations, sensations of clenching, tightening, relaxing, yearning, arousal, aches and pains, movements of breath, or anything else that is there.

---

39 ChelseyFasano.com

It's like listening to your favorite song and really getting into the feeling of it—let your attention be immersed in yourself the way it would be in a song you love. Direct your attention to what is happening in your body, and use your breath and movement to fan the flame of sensation. Concentrate on feeling what there is to be felt, even if it's barely there at first, and focus on relaxing your body around the sensations, rather than tensing. In time, you will develop the capacity to feel more and more sensations as your attention and relaxation increase.

Once the sensations in your body get stronger, practice allowing your body to move as an expression of the sensations as they arise. Set aside time where you let your body's signals be in the driver's seat, whether that is by dancing, focusing on your breathing, massaging yourself, or rolling around on your bed alone. You can even do things that feel semi-silly, like pretending to be an animal by crawling around your house, making different animal movements and noises. Allow yourself to experience the range of movements and noises your body is capable of, and tune into your senses. This stuff can be subtle and sweet, or ridiculous and wild. The point is to give your body time in the driver's seat.

Chelsey learned almost everything she knows about this subject from her teacher, Michaela Boehm, author of *The Wild Woman's Way*.[40] Michaela has tons of resources, including courses and workshops for men and women, to help anyone learn the full mechanics of how to engage in this process, which could constitute several books in itself.[41] What I'm presenting are just the

---

40   Michaela Boehm, *The Wild Woman's Way: Unlock Your Full Potential for Pleasure, Power, and Fulfillment* (New York: Atria Books, 2018).

41   MichaelaBoehm.com

basics. Scan the QR code that follows to go to Chelsey's site and learn more about this process and her work around embodiment and deep feeling.

One of the best times to practice moving through sensations is in sex itself. Focus on the sensations that occur during arousal that are more subtle, moving your body and breathing in ways to increase these sensations. Rather than thinking of sex as a performance, think about it more as a way to sense your own (and your lover's) body in ways that you normally do not. Allow yourself to become aware of more and more nuance in your sexual sensations and see if you can let your body move with them as they come up. This is the key to learning how to feel pleasure in deeper places that connect to visceral nerve fibers through the core of the body, like the prostate, G-spot, and cervix.

I sometimes joke that if you want to understand the vulnerability involved in receiving and feeling these deep core sensations, try playing with your prostate! Behind this "joke" is a serious piece of advice: being able to feel the physical sensations requires that you also be able to feel the emotions and vulnerability that go along with them. Once you understand the subjective differences in feeling between the visceral sensations and somatic ones, you'll understand how your partner's sensory experiences vary between clitoral stimulation (which is mostly somatic) and deeper G-spot or cervical stimulation (which is mostly visceral). You'll also get a sense of what comes up for your partner when you touch a deep nerve and how it feels to be penetrated—something that is hard to understand unless it's been done to you.

Be-Do-Have

Lowering inhibition is required for great sex. When you do the work of reconnecting with your emotions, you'll see huge benefits in your sex life. Technique is only part of the equation; it's the connection to our partner—and even more importantly, to ourselves—that makes for great sex.

In my twenties, I learned the concept of Be-Do-Have: we have to *be* a certain way in order to *do* the actions needed to *have* the results we want. If we want to have mind-blowing sex, and we know our partner has to be willing to be vulnerable enough to go there, we need to be vulnerable first so our partner can join us. We are human *beings* after all, not human doings.

If we want our partners to be unselfconscious, we need to be able to allow all our natural emotions and bodily functions to come up unselfconsciously. If we want our partner to be able to relax, we need to be able to embody calm. If we want our partner not to stress out about whether she's going to orgasm, we need to stay unattached to orgasm as a goal. When we're able to embody these traits and be in the moment, we open the door for our partner to join us.

So how do we do all *that*? Well, we can emulate Bruce Lee and learn from many traditions and schools of thought, developing a range of soft skills to help us be our best self in sex. As he says, "Absorb what is useful, discard what is useless, and add what is specifically your own." The best lovers do this not just with the outer skills required to be a good lover, but the inner skills as well, becoming a mixed martial artist of sex.

The Science of Training Sensations

Mindfulness training, like we talked about in Chapter One and in the section above, can increase the brain's ability to experience pleasure. If you look at ancient wisdom around sacred sex, like the sexual techniques developed in tantric traditions, many of the practices are designed to hack the sexual experience through paying more attention to sensation. The kink scene, on the other hand, maximizes the physical side with intense sensation. Both of them create a fine art out of sex. From the ancient wisdom of Eastern traditions, to Japanese bondage, to Victorian-era vibrators, sex hackers have been around for millennia. Western science is just starting to catch up, and new exciting studies are coming out to better understand how orgasm works in the brain and the body.

Earlier we talked about taking off the brakes and putting our foot on the gas as two different aspects of how to build sexual pleasure. While there are lots of techniques available to increase the gas, so to speak, ramping up intensity of sensation, there are not as many well-known ways to take off the brakes. And what's even less well-known is why this is so important.

My friend Chelsey Fasano, who we mentioned above, studies the neuroscience of meditation and attention at Columbia University, and she helped me understand how this works. When we pay attention to a sensation, the sensory processing areas of our brain in which neural activity occurs as a result of the sensation actually fire *more*. This causes a subjective sense of the sensation being focused on *increasing*.

On the other hand, we could be adding tons of stimuli, but focusing on something else, and our sensory processing areas could remain relatively inactive. Our brains are designed to conserve energy by deactivating things we don't focus on, even to the extent of pushing them out of awareness altogether. Have you ever been engrossed in a book, and someone says something to you that you literally don't hear, and have to ask them to repeat? If we are focused on something besides sex, we can tune out sexual stimuli in exactly this way, becoming "deaf" to the sensations in our own bodies.

We have all had the experience of some kind of stimuli evoking intense feeling in us, whether it was a beautiful sunset, a delicious piece of food, or a song that hits us in just the right emotional spot. What we often don't realize is that it is not only the nature of the stimuli that makes us enjoy it so much, but the fact that we were able to so exclusively focus on it at that moment that made it so absolutely exquisite. Our ability to focus on sensations can actually magnify and amplify them.

Of course, the best of both worlds is a blend of competent stimulation and mindful attention. In Chinese, "kung fu" refers to embodied mastery; it's not a martial art in and of itself, but a mastery over one's craft. The best sex involves inner and outer skillsets—an inner and outer kung fu. This is not something you can simply understand intellectually; you have to practice to acquire skill and competency in both of these areas. To help you with acquiring your inner and outer kung fu of skillful sex, Chelsey and I have developed a private coaching program that combines my personal training and sex coaching background with Chelsey's extensive training in yoga, meditation, and tantra. Use the QR code that follows to learn more. We pride ourselves on designing programs that not only educate students, but actually help them master the skill in an embodied fashion. Knowing intellectually and knowing in the body simultaneously is the best combination.

Beyond Satisfied
Coaching Program

In addition to mindfulness, the other major factor in how we experience pleasure is our biology. The diversity in neural layout we discussed before, combined with our preferences and habit patterns, results in a huge array of preferences. Some people love cervical stimulation; some people hate it. In Chapter Two, we laid out the most popular spots where women tend to like stimulation, but everyone varies in what they like touched and the amount of stimulation they need.

How quickly a person reaches orgasm also depends on how fast their system switches between the parasympathetic and sympathetic nervous systems, like we talked about in Chapter Three. It doesn't take much stimulation for some people to flip their switch, but for others the switch can be sticky. This is true for men and women, and culturally, we shame men for having fast switches and ejaculating "prematurely," and we shame women for having slow switches and taking "too long." In both of these judgments, we're trying to force biology to fit a cultural paradigm of what sex should look like. Meanwhile, biology doesn't give a fuck what society thinks.

Our culture also overemphasizes penis-in-vagina sex as the ultimate intimate act, even though, as we've previously seen, only 18 percent of women report being able to orgasm with penetration alone.[42] We demonize the idea that women might need to stimulate their clits during PIV sex—yet imagine expecting to get off by having your partner touch only your prostate and never touch the head. Only a low percentage of men can cum from that kind of stimulation.

When we're seeking to experience optimum pleasure, it's helpful to combine a wide variety of sensations. Our taste buds can pick up on a wide range of flavors, and the more flavors we're exposed to, and the more often we taste them, the more we broaden our palate. Similarly, our bodies are capable of experiencing a huge range of sensations, and we have different thresholds for how much stimulation we need for a sensation to register as pleasurable.

We can train these thresholds by building our capacity to pay attention to sensation. The more we pay attention, the more we can feel nuances. The better we get at paying attention to those sensations, the more we can turn a pleasurable sensation into an orgasm-inducing

---

42 Debby Herbenick, "Women's Experiences with Genital Touching, Sexual Pleasure, and Orgasm: Results from a US Probability Sample of Women Ages 18 to 94," *Journal of Sex & Marital Therapy*, August 9, 2017.

one. When we learn to pay attention, feel the nuances of our experience, add lots of flavors to our sex, and be open to new sensation, we can begin to broaden the range of our orgasmic experiences.

Misconceptions about Orgasm

One of the incredible upsides to learning more about sexual technique and experience is that we can train ourselves to help us become more receptive to pleasure. For people who have a hard time orgasming, this is great news—we can build this capacity with deliberate practice. But first, we have to understand it's possible, and adopt a growth mindset towards pleasure. Let's tackle some of the misconceptions many people have around orgasm, and how to overcome them.

Orgasm Is the Only Goal of Sex

You know the experience of gritting your teeth through a sleepless night? You lie awake, thinking about how you can't fall asleep, and the more you think about it the further away sleep seems. Orgasm is the same way. It's the animal in the brush. The more you chase it, the farther it runs away. A skilled hunter doesn't go straight for the prey; they follow the signs and watch patiently for the right moment to move in.

Anxiety creates a deflection. When your partner is worried about whether she'll orgasm, she may focus on the fact that she's not cuming yet instead of focusing on the pleasurable sensations she's feeling. Set aside the "goal" of orgasm, and you can both focus on the signs from your partner's body. Track which sensations she finds pleasurable and stay with the ride. For this to work, you have to truly believe that the journey is as important as the destination. Stop and smell the flowers, enjoy the ride, and you will help your partner do the same.

It Takes Too Long to Get There

Many people get stuck in anxiety over how long it takes them to cum. They worry their partner is getting impatient and just waiting for them to finish. It's not hard to see where this misconception comes from: in porn, the actors make it look so easy, and some women seem to cum almost instantly. (Remember: Porn stars are actors.) In real life, your partner is lying there, distracted from the sensations in her body because she's worried she's taking forever. The more she chases the idea of orgasm, the more anxiety builds, and the further away orgasm seems.

Often, it doesn't actually take longer for women to cum than for men. It just takes longer to dial in the sweet spot. If your partner isn't getting the physical sensations or the mental stimulation that works for her, she won't climax. Take time to explore lots of different sensations with your partner and calibrate the speed and pressure she needs. When you find the sweet spot on the sensations she loves, she may be pleasantly surprised at how fast the switch from arousal to orgasm can happen.

Men and Women Should Have Equal Numbers of Orgasms

When your partner is primarily concerned with getting you off, she's not fully focused on her own pleasure. Sex is a give-and-take, and each partner has to allow themself to receive fully. As you know by now, men's and women's orgasms don't happen in a one-to-one ratio. There are multiorgasmic men out there, but they're few and far between (and usually they've done a lot of fucking training to get there).

In general, your partner is capable of having far more orgasms than you. If she expects that she'll have one orgasm and then she'll help you get yours, she may be cutting herself short on her orgasmic potential. An adult can eat more than a kid can; you wouldn't feed them both the same size portion. Encourage your partner to eat until she's satiated. No kid's meal for her.

If I Lose Control in Orgasm, I Will Die
(Or at Least Severely Embarrass Myself)

Despite the popularized French expression *le petit mort*, no one has ever died from orgasm alone. And yet, it's an incredibly common fear that grips many people, that if we fully let go and give into pleasure to the point of orgasm, something very, very bad will happen.

This may seem ridiculous to our logical brains, but to the nervous system it makes complete sense. Remember that when we're on the verge of orgasm, our brain switches from the rest-and-digest mode to fight-or-flight. To the nervous system, an orgasm is dangerous, thrilling, and overwhelming. On the cusp, when we're in the grip of our body's fear instinct, it's a natural response to want to quit stimulation rather than give into an experience that might be too much.

Sometimes, when I'm with a partner who is experiencing that sense of fear, it's enough to hold their hand and say, "You're not going to die. Let it happen. I'm here." That little nudge can often establish enough safety for my partner to go on.

For some people, it's not death they fear, but embarrassment. They worry that by letting go completely, their body may do something fully involuntary—spasm, fart, pee, or any number of bodily functions—that they will feel ashamed of. The ironic thing is that one of the most fun things about sex is getting to play with control and the loss of control.

The more we can tune into our bodies and encourage our partners to ride the waves of sensation they're experiencing, the more skill we can build to navigate the border between control and letting go. When you're helping your partner get comfortable with letting go, pay attention to whether they're rushing and encourage them to take their time. If they're holding back from moaning, tell them to moan louder. If they're enjoying a particular sensation, encourage them to take a couple more bites. Watch for signs that your partner is close to losing control and encourage them to lean into the sensations that are taking them over the edge.

Star Players (and Their Helpful Teammates)

We each have our own set of go-to techniques to get off, and we often end up treating these reliable sensations like Megan Rapinoe on the US women's soccer team: we rely heavily on one star player, one technique, to kick the ball in the net.

But that one player isn't the only one helping the team score; there are ten other players passing the ball and advancing it down the field. Similarly, we can combine different sensations to broaden the brain's idea of what is pleasurable. For many women, the clit is the star player, and a certain stimulation may bring her to orgasm every time—but you can layer in stimulation to the G-spot (or the A-spot or the P-spot or the cervix) to create new combinations.

Ultimately, pleasure comes down to personal preference. Some people are satisfied with only one way to cum. Others may try a million different techniques and discover they like a wide array of different sensations, but only want some techniques once in a while. For most, a small handful of sensations often become the star players.

By exploring your partner's body and testing out lots of different types of touch, you can learn where her thresholds are, and possibly even expand them to find a new winning player your partner has never seen before.

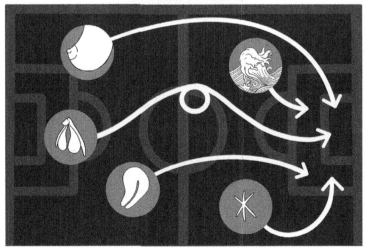

Multiple Orgasms

As we discussed above, just because most guys are "one and done" doesn't mean that women's orgasms play by the same rules. In fact, 47 percent of women have had multiple orgasms.[43] After a warm-up period, the body gets aroused and the genitals get engorged, all the way up to the peak of orgasm. After the first orgasm, arousal drops back down—but not all the way down, if there is some stimulation and you stay engaged.

How low the dip goes and how long it lasts is different from woman to woman. One woman could need ten seconds after an orgasm to recover and be ready for more stimulation; another woman could need sixty-second rests, timed almost like a workout. Still others (about one in seven[44]) can have rolling orgasms, with one right after the other.

In *Orgasm Unleashed*, author Eyal Matsliah talks about orgasm potential as a set of peaks and valleys that's unique to each partner.[45] Some orgasms are discernible, clear climaxes, while for others it's difficult to tell where they begin and end.

There are three general patterns of multiple and extended orgasms. The first is what I like to call "popcorn," where a woman has orgasms throughout a longer play session at random intervals. She may have one after ten minutes, another after five more minutes, a third at the half hour mark, and so on.

---

43 Debbie Herbenick, et al., "Women's Experiences with Genital Touching, Sexual Pleasure, and Orgasm: Results from a US Probability Sample of Women Ages 18 to 94," *Journal of Sex and Marital Therapy*, 44:2, 201–212

44 Ibid.

45 Eyal Matsliah, *Orgasm Unleashed: Your Guide to Pleasure, Healing, and Power* (Intimate Power, 2015).

Popcorn

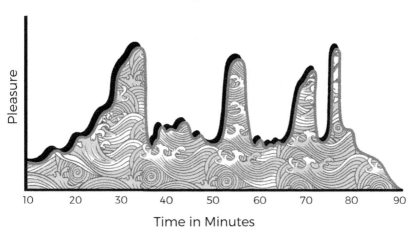

The second pattern is "back-to-back" orgasms. As soon as one orgasm ends, it begins to build right back up to the next one. Sometimes the next orgasm comes in as short as a few seconds, or it can be about a minute later. Nevertheless, these orgasms occur in sequence, very close together.

Back to Back

The third pattern is an "extended orgasmic wave," and is like an erotic trance state. Women describe this experience as one long rolling orgasm that ebbs and flows slightly but stays at an orgasmic level of pleasure for five minutes to as long as a half hour. If you want to know which pattern your partner tends to fall into, ask them about their masturbation habits or past sexual experiences. Many women know the answer to this but have just never been asked!

Extended Orgasmic Wave

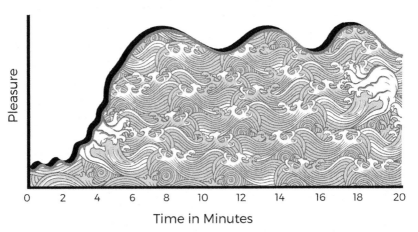

When one nerve ending is tired out and overstimulated, I like to move to other areas. If the clit needs a little recovery, I like to play with the G-spot, for example, to keep my partner's arousal up. When the clit is ready for stimulation again, I add it back in. Mixing up sensations on different body parts keeps my partner guessing at what new excitement is coming next. It also helps me stay engaged and lets me rest if my tongue or fingers or arm are getting tired.

Sometimes I use erotic narrative to help get my partner to the next peak. If we're doing a kinky domination scene, for example,

I might tell my partner just after an orgasm, "Did I say you could stop? Don't you fucking stop." A command like that kicks the receiver back into fight-or-flight mode, which helps them stay in their orgasmic high.

As a giver, your job is to surf the waves of your partner's pleasure. When we stay fully in tune with the moment, it's sometimes possible to help our partner break through to a new, unprecedented experience. We only conceive of what's possible through our own lived experience, and for some women, one orgasm (or none) is their baseline.

It's great if your partner only wants to have one orgasm. But many people don't realize it's possible to train our bodies to break through the ceiling of our experience. They don't realize how high the ceiling can go. With practice, we can open up to new peak experience.

All that said, it's important to keep your own ego out of your partner's experience. If your partner is having performance anxiety over orgasming, and you're feeling determined to make multiple orgasms happen, you'll both end up fucking up the experience by putting too much pressure on the end goal. Like Eyal says, counting orgasms is for amateurs.[46] A pressure-free environment provides the highest likelihood for optimal pleasure.

The idea is not to force the body into a multiorgasmic cycle of peaks and valleys. Instead, think about how you can help your partner remove any blocks they have on their pleasure. Set the right environment and conditions for the full force of their sexuality to emerge naturally, exactly as it is.

There's nothing linear about building capacity. If you want to get stronger at the gym, you might show up every day, but some days

46   Ibid.

you feel stronger and some days you don't. Sex works the same way. Some days your partner might respond to a certain kind of stimulation, some days she won't.

The above chapters on anatomy, neuroscience, and orgasm potential provide a lot of information, but my favorite part about knowing all of this is the way it informs my ability to learn and help my partners learn to experience more and different kinds of pleasure.

Every time you or your partner have a "beyond satisfied" moment, you create a new reference level for the kind of pleasure that is possible. Think of the best meal you've ever had, or the best place you've ever traveled to: with these experiences, your paradigm shifts. You can create innumerable peak sexual experiences across your lifetime, and with each one, your capacity for pleasure grows.

Because of the way our neurology works, sex gets better through having more peak experiences—which for many people means sex gets better with age and exploration.[47] Women in their sixties report having more pleasurable sex than when they were in their twenties.[48]

As you can see illustrated in the graphic that follows, our subjective reference point for "the best sex ever" increases through the lifespan, as long as we continue to grow, learn, and explore. The more pleasurable peak experiences we create with our partners, the more pathways for pleasure are created and strengthened in our brains. Rather than waiting until you're sixty, use sex hacking to accelerate your process of sexual growth and discovery now.

---

47 Peggy Kleinplatz and Dana A. Menard, *Magnificent Sex: Lessons from Extraordinary Lovers* (Milton Park: Routledge, 2020).

48 Shere Hite, *The Hite Report: A Nationwide Study of Female Sexuality* (New York: Macmillan, 1976}.

What we know about sex and who we think we are sexually is not static, but is malleable and open to expansion, if we let it be. As Dr. Pfaus says, "The erotic body map a woman possesses is not etched in stone, but rather is an ongoing process of experience, discovery, and construction which depends on her brain's ability to create optimality between the habits of what she expects and an openness to new experiences."[49]

BEYOND SATISFIED

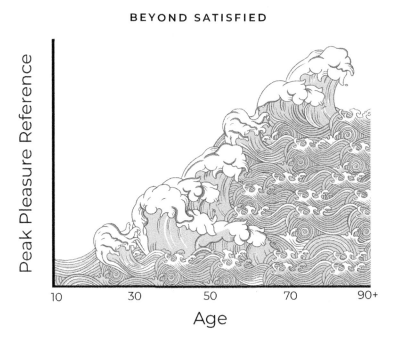

49   James G. Pfaus, Gonzalo R. Quintana, Conall Mac Cionnaith, and Mayte Parada, "The Whole Versus the Sum of Some of the Parts: Toward Resolving the Apparent Controversy of Clitoral Versus Vaginal Orgasms," *Socioaffective Neuroscience and Psychology*, October 25, 2016.

7

Psychological Arousal and Erotic Context

What do you fantasize about? What gets your partner going? Setting the erotic context can be as simple as leaving an erotic novel and a flogger on the bedside table with a note that says, "See you at seven." Or it could be a text sent from the restaurant bathroom that says, "Hey, it's really roomy in here."

Everyone has their own personal turn-ons that make them go crazy (and for better or for worse, a lot of our desires aren't a conscious choice). Sometimes a couple of dirty words will do the trick. Sometimes novelty adds excitement, and a new toy or a new place to fuck can be a special ingredient to elevate the experience.

The sensations we feel during sex are only part of what turns us on and brings us pleasure. The other part is the erotic narratives that play through our minds during sex. Erotic context is the meaning we place on the experience.

Two people can have very different responses to the exact same activity. Take spanking: a smack on the ass could be highly erotic for a partner who wants to play with a fantasy of being a naughty, dirty girl, while another woman could find it super hot to be a goddess worthy of worship, who would never allow a man to bend her over his knee or hit her. The erotic context stems from the relationship your partner has with that activity.

Sometimes our partners need us to help nurture their fantasies in order to lose themselves. *Tell Me What You Want*, by Dr. Justin J. Lehmiller, explores common fantasies like group sex and power dynamics, and it's an excellent resource to learn more about the power of fantasy in our sexual lives.[50]

In the book *A Billion Wicked Thoughts*, authors Sai Gaddam and Ogi Odas analyze search engine data in an attempt to discover what turns women on. Want to know the five cliché characters that seemed most sought after by women? Surgeon, pirate, billionaire, vampire, and werewolf.[51] You don't have to transform yourself into a character to turn your partner on, but the more aspects of yourself you can bring out to play—including your assertive side, your tender side, your geeky side, and all the other parts of you—the richer your experiences can be.

---

50 Justin J. Lehmiller, *Tell Me What You Want: The Science of Sexual Desire and How It Can Help You Improve Your Sex Life* (Boston: Da Capo Lifelong Books, 2018).

51 Sai Gaddam and Ogi Odas, *A Billion Wicked Thoughts: What the Internet Tells Us about Sexual Relationships* (New York: Plume, 2012).

Authenticity Is the New Sexy

So how the fuck can you become more authentic? As I started to deconstruct the techniques and elements of great sex, I connected with sex
researchers who were looking into the same questions. Dr. Zhana and
I developed a model to understand where sexual authenticity comes
from. The Sexual Authenticity model is a simple Venn diagram with
three intersecting components: desires, values, and behaviors.

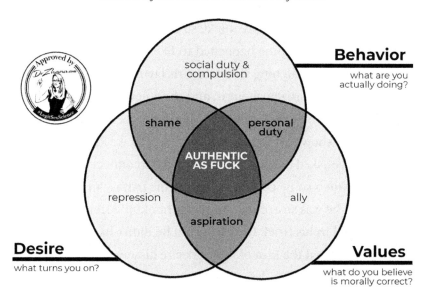

SEXUAL AUTHENTICITY MODEL
Created by Dr. Zhana & Kenneth Play ©2016

When we separate these three elements, we can start to understand where they intersect, where they don't, and what effects that
mix creates in our sex lives.

Desire is defined by what we want and what turns us on physically, mentally, and emotionally. Our wants can range from simple

physical desires—for example, I really like boobs—to complex fantasies. Desire is like appetite: much of it is innate and subconscious, and largely outside of our control. However, some of it can be changed over time with experience and exploration. For instance, most adults learn to like many more types of food than they did as children—though taste buds vary in their genetic expression, we also learn to like different kinds of tastes as our repertoire of possibilities expands. Additionally, we can intentionally learn to feel hungry or not at certain times of day by eating on a specific schedule. Like most things in sexuality, desire is some combination of biology, developmental factors, and conscious and unconscious habits and patterns.

We also don't truly know our desires until we've lived them. A friend of a friend of mine happened to like a rare kind of porn: he was turned on by watching videos of girls farting. He told my friend how much he fantasized about it, and she'd never seen that kind of porn before, so he sent her a clip. My friend checked out the clip, and then she showed it to me—and we realized we knew the girl in the video. We asked the guy if he wanted us to connect him with the girl in the video so he could experience his fantasy in real life. He agreed, and he was so excited...until the hookup. After all the fantasies he'd held in his head, he discovered he didn't like the reality at all; he'd only liked the idea of it. His desire dissolved.

Dr. Justin Lehmiller describes how our psychological turn-ons don't always match up with our physical cravings.[52] It's when we start to experiment with our desires that we can understand them and finally put them in perspective.

---

[52] Justin Lehmiller, *Tell Me What You Want: The Science of Sexual Desire and How It Can Help You Improve Your Sex Life* (Boston: Da Capo Press, 2018).

The second component of our authenticity is our values, which include our sense of good and bad, right and wrong. Our values come from our own internal compass, and they also come from our culture and community.

It's not always easy to identify the beliefs we hold around sex and pinpoint where they come from. In the early days of the internet, before porn was widely available, if a kid found an issue of *Playboy* or an illicit VHS tape, he shared it with his friends. Boys would watch porn and masturbate together, not necessarily because they were interested in masturbating with other boys around, but because there was porn playing. But if they bought into society's myth that anytime men do something sexual around each other, they must be gay, those same kids might look back and think, *That was so gay— was I gay?* (For me, looking back on those memories reminds me I always enjoyed group activities.)

Desires and values can conflict: whatever rules we may try to impose on our sex lives, our sexuality doesn't give a fuck. Think of a gay boy growing up in a conservative Mormon family. His values may dictate that he should find a girl to marry and have a family with, but he desires and is aroused by other men. Depending on to what degree he internalizes the value system he was raised in, he could either suppress his desires to be with men, believing that this is the right thing to do, or he could actively challenge the value system by working through his internalized desires so he can live a more authentic life.

The third component of authenticity is our behavior—what we actually end up acting on. The Mormon boy who secretly lusts after men might allow himself to fantasize about them while he jerks off in the shower, but never acts on his desire with another person. He ends up following his values and acting on what he thinks is right, but because he still has a desire for men, he believes he's bad. On the outskirts of our Venn diagram, where desires, values, and behaviors don't align, we experience shame.

But at the center of the Venn diagram, where desires, values, and behaviors are all connected, we feel authentic as fuck. We're most satisfied when we experience desire, believe it's good, and act on it—or when we don't experience desire, think something is bad, and don't act on it.

Of course, that magical alignment doesn't always happen. You might value monogamy but desire to fuck other people. In that case, you have a choice to make: act on your values, or act on your desires. The guiding principle here should be to maximize pleasure and minimize harm. Only you can know what the best way to do that in your life is.

We face these kinds of complicated choices all the time, and there's no prescriptive way to make these decisions. The gay Mormon boy has to decide whether his faith and community are more valuable to him than his suffering. It might be worth it to him to stay in Utah. Or he could say fuck it to religion, move to New York City, and be gay as fuck. Sexual wellness depends not on always acting on our values or always acting on our desires, but on making conscious choices that feel good to us.

Our desires can also be bounded by a lack of opportunity to fulfill them, or by lack of skill to make them happen. We may want to try something new in bed, and our desire may align with our values, but if we don't have the skills to try a new technique, we may still get stuck in frustration and resentment. Our desire will remain aspirational until we develop the skills to act on it.

Trauma can also fuck up the synergy between our desires, values, and behavior. A woman might have been molested by a family member while she was growing up, but her body still experienced physical pleasure. When she experiences pleasure as an adult, she may trigger the memories of abuse. She may feel pleasure, guilt, and repulsion simultaneously, because those emotions became wired together during the abuse. As a result, she may have an involuntary response to intimacy that doesn't line up with what she actually values. The same thing can happen to men, of course, and is equally as complex (I recommend the book *The Mask of Masculinity* by Lewis Howes as a resource for men on this topic.)[53] We won't go into depth on trauma in this book; a good sex therapist can help navigate the complexity of a traumatic sexual history.

Take the time to examine your value system around sex. Consider what factors shaped those values, whether they came from your family, your religion, your community, or yourself. Understand how important those values are to you. Then get honest about your desires. Think about what you already crave and what you've always wanted to explore. Then take an inventory of your current and past behavior and patterns. By taking the time to understand yourself, you can more consciously choose your behavior. You may even find that as you explore, you'll develop more tastes and expand the center of your own Venn diagram, where desires, values, and behaviors converge. Once you understand yourself, you'll be able to support others in their exploration and bring more curiosity to your partner's unique Venn diagram.

---

53 Lewis Howes, *The Mask of Masculinity: How Men Can Embrace Vulnerability, Create Strong Relationships, and Live Their Fullest Lives* (Pennsylvania: Rodale Books, 2017).

Mining Your Sexual History

Where do our sexual needs and desires come from? The things we crave and require in sex are a result of our sexual conditioning, which is a combination of nature, nurture, and life experiences.

You can think of sexual conditioning in much the same way as physical conditioning. Your innate genes are major factors in what your body is able to do. But if you've never worked out a day in your life, you'll have no idea what your body is capable of. If you've never seen a physical transformation in yourself, you might hold onto a static label like "I'm big boned" that you use to describe your body. Your experiences inform your perception of yourself.

Everyone has active and passive habits based on their experiences and conditioning. If you grew up in a food desert with limited options for healthy eating, and you never learned to cook, you may have poor eating habits that developed passively from what was available and taught to you. You also have habits you've actively cultivated through discipline, like a workout regimen. In our sex lives, we have passive and active habits as well, and we'll discuss that in more depth in the next section.

Another factor that shapes our sexual makeup is our personal histories, which solidify the myths and beliefs we form about our sexual identity and desire. Think of the most significant moments of your sex life:

- When did you discover desire?
- How did you learn about sex?
- Were you ever shamed for your desire? When, and how?
- When did you lose your virginity?

- When was the first time you experienced mind-blowing sex?
- When did you have the worst sex of your life?
- How did each of these moments influence you?

From this sexual history, we can begin to understand the narratives we've formed from these experiences. And fair warning: some of the shit we uncover in this exploration can get dark. Many of us have trauma that affects our story and creates mental or physical blocks in our sex lives.

These blocks can come from our personal experiences, or they can come from the cultural stories we've inherited around sex. For example, it's common for someone who was told that penis-in-vagina intercourse is a sacred experience to build up tremendous hype about this particular sex act, and then they think something is wrong with them when they cannot experience orgasm from this particular activity.

Because most of us live in a sex-negative culture where comprehensive, pleasure-based sexual education is extremely rare, most of us have shame attached to some part of our sexuality. Think of a girl who at five years old discovers that humping her teddy bear brings her pleasure. There's no erotic or sexual narrative to this act at such a young age, but she returns again and again to this humping habit because it feels good. It creates a pleasure-based habit loop. Then one day her grandmother walks in and catches her humping a teddy bear and tells her, "Only dirty girls do that." This belief may not be one the grandmother created herself; she probably grew up in a sex-negative culture and heard the same kinds of remarks from her own mother or grandmother.

In that moment the little girl hears this comment, masturbation transforms from pleasurable to disgusting, and the girl may even start to carry a story that she's a "dirty girl." That story will inform how she thinks about herself and what she wants to explore in sex, with many different possible outcomes. She might become identified with being "dirty" and become kinky later in life, or she might identify as a "good little girl" and repress her pleasure. This single story could take her in a number of different directions, depending on how she incorporates it into her sexuality.

Habit Loops That Rule Our Sex Lives

Neurons that fire together wire together. Each time we practice something, we cause neurons to light up a pathway in our brains, and that pathway becomes stronger and stronger. The more we travel along that path, the easier it gets to travel it. Eventually, it's like when you're driving home from work the same way you do every day—at some point you no longer need to pay conscious attention and you get there without even noticing.

Whether we realize it or not, we passively create habits in each moment, and it can take active effort to undo those habits. What's more, we identify with our habits, and our behavior habits feel like part of us, as if, *That's just me, I'm just like this.* It can feel strange or even a bit inauthentic when we start breaking those ingrained habits. If you're a couch potato and are trying to develop the habit of going to the gym, you have to adopt new behaviors—going to the gym and working out—but you also have to change your identity from couch potato to athlete.

We develop the same grooves around our sexual habits. The more you masturbate in a particular way, the more deeply engrained a particular pathway to orgasm becomes, and our sexual identity forms around it.

Our habits create a fast track to pleasure, and they can put up roadblocks. If you think sex is dirty, you'll spend a lot of time practicing (usually unconsciously) rejecting certain sexual feelings. In the example of the girl with the teddy bear, as soon as she feels the desire to hump something, she might block it: *I'm a good girl; I should never think this way.* Or conversely, she might get turned on when her partner humiliates her and calls her a dirty girl. Her experience and her story shape her access to pleasure.

Through our sexual practices, we also shape how our bodies respond to different kinds of pleasure, both in terms of our mindset and our physical response. Think of your sex life in terms of hardware and software. The "software" includes mindset patterns that are reinforced by your perspective and beliefs about sex. For example, if every time you had sex with your partner, you focused on how you were only doing it to please them, you'd reinforce a thinking pattern that tells you sex is for your partner, not for yourself. Your software can be updated with the techniques we discuss in the next chapter on authenticity. Then there's the "hardware," the physical patterns that develop as a result of your experience, such as the way you masturbate and the kind of touch you most enjoy.

Since the invention of sex tech, women have been able to use vibrators for a specific kind of pleasurable stimulation that can't be directly recreated with fingers or tongues or penises. The more they use a vibrator, the deeper that pathway to pleasure roots in their brains—and some women, unfortunately, end up feeling fucked up about having a dependency on their vibrators.

In reality, their "dependency" is just a habit loop. We become sensitized and desensitized as a result of our habits. Imagine you're used to listening to your headphones at their highest volume. That level becomes your set point. If you want to wean off that level (and preserve your hearing), you have to give your ears time to adjust to a lower volume. When you initially crank the sound down from 100 percent to 50 percent, the new level will seem almost inaudible. But give your body some time, say a couple of weeks, and your ears will adapt to the new set point.

So it is with our sexual habits. We can break our habit loops by turning down the volume on them for a while. We can put the vibrator away or relax the death grip on our penises. When we masturbate in different ways for a couple of weeks, we start to rewire our habit loops, and we can learn new ways of getting pleasure.

That's not to say we shouldn't have our habits and preferences. If I like to put a lot of salt on my food, and my blood pressure is fine, there's no reason for me to force myself to get used to having less salt. It's not killing me, and it tastes good. Similarly, there's nothing wrong with loving the high intensity of a vibrator. Why would sex need to be vibrator-free? As we decide which of our sexual habit loops to keep and which to break, we have to consider what we value and what we want our sex lives to look like.

When we arrive at partnered sex, we bring our own habit loops to the encounter, and our partner brings hers. To create great sex together, we have to know our own desires and pleasures. Then, we ask our partners what they like—or, even hotter, ask them to masturbate for us—so we can each learn each other's habits.

Pleasure Personalities

As someone *Playboy* named the "personal trainer for pussy," I have no problem adapting my style to satisfy my partners. I have Bruce

Lee to thank for my adaptability. Bruce Lee's philosophy around martial arts was to absorb what is useful and discard what is not. He wasn't beholden to any particular tradition, but instead utilized the techniques from each tradition that was most suitable for him, his goals, and his desires. In any given fight, he didn't just stick to a single style; he pulled out the techniques he needed to match his opponent. He was able to stay mindful and bring forward whatever he needed in himself to succeed.

Similarly, when I'm fully engaged with a partner, I become a style bender. I'm able to employ many different techniques—but it goes deeper than that. I'm familiar with a lot of different aspects of my personality and my energy, and I can call on the part of myself my partner craves most.

The upside is that I have a lot of great sex, and my schedule is perpetually full of play dates (seriously, it's a problem sometimes). The downside? I can get caught up playing the chameleon and lose sight of my true colors. Sexual satisfaction comes from more than just pleasing your partner; it comes from knowing yourself and being able to express all parts of yourself to connect with your partner.

From Sheep to Lion

In my own sexual life, I'm often a dom (dominant). I sometimes switch to the role of the submissive, but I mostly play the dominant role. This is a reversal of my adolescent sexual experiences. When I was a kid, I always got "friend zoned" by the girls I was interested in. I made myself harmless and helpful; I was the ultimate nice guy.

Eventually, I realized that was bullshit. The way I portrayed myself on the outside didn't match what I felt inside. I didn't want to just be friends with these girls; I wanted to have sex and a girl-friend. By putting up a "nice guy" act, I was actually being insecure and manipulative. I was being inauthentic, pretending to be sweet, and it was creepy. I worried girls wouldn't like me, so I brought them lunch and let them cry on my shoulder and never let on I liked them.

I started to realize that in order to be myself, I needed to have a spine. When Dave Chappelle accepted the Mark Twain Prize for American Humor, he said, "I'm a sheep, but sometimes I have to act like a lion so I can go back to being a sheep." There's something sexy about a man with principles and values, a man who can't be fucked around with. There are virtues to being a sheep, but I wanted to learn how to become a lion, too. I needed access to both of these sides of myself.

Sex appeal comes from the ability to move fluidly back and forth between all the different parts of yourself. To not get stuck being just the pirate bad boy or the helpful friend. Think of the yin and yang symbol: in a dark swirl of black, there's a dot of white, and vice versa. We can fully inhabit our sheep tendencies without losing our spine. We can fully inhabit the lion without losing our tenderness.

By moving fluidly between these elements in ourselves, we can access the qualities that best complement our partner in the moment. When your partner is soft, you can be strong. The vacillation between these polarities can become a dance between ourselves and our partners. Like in any dance, there may be a leader and a follower, and the roles may switch (I've realized I have a tendency to lead too often, and I sometimes need to chill the fuck out and just follow my partner—I imagine I'm not alone). The goal is not to impress or overpower your partner, but to watch her, communicate with her, and match what she needs in the flow of the moment.

When we have awareness of all those parts within ourselves, and the facility to tap into each of them, we expand our ability to weave an erotic narrative with our partner.

What Is Your Pleasure Personality?

All of us are attracted to different archetypes that we find arousing. The more aware you are of your pleasure personality, the easier it is to find a partner who wants what you have to offer—or to work on expressing parts of yourself you're less familiar with. If, for example, your partner is turned on by domination, but you're the empathic hippie type, you may have to dig deep to access the more assertive director in you. Or you might realize you'll fit better with a type that's more aligned to your own. The more aware you are of your sexual style, the better you'll be able to complement (or contrast!) your partner's type.

By blending psychology research on personality with pop-culture archetypes, I've identified five "pleasure personalities" that can help you reflect on your own traits and understand how women view your type. See if you can pick out your own type from these descriptions, and you'll understand your natural strengths and the areas you can work on to round out your appeal. You can use your self-awareness to work on your weak areas and win a broader variety of people over, or you can lean into your strengths and go after those who are compatible with your type.

I developed a quiz to help you find out which pleasure personality fits you best. However, it's not an exhaustive list. If you want even more information, check out Dr. Nan Wise's book *Why Good Sex Matters*,[54] Jaiya's five erotic blueprints (which can be found on her website, missjaiya.com), and Jack Morin's *The Erotic Mind*.[55] All of these people's work inspired me greatly while I was creating this. Use the QR code that follows to take the quiz online, and figure out what your pleasure personality is.

The Director

You're a natural leader and a confident dom who's equally at home in a dungeon or a boardroom. You command attention in life and in bed. You understand how to create the perfect sexual scene, and your erotic storytelling abilities are unparalleled.

- **Who you appeal to most:** Submissive women love you, and those who are used to being in charge and leap at the chance to surrender control might love you even more. Women who are looking for a relationship might find you inflexible and stubborn, and sensitive women who need a gentle touch may steer clear.

- **Your secret pain:** Some women love your commandeering style, but some women fear it. In our current culture, male

---

54 Nan Wise, *Why Good Sex Matters: Understanding the Neuroscience of Pleasure for a Smarter, Happier, and More Purpose-Filled Life* (New York: Houghton Mifflin Harcourt, 2020).

55 Jack Morin, *The Erotic Mind: Unlocking the Inner Sources of Passion and Fulfillment* (New York: Harper Perennial, 2012).

sexual dominance can easily be perceived as toxic. If you're sensitive to the times, you may be uncomfortable fully expressing yourself erotically. You may not be able to let go to receive or let your partner take the reins.

- **How you can level up:** Work on your communication skills and kink negotiation skills and learn to calibrate to your partner in order to make your dominance even sweeter. Develop your aftercare game to complement the intensity of your sexual play.

- **Examples:** Erik from *True Blood*, Lucifer Morningstar from *Lucifer*, Professor Marston from *Professor Marston and the Wonder Women*, Don Draper from *Mad Men*, Winston Duke from *Black Panther*

The Athlete

You can pick your partner up and carry her over your shoulder. You have excellent endurance, and you fuck like a beast. Your body is beautiful and you know just how to move it; your energy is primal; and the combination is delicious to most women.

- **Who you appeal to most:** Women with a high sex drive will feel they've met their match with you. Physically strong, intimidating women will delight in feeling you can handle them with ease. Women who want slow, sensual sex may feel disconnected from you, and women who prefer a lot of negotiation may be put off by your quick tactics.

- Your secret pain: You're skilled at intense sex, and you are skilled at fucking hard and deep, but while your style brings some women pleasure, it can bring other women pain. Fucking her like she's a CrossFit workout can get old quickly. As a result, women's pleasure can seem confusing, and you wonder why you get ghosted after porn-star-level sex that seemed to go great.

- How you can level up: Expand your skillset with foreplay so you can get your partner fully warmed up for your intensity. Stretch yourself to communicate more with your partner in order to create a deeper emotional connection during sex, and your awesome talents will have the context they need to fully shine.

- Examples: The Rock, Jason Momoa, Channing Tatum as *Magic Mike*, Idris Elba, Kumail Nanjiani

The Technician

The technician has the game of pleasure down to a science. You collect techniques that give you a cutting edge, you use biomechanics to your advantage, and you love to improvise with new positions to give your partner pleasure she's never felt before.

- Who you appeal to most: Self-aware women who know their own bodies and their power well will feel respected and understood by you. Intellectuals will love to hear the science behind your skill. Women who are looking for an emotional connection may find you hard to relate to, and women who are kinky or animalistic may be frustrated by the time you take on the technicalities you love. And of course, you're a hit with the Comic-Con crowd.

- **Your secret pain:** You can come off as clinical or mechanical and miss out on showing partners your sensual side. You know all the right moves, but you might not always be clear on the best context in which to apply them. You might have adopted the Technician style because you don't have the sharpest sense of social cues, so you've made up for it in the technical aspects where you know you can shine.

- **How you can level up:** You're like a technically skilled dancer who's missing the heart of the dance. Learn to express your feelings and get more vulnerable with your heart. Remember that while strong technique is one element of sex, there are presentation values that elevate your partner's experience too. Setting the mood, smelling good, and looking your best can all go a long way towards orchestrating better sex. No one cares how well you can finger a G-spot if you have dirty fingernails and bad breath.

- **Examples:** Bruce Banner, Trevor Noah, Sean Connery as *James Bond*, The Flash, Iron Man

The Romantic

A classic Casanova, you know how to use romantic gestures and sweet words to make your lover's body melt. You're thoughtful and considerate, and you pay attention to your partner's prefer-ences in detail. You're quick to say what your partner is longing to hear. You can rescue your partner when she's in a bad mood, and you know how to shift her mind to sex no matter how stressed out she is.

- **Who you appeal to most:** Die-hard romantics are your prime market, but creative, artistic, and mystical types also love the ease of connection they have with you. Athletes and intellectuals may need proof that you're not just wooing them to get an ego boost.

- **Your secret pain:** You're baffled when your partner wants to be treated like a princess in real life but wants to be a dirty slut in bed. You sometimes come off as a player or a pick-up artist, and while you easily fulfill your partner's needs, you struggle to be direct about your own.

- **How you can level up:** Access your primal side and rough up your sexual style a little bit. Add some kink techniques to your sexual skillset, including good negotiation with healthy boundaries, and you'll be able to bring a wider variety of flavors out for your lover to swoon over.

- **Examples:** Ryan Gosling in *The Notebook*, Leonardo DiCaprio in *Titanic*, Wesley from *The Princess Bride*, John Cho, Enrique Iglesias

The Empath

The empath's superpower is that you are incredibly present. You're comfortable with your emotions as well as your partner's, and your patient and gentle nature helps your partners feel safe around you. Women tend to soften in your presence. You know how to transform sexual energy into a mystical experience.

- **Who you appeal to most:** Spiritual types as well as artists and free spirits who meet you will feel they've finally found a man who shares their values. Romantics can get quickly attached to your vulnerability. Intellectuals and athletes may feel bored by your slow, quiet way of being. Kinky girls will find your love and light unbearable.

- **Your secret pain:** Some people mistake your kindness for weakness or expect you to be more aggressive than you naturally are. You're a master of foreplay, but your sensual skills may not translate into electric sex. In the quest for spiritual connection, you may have lost your groundedness and might even come off as self-involved. You secretly struggle to develop an authentic interpersonal connection with the woman in front of you; be willing to see her and yourself as you both are.

- **How you can level up:** Add some spicy flavors to your sweetness. You live in your body—so learn to operate your inner animal! You can access the degree of trust and surrender you like to reach with your partner through bondage play—learn some technical skills, and when your partner is tied up your emotional connection will especially shine.

- **Examples:** Young Professor X, Russell Brand, Neo from *The Matrix*, David Bowie, J.P. Sears

Style-bending

The more flexibility you have in your style, and the more access you have to the different types in yourself, the more different types of partners you'll fit with. If you're entrenched in one particular type, try on a different style to expand your self-expression.

Like the other sexual habit loops we learned about in this chapter, your style is a collection of the habit patterns you're used to acting in—but there's nothing keeping you from expressing other aspects of yourself. It's okay to be awkward and clumsy when you're trying on a new style; awkwardness is part of the process of breaking an old habit to learn something new.

Coaching and mentorship can help you access new facets of your personality. If you want to get fit, it helps to hang out with fit people to experience their habits. If you want to be more of an Empath, hang out with spiritual people. If you want to be a Technician, look for the rope bondage experts.

As you expand your personal expression, you can become more well-rounded and capable as a partner. The more you explore your own styles, the more you'll learn how to accurately read your partner's signs and tailor your approach to fit the moment for the most pleasurable experience possible. Your cognitive and emotional flexibility will make you a master at juggling your partner's contradictory desires.

But don't seek out a new style only at the request of a partner. Follow what feels good to you and helps you build a fuller, more authentic sense of self. Then seek out partners who are compatible with your style—and who find you delicious.

When you take the time to examine your values and desires, you can find the people who match what you want and what you have to give.

Sex Market Fit

The game of dating is in part about finding the right "market fit." The more you invest in yourself, and build your skillset around what you most desire, the more attractive you'll be in the market of that desire.

Firstly, you have to know which dating market is available to you. For example, if you live in a more conservative, religious culture, the choices are quite limited. But, if you happen to live in a more progressive, liberal part of the world, you have far more options than most people realize. For instance, in terms of relationship style, monogamy is definitely not the only option. You can figure out how to live a sexually adventurous life without ruining sex and commitment. But you'll need to find a partner who wants the same. It's a really good idea to figure out what you want, so that you can look for partners who match your desires. Scan the QR code that follows to check out Dr. Zhana's open relationship course, Open Smarter, to figure out which relationship type is right for you.

In the end, authenticity is about loving yourself, expressing yourself, and working with what your mama gave you. If you have a micropenis, you probably won't have much luck going after size queens (unless you're interested in investing in a giant strap-on). But there are people out there who value micropenises, or who are attracted to men but don't enjoy penetration. If you don't go after that market, you end up rejecting on accident the people who would be most interested in what you have to offer.

If you want to fuck a supermodel, ask yourself: Am I the kind of person a supermodel would date? Am I in the market where supermodels hang out? You're not entitled to any particular market or any particular person's attention. But you can cultivate the attributes and skillsets that are attractive to the type of person you want to be with, as long as you are true to yourself. You can work with what you've got and find the market with the highest odds of making a match.

The worst thing you can do is to enter into a perpetual penis-measuring contest with the world. Rather than measuring yourself against other people, it's far more useful if you measure yourself against you. Am I on the way to becoming the best version of myself? Am I better than I was yesterday, last week, last year?

On my own journey to self-acceptance, I came to understand that I was rejecting myself in order to spare myself rejection from others. When I chose to stop cockblocking myself, and uncovered my desires, I started to understand myself more authentically. I'd been chasing the "best version" of myself that society told me I should be: a rich guy with a big cock. When I entered the sex-positive community, I was able to let go of that. I became the best version of myself that I chose to be—the version of myself that was aligned with my values. And I found that the more authentic I was around potential partners, the more desirable I became.

Self-development is one of the most attractive qualities you can display to your partner. There's nothing like the feeling of earning true respect and admiration from your lover in the bedroom and in life—you can't fake that shit! Being good, kind, and capable is the best way to satisfy your partner.

But to make yourself irresistible, you'll also need to fuck people well. Even if you can attract a great partner, you'll still need great sexual skills to give value to your partner and keep her coming back to bed. That's why we devote Part Three to the techniques for great sex.

PART III

Sex Hacking Techniques

8

Hack Your Sexual Performance

B efore we get into some of the more hard-core sexual skills, I want to speak about sexual performance. The words "sexual performance" have gotten a bad rap in recent years, because we associate them with porn stars performing for the camera. We think that sexual performance is about faking it, trying to be someone you're not, or showing up to the bedroom as an act of proving yourself. In this formulation, you're performing sex for some reason that might not be the best reason. Porn stars are performing for clicks and popularity, bros are performing for their own ego, and insecure guys are performing to soothe a nagging, self-critical sense of inadequacy. We therefore associate performance with these negative impulses.

But you can perform to be your best self like an athlete would in a game. You can perform out of love for your lover, or out of the desire to share the most pleasure possible. You can perform like an artist trying to express yourself most astutely. You can perform to be immersed in flow and commune with something larger than yourself. I want to reclaim the word "performance," extracting it from its common associations and making it more like how we think of athletic performance.

After spending a decade and a half as a personal trainer who taught complex movement, body awareness, and how to change and transform people's fitness lives, I'm aware of just how much people can grow when it comes to using their bodies. But for some reason, as a culture, we don't apply this same mindset to sex.

It is widely known in athletics that even people with raw talent need training. The story of David and Goliath is well known for a reason: people understand that a talented but less-gifted competitor can beat an untrained brute when it comes to athletics and fighting. A well-timed triangle chokehold is mightier than any punch.

In the domain of professional sports, we've developed whole protocols and exercise science programs aimed to continuously improve athletic performance. And because of it, we've broken more world records in recent years than ever before. We have special shoes, performance-enhancing supplements, and personal trainers at gyms on every block. We could do this exact same thing for sex, but because it's taboo, we view it as forbidden knowledge.

All the sex myths I mentioned earlier in the book contribute to creating a culture in which we can barely talk about sex, let alone develop sophisticated protocols for improvement. I'm committed to changing this. I want sex to be a domain where we can explore our human potential!

We use sports to explore ourselves and engage in a process of self-mastery. We could do this with sex, too. We should be devoting just as much attention and as many resources to sex as we do to athletics. After all, if you asked most people what their top priorities in life are, sex would be in most people's top five.

Having said all that, here are the techniques of sex. As you're reading them, try to think about mastering them as you would a new sport, or leveling up your athletic performance. Don't expect perfection on the first attempt, and try not to link your entire sense of self-esteem to your performance. Instead, look at this as a process of growth and skill acquisition.

If something isn't working, think of it as an opportunity to learn more. If you get confused at any point, my video course, Sex Hacker Pro, is out there to help you. Use the QR code that follows to access a special discount just for readers!

I did the best I could do in this book to describe things in words and pictures. However, videos are infinitely more informative when they include real demos, just like a personal trainer would show you how to squat instead of describing how to squat. The course covers significantly more than I could cover in this book, with over seventy videos, twelve hours of content, and nine life-changing modules. The take-home lesson is: there's usually an answer, and the answer isn't usually about anyone being broken or fundamentally flawed. Most people are doing just fine; they just need a little education and practice! And unlike helping people lose weight, which takes forever, sexual skills can be learned pretty fast and are immediately pleasurable to master.

Building Body Awareness

Some of the same things that dictate natural prowess in sports apply directly to sex. We all have different levels of hand–eye coordination, and dexterity of movement comes more easily to some people than to others. I saw this very clearly when I was teaching a squirting workshop, walking up to different couples and showing people how to move their hands and bodies. Some people took to physical direction very quickly, while others needed practice to get the right movements and positioning down. This comes down to different levels of body awareness.

In order to do any movement well, there are three capabilities we need. The first is *proprioception*, which is our ability to perceive or be aware of the position and movement of our body in space. In terms of dancing, this is the ability to execute dance moves accurately—we can move our feet without looking at them, for instance.

You can gauge your proprioception with a simple test: close your eyes and touch your index finger to your nose. This is a demonstration of your ability to orient where your body is in three-dimensional space.

You also need *kinesthetic awareness*, which is your ability to interact with the environment and the people in it. A dancer needs a lot of kinesthetic awareness to dance with another person, continuously monitoring the other's movements and responding to them in rhythm. The reason many women intuitively feel that a man who can dance well can also fuck well is because it demonstrates this skill. Kinesthetic awareness allows you to move harmoniously, synchronized with your partner's movements.

The third element we need for body awareness is *interoception*, or the ability to feel sensations inside your body. This is part of what martial arts traditions call "inner kung fu." This is the most underrated sexual skill we have, so I'm going into full-on sex nerd mode to explain this. There are many reasons why interoception matters, and all of them are important.

Firstly, if we can't feel our own bodies, it's very hard to experience the full range of pleasure that is possible for us, as we discussed previously in the Chapter Six section "Letting Your Body Guide You." But secondly, if you can't feel your own sensations, it's very hard to sense your lover's sensations and emotional state. The reasons for this lie in a part of our brain that relates to movement and senses the motivations for movement. In this part of our motor cortex, we have specialized neurons called "mirror neurons."

My colleague Chelsey Fasano explained that in neuroscience studies where they tracked the firing of these neurons, they found that these specialized neurons fired not only when we ourselves move in a certain way, but also when another person moves in that same way. In other words, these special neurons do not differentiate between ourselves and others—they simply indicate movement.

Neuroscientists believe this was an evolutionary adaptation to help us predict and understand others, in order to avoid threat and engage in pro-social behavior. The long and short of it is: we feel what other people feel, and we feel the likely motivations behind their movements in our own body as if they were our own.

One of the best ways to sense anyone else's feelings and desires is through our own body. As Om Rupani, a teacher of mine, says, "The key to feeling your woman is feeling yourself." This is probably why Floyd Mayweather can avoid being punched by the best fighters in the world and predict his opponent's behavior in a way that verges on magical. He's practiced tapping into this part of his nervous system. He can sense when his opponent is tired, afraid, or losing confidence, and that's the moment he chooses to strike.

You might think this is a foreign concept, but most of us have had this feeling while watching a movie! Think of a time where you were super engrossed in the plot of a movie and found yourself laughing and crying along with the actors. This is because you've directed your entire attention to the actor in the film, and your mirror neuron system causes you to feel the same emotions the actor is displaying.

There's an extra element here beyond just feeling things, as well; you need to develop a framework to make sense of the feelings to put them in context. Because you've been following the character in the movie you're watching and have a sense for the context in which their emotions occur, you can interpret the sensations in your body in light of the plot.

It's the same with your lover. You have to develop a context for the feelings you are picking up on. To be a good lover, you have to be able to interpret erotic cues within a framework of possibilities. This is why the more you understand how your lover interprets the sensations they are experiencing, the better you can predict what they are feeling. You could say that, in a sense, people who are great at reading others are good at predicting not only how other people are feeling, but how that person interprets those feelings.

A little-known fact about Bruce Lee is that in addition to his famous talents, he was a cha-cha dance champion in Hong Kong. I think it's likely that he was a great martial artist, dancer, and filmmaker because he had the combination of proprioception (executing dance moves and fighting skills), kinesthetic awareness (flowing with his dance partner or fighting an opponent), and interoception (using the data from his own body to predict the emotions and motivations of other dancers and fighters).

9

Foreplay

The Necessary, Often Missing Ingredient

I *don't mean to brag with this next story*. Really. I just want to show you how awesome sex can be when you pay attention to all of the elements of the experience and get into a flow with a partner. Because great sex isn't just about the sex acts themselves—the actions are just the mechanics. Great sex is an erotic art form that incorporates all the senses, blends them with narrative and unexpected pleasures, and can deliver pleasure your partner has never been able to experience on her own. That's the art and science of sex. Great sex leaves us gasping for air. When someone can touch you better than you touch yourself, it's fucking mind-blowing.

When we host events at Hacienda Villa, our sex-positive community, we always make sure they're great parties first and foremost,
and sex is secondary. We curate art on the walls and performers in
open spaces, and we serve delicious food. Scan the QR code that follows to check out everything Hacienda has to offer, from awesome
sex education events of all kinds to legendary sex parties.

At one of these epic sex parties, I was cooking for our hundred
guests when I was approached by a woman and her friend who had
questions about squirting. The woman was reserved and polite, and
something about her demeanor made me very curious about her.
She was asking questions like a valedictorian, but here she was at a
sex party.

I asked if she'd ever been to a party like ours, and she said she'd
only been to swingers' parties where there were cocktails and a
mattress in the middle of the room and a lot of pressure for people to fuck. She said she liked that this party's atmosphere was so

intentional, focused around art and an enjoyable experience, not just sex. She was having fun hanging out with people.

On a whim, I said, "I know this is a little sudden, but I'd love to make out with you for five minutes before I get back to cooking." She seemed stunned for a moment, and then she said, "That sounds good."

Within a few seconds of kissing her, I realized she was super sensitive and responsive; kissing her was like driving a Ferrari. In the moment we started some negotiations. "Can I touch you and caress you a little bit more?" I asked, and she said yes. "Can I count on you to let me know if you don't like anything?" She said yes. After caressing her for a little while, I put my hand on her throat. She moaned. "Are you kinky? Do you enjoy being submissive?" I asked, and she said yes. When it was time to go back to cooking, I made the separation a game. I told her she needed to sit and wait while I cooked, and no one was allowed to touch her while I was away.

Every moment I could break away from cooking, I told her what I wanted next. "I want to spank you. I want to drizzle hot oil on you. I want you to close your eyes while I massage you." I'd play with her for a few minutes at a time and then turn back to the stove to make sure I didn't burn the potatoes. It was a built-in distraction that heightened the tension.

I noticed that every time I started talking to her to negotiate, she came out of the experience. She was the appropriate valedictorian again. I realized the real game was to keep her in a submissive head-space. After I learned that she had some experience with kink, we stopped and took our time to negotiate the kink we wanted to do together, so we could stay in the game. When the cooking was done, we transitioned out of the kitchen and into the main room to play with more toys.

I tied her up, spanked her, and went down on her, and she was super orgasmic from the get-go. It was like goddamn Christmas. If she got distracted by the party, I told her to pay attention to the sensation I was creating. I made a game out of orgasm denial and told her she wasn't allowed to cum until I let her. I was able to calibrate quickly without conscious effort, just by noticing her response to different kinds of pressure and speed. I felt like fucking Bruce Lee. That night at Hacienda Villa, I realized I could employ those skills without being consciously aware of them. I'd entered the flow state.

Our scene got so hot and beautiful that everyone in the room stopped fucking to watch. We weren't trying to put on a show; we were just so engaged with each other that we magnetized all the attention to us. The praise people gave me afterward actually made me feel a little embarrassed. It wasn't the recognition I wanted; the real reward for me was being able to access the flow state and create a peak experience for my partner and me.

Flow state comes from practicing your skills so much that you stop thinking about how to do something and just do the right thing at the right moment—which is why it's so important to get hands-on experience with everything you're learning in this book. But the other aspect of flow state, and the art of sex, is being able to incorporate sensual details from your environment and respond to subtle feedback from your partner.

As I mentioned previously, you don't go to a Michelin-starred restaurant just to satiate your hunger; you can do that with a hot dog. You go to an upscale restaurant to have an incredible experience. From the atmosphere, to the sound of food cooking and glasses clinking, to the colors and smells of the food on your plate, to the nuanced and surprising tastes, a great chef curates every element to amaze his guests. Similarly, you can curate each element of a sexual experience, from the environment, to the toys, to the pace of play, to please and delight your partner.

Designer Foreplay

Everyone has their own specific preferences for what turns them on and gets them in the mood. For some people, a massage helps get their system in a relaxed state for arousal; for others, the best foreplay is getting bent over and slapped on the ass. Like we learned in Chapter One, the important function of foreplay is to help your partner feel safe enough and excited enough to get aroused. Part of establishing safety is negotiating with your partner, which we discussed in Chapter Four.

Just like the warmup for a workout, foreplay prepares both partners psychologically and physically for sex. To get your partner in the right headspace, it's important to set the mood that's right for the individual.

Setting the Scene for Sex

For many people, setting the right mood means cleaning your space, changing the sheets, playing music they like, and making sure the temperature is comfortable and the lighting is soft—all of these tools become part of the foreplay before foreplay begins.

Of course, some people are turned on by a dirty bathroom in a seedy bar. Or a sterile dungeon full of uncomfortable instruments. Most people relax better in a comfortable environment where they feel cared and provided for. There's a reason why candles and bubble bath products sell so well!

Attention is a finite resource, and if your partner is worrying about whether she has what she needs at your place, or whether she can trust you to care for her well-being during sex, she won't be able to pay as much attention to her body. Be a good host: keep tampons in your bathroom and put out extra towels on the rack. Clean your room and make your bed. This includes making sure you have a relatively fresh pair of sheets on the bed. You don't have to go full-on OCD, but basic cleanliness and tidiness go a long way, as well as having a sense of manners. Ask your partner if she wants a glass of water or wants to use the restroom before you start.

Paying attention to your environment, clothes, and other aesthetic elements is one of the best ways to communicate your mating value to women. Women don't like to hear how great you are; they want to *see* how great you are. If you need help in this department, read Chapter Thirteen, "Styling and Profilin'," of *Mate* by Tucker Max and Geoffrey Miller PhD.[56] If you take care of all the basics by making sure your partner has everything she needs, you can help her shift her focus to pleasure.

From Make Out to Mating

Foreplay is a great opportunity to get a feel for what your partner likes and what they're ready for. Pay attention to how they kiss. Do they start with small pecks or an open mouth? Do they use a little tongue or a lot? Kiss them back the way they kiss you. If they're giving you pecks, they're not going to welcome a tentacle-porn kiss, so

---

56   Tucker Max and Geoffrey Miller, *Mate: Become the Man Women Want* (New York: Little, Brown and Company, 2015).

don't shove your tongue down their throat unless they're putting all of their tongue in your mouth.

From a mating science perspective, kissing is one of the first stages where we start to evaluate—mostly unconsciously—whether our partner is a worthy candidate for sex. We're paying attention not just to what their body feels like but to how responsive they are to us and our needs. When our partner demonstrates care and attention towards us, it's easier to get a sense of safety and to relax into sex.

So, definitely don't go in with your mouth open unless you already know the person and know this is what she likes! Like everything about sex, it is better if you tease her until her body and verbal cues (both words and sounds) invite you deeper. Start with regular kissing, and slowly get deeper as she opens her mouth to be kissed more deeply. Just because she wants your tongue deep in her mouth at one point doesn't mean you should spend the entire make out like that. It's the mixture between types of kisses and the dance between deep and shallow that usually makes for the best make outs. Like music, you want to dance through a symphony of different notes—high, medium, and low—and different rhythms, to create the best experience.

The most important thing to keep in mind when you are kissing someone with tongue is to keep your tongue relatively soft, even if it is in your partner's mouth. No one likes to be jabbed with a pointy tongue. There's an art to keeping lip and tongue soft while they are active.

Which kind of tongue works best depends on who you are kissing. Some women like you to really penetrate their mouths, others prefer to meet in the middle, and others will want to put their tongue in your mouth. Wherever it is you meet with the tongues, a good way of doing things is to massage her tongue with yours gently. Then, end by taking your tongue back and transitioning into a regular kiss, so she experiences some of your lips, too.

If you are feeling experimental and it seems like she'd be into it, you can also get her tongue in your mouth and suck on it, which can feel really good, or let her suck on yours. And if she's really into sucking cock, having your tongue super deep in her mouth and massaging her tongue while it's more in the back of her mouth can mimic the sensation of cock sucking. However, this is not for all women, so use her nonverbal and verbal feedback to figure out if what you are doing is working.

While you are kissing her, caress and touch her. Touch her hair, face, and neck. Put support on the back of her head or nape of her neck. Pulling her hair can feel nice if it's done right. Grab a big handful and squeeze, rather than pulling her head backwards—the more hair in your hand, the less likely it is to actually hurt her. It will feel like more of a firm pressure against her scalp, which displays competence and assertiveness, while displaying desire.

The important concept here is to pace things. If you are caressing her and she is not caressing you back, maybe back off a little, even kissing her more gently until she comes your way. When she's into it, she will likely start doing the same things to you. Also, don't forget about eye gazing—staring deeply into each other's eyes creates tons of intimacy and lets her know you are truly present with her. This is also a great time to slip in an artful compliment. Something genuine about how she looks, tastes, or feels, like, "Kissing you is so delicious."

But what do you do if things are just super off, and you can't pick up on her signals? If it feels like you two are really out of sync you can try this: tell her you want to play a game to get to know how she likes to kiss. Position yourself in a way where you are beneath her or on her level, with her either straddling you, on top of you while you lie beneath her, or somehow come down to her level if you're taller. Then, tell her you are going to follow her lead completely while she kisses you. Let her take the reins and do your best to follow her rhythm and movements. If she kisses you with her mouth closed, do it back, and whatever pace she sets, follow so you can learn her movements. She will usually kiss you the way she wants to be kissed, and this is the way you can learn most easily.

Most importantly, women smell your breath and taste your mouth to see if you are healthy and make sexual decisions based on how you smell. This is an evolutionary adaptation to find mates who are fit and have good genes, so keep up your oral hygiene![57] You can get everything else right, but if your oral hygiene game is weak and your breath smells like trash on Thursday, you lose the whole game!

And finally, don't forget that kissing can be just for kissing's sake! It is an event unto itself. Don't just use it as a way to get to the next base. Really enjoy and savor the experience. Linger there and focus on it. Make it an art. One of my lovers even had an orgasm once just from me kissing her. While this isn't super common, it just demonstrates how amazing kissing can be when you really give it time and let the erotic charge build.

---

57   If you happen to be in Brooklyn, my dentist and oral surgeon, Dr. Konstantin Rubinov, is the sexiest dentist in the city. Look him up at WilliamsburgDentalArts.com/provider/Konstantin-rubinov-dmd-ficoi.

Undressing

In the early stages of foreplay, we're also paying attention to how competent our partner is. It's important to learn to pop a bra, because clumsiness will pull her out of the moment during the important early stages when she's still assessing you. Fumbling with a bra is easily forgivable, of course, but the better you get at it, the more you can demonstrate overall competence.

Undressing is an opportunity to get a little more physical with her body and show her you know what you're doing. If you want to push her up against the wall before taking her shirt off, think of the biomechanics involved: she could bang her head on the wall and turn a sexy moment into a painful one. Put your hand on the back of her head as you push her against the wall, and your arm will hit the wall rather than her head. She gets the same sense of impact, but it comes with the care and softness of your hand. Then you can rip her pants off.

As you take off your partner's clothes, you can infuse the moment with different kinds of energy. There's the classic lustful undressing, for example, where you and your date walk into a room and can't keep your hands off each other, so you rip each other's clothes off and throw them everywhere. (Don't lose her fucking underwear—losing track of her clothes shows you don't care. I keep a basket by the bed to toss smaller items in.)

You can also play with kinky versions of undressing: you can command your partner to strip off items one at a time and fold them neatly, and then point to the spot where you'd like her to set them. If she has long hair, you can make her sit still in front of you while you pull it up and tie it the way you like it.

As you take off your partner's clothes, you can get a sense of the kinds of narratives that turn her on. Get a little theatrical and explore the kinds of roles and characters you both find sexy.

Grounding Touch

In the beginning, use firm, steady touches to help your partner ground her attention. Grounding touches with firm pressure help to relax the nervous system—think of the effect a gravity blanket has on helping you feel your body. Place your hand on your partner, and don't move it. Take a breath, get into your own body, and then begin to slowly move your hands to explore her back, shoulders, neck, and hands. If you keep taking deep breaths, you'll not only ground yourself, but you'll likely entrain your partner's breathing cycle to synchronize with yours. You want to be calm and steady so she can be calm and steady, which allows us to tap into the parasympathetic nervous system, as we discussed earlier. Plus, there's something really sexy about taking your time and demonstrating control.

Before I even touch my partner's vulva with my hand, one of my favorite techniques is to press the softest part of my thigh against her vulva. I vary the amount of pressure, starting light and giving more pressure as I kiss and caress more intensely. If she's ever humped a pillow or a teddy bear, she knows what's up.

In the kinky version of this technique, I hold my partner by the neck, look her in the eye, and in a sexy, forceful tone I say, "I want you to grind your pussy on my leg." If she's familiar with the sub role, she'll respond, "Yes, sir." God, it's so hot.

As she becomes more responsive to touch, you can begin to tease more sensitive body parts. Caress her vulva with your fingertip to create anticipation. Anticipating the next subtle touch is like activating her spidey senses. Think of this part of the encounter as the time to build craving. A psychological thriller wouldn't be thrilling without the foreshadowing! Wondering what comes next changes our experience of the event when it finally does come.

As you try new types of touch, pay attention to whether she moves away from you with hesitation or towards you with yearning. If you're unsure, ask her, "Does this feel good or bad?" If you give your partner options to pick from, like a yes or a no, you'll make it simple for her to give you feedback. You can also ask questions to calibrate: "Do you want it softer or a little harder?" Make a mental map of the parts of your partner's body that incite pleasure.

I wait to advance until my partner is engaging more actively rather than passively. If she's still kissing me politely back at first, I keep going slow until she's *really* kissing me back. I wait to touch her nipple until her nipple is erect and ready to be touched. I tease around her pussy until she squirms around a little bit, trying to move her pussy closer to my hand.

Breast Play

I love breasts, and I love to give my partner a breast massage as we're warming up. Most women dislike having their nipples tweaked right away, or having their breasts grabbed and honked like a teenage boy would. Instead, start by caressing along your partner's bra line, across her ribs, up her sternum, and around the sides of her breasts. Massage the entire breast with a firm touch to give a sense of compression.

When your partner's nipples are erect and you're ready to touch them, you can move in to squeeze her nipples between your fingers while still giving compression with the rest of your hand. Nipple sensitivity varies a lot in women, so pay attention to her feedback and ask how she likes to be touched.

Try sucking on her nipple, around and beneath the areola. Stimulation of the nipples creates peripheral oxytocin release, and it takes time—at least a few minutes—to feel really good. This oxytocin release creates contractions in the uterus and vagina. In the brain, the nipples are represented in a region of the somato-sensory cortex that is a neighbor to the clitoris and vagina. When you play with her nipples for extended periods of time, the increase in stimulation can cause her to have strong sensations of genital arousal, as well as a serious increase in lubrication. Nipple play is an amazing sex hack to get her clitoris fully engorged and begging to be touched. Think about how much more amazing it feels to be touched when you are fully erect, rather than someone trying to stimulate your soft penis. You want to get her clit fully engorged before you ever touch it. Breast play and kissing are amazing ways to do this.

Pussy Tease

As your partner warms up, pay attention to how her pussy changes as it becomes engorged. You can mix techniques to create a variety of sensations. Give her a grounding touch with your whole palm covering her vulva, using some pressure and a little movement. I call this a "pussy hug." It helps bring a calming sensation to her genitals without creating stimulation right away.

When your partner is ready for more stimulation give light strokes around her labia. Lick your fingers so your saliva lubricates them; otherwise your dry skin might be too much friction too early. Be intentional rather than shy about your teasing.

Because the clit is incredibly sensitive, it usually doesn't like to be touched directly right away. You can tease the clit by pinching the outer lips of her labia around your partner's clit and hood to make a sandwich. Use your fingers to lightly squeeze and massage the layers of tissue, and you'll be stimulating her clit at the same time.

Find Your Stride

We're all sensitive in the beginning of sex, and we're more easily turned off early on in sex. That's why it usually doesn't work to go straight for the nipples or the vagina; if these body parts aren't warmed up, the body's response is one of aversion rather than pleasure.

As we get more aroused, our subjective perception of the same actions changes greatly, and what once felt like too much feels just right. During foreplay, you and your partner are testing the waters, and that process takes different amounts of time for different people.

Gauge your pace based on how your partner is reciprocating. Learn to dance with your partner. Pay attention to her responses and pay attention to your own feelings. Smell her, caress her, and focus on what those sensations feel like. The more sensitive you can become to both of you, the better the dance can be, and the better you'll be able to dial in the right pace. If things feel awkward or you sense your partner is pushing back, slow down. If the energy is dying, move a little faster to build the heat back up.

Add a Little Drama

Once my partner is comfortable, I like to test the waters with a little power play and see how she responds. I might show a little dominance by asking her to put her hands behind her back. I run my fingers through her hair and pull it back a little when I kiss her. I never reach out to choke a partner right away, but I caress her neck with my hand over her throat without any pressure to see if she gives a positive or negative response. Not every guy needs to be dominant or kinky, and not every girl likes this, but it is a popular archetype. This is why *Fifty Shades of Grey* sold so many copies.

If I get a positive response with these gestures, I move forward with more of that kind of touch. If she tells me she doesn't like it, I back off. If she gives no response at all, or I'm unsure what her signals mean, I ask whether she likes that kind of touch. I only use her positive signal as feedback to move forward with that type of touch, not as license to do whatever kinky thing I want. Just because she likes her neck to be caressed doesn't mean she wants me to slap her face. But through initiating small gestures and getting feedback, I can make educated guesses about what she likes, and it opens the door to ask about her preferences.

A caveat here: while I use foreplay to feel out what my partner likes and do a little bit of negotiation, I don't go from there into a heavy kink scene. It's too difficult and risky to negotiate a full-on scene when foreplay is already in motion, because at that point my partner is compromised a little bit by being aroused. If I know I want to do a kink scene with her, I negotiate the scene before we begin to play. But for lighter kinds of activities, I'm comfortable asking if my partner would like me to be a little more kinky, and I tell her a few of the things I enjoy, and invite her to talk about her desires.

I like to use kinky touches not just because I like kink, but because I like to mix rough and gentle sensations. There's incredible drama in contrast notes, like giving my partner the sweetest kiss while I pull her hair. Variety allows her to access different parts of herself: the part that wants to be a good girl, and the part that enjoys being a slutty whore. You can create a space where all those parts are welcome and give her freedom to express herself fully.

Sensory Immersion

I like to have my partner wear a blindfold and physically pose her body as I observe and compliment her. I tell her how beautiful her back looks when she arches it, and I run my hands across her body. Restricting her sensory input with the blindfold is a wonderful hack that puts a spotlight on the sensations she's feeling across her skin.

From there, I like to have a warm bottle of coconut oil at the ready. With my partner still blindfolded, I drip the warm oil on her, arcing it across her body and playing with dripping it closer to her vulva and farther away. She doesn't know when or where the next drop is going to hit, which builds anticipation and a sense of safe risk. When the oil hits her skin, she can feel the warm temperature and the silky liquid, and I can use the oil to massage her.

> **PRO TIP**
>
> An easy sex hack is to use a cup warmer to keep the coconut oil at the right temperature.

This is one example of layering different sensations to create a rich erotic experience. Think of different sensations you can incorporate:

sights, sounds, textures, temperatures, tastes, and smells. Consider what elements you can restrict to pull your partner's focus to a particular sensation. You can restrict her vision with a blindfold or restrict a little bit of movement with a simple tie.

Of course, you're not going to put on a whole big show every time you have sex, just like you don't go to a fancy restaurant for a nine-course meal every day. Sometimes you just want to order pizza. To be a great lover, it's important to know how to do both, and adapt to your partner's desires in the moment. Foreplay is really about paying attention to your partner and the moment and playing together in a way that gives you both time to relax and get aroused. The more senses you involve, the richer the experience will be.

Imagine that each of the things you do to prepare for sex adds another layer of experience you can use to create a complex and exquisite flavor that is unforgettable. From the organized and welcoming space to the softness of your duvet, to the ambient lighting, to the variety of types of kisses and the way you hold her, to the kinds of words you say and how you compliment her, to the blindfold and oil, you can caringly invite her out of the everyday world and into the world of her senses. You can be like an erotic artist that creates a spellbinding experience she will never forget.

Roller Coaster of Pleasure

Think of how many different designs there are for roller coasters. Some of them go up a big hill, building tension with each tick of the gears, until finally they crest and take a thrilling plunge. Others have loop after loop after loop. Some have just one dramatic peak; others have multiple twists, turns, rises, and dips.

Sex is like that, too. The more sexual skills you have, the more you have to offer and the more different kinds of experiences you can design. That's why Part Three of this book is devoted to helping you build your technical skills—and those skills can be mastered quickly, in about the time it takes to complete a semester-long course.

How you choose to employ those skills comes down to what you're observing about your partner's turn-ons. As you transition from foreplay to sex, keep paying attention to your partner's responses. I like to start sex with fingering and oral, because I can pick up a lot more data this way. It's way easier to sense nuances with your fingers and tongue than with a penis. Also, your head is nearer to her genitals, and so you're able to sense her responses with more clarity. In addition, your own pleasure and needs are not involved yet, so you can see what works for her without your own sensations getting in the way. Like Ian Kerner says in *She Comes First*, sometimes "the tongue is mightier than the sword."[58]

Does she like when I use a flat tongue or the tip of my tongue? Does she like sucking or licking? How deep are her A-spot, P-spot, and G-spot? How does cervical stimulation feel to her? Like we talked about in Chapter Two, I make a mental map of the stops I find that are pleasurable to her—and I also use the opportunity to give her a few warm-up orgasms. (We'll talk more about multiple orgasms, and how common they really are, in the next chapter.) I can pin down her likes and dislikes, learn which points on her body are the most sensitive, and discover what types of touch induce orgasm.

---

58   Ian Kerner, *She Comes First: The Thinking Man's Guide to Pleasuring a Woman* (New York: HarperCollins, 2009).

I find I can learn more by using my hands than by going down on my partner, because I have more options for the type of touch, as well as the pressure, speed, and friction I can create. And of course, there's always the option to do oral and fingering at the same time.

Above all, be responsive. Some women want to skip all this shit and get straight to fucking; some women want to take a break from their own pleasure and give their partner head for a while. There are many different roller coasters to ride.

🔟
Fingering

I've made more women cum with my hands than with any other tool. Hands down (no pun intended), fingers are the most effective, underrated tools for learning how your partner's body responds to different kinds of sensation.

My fiancée and I joke that in the same way Pamela Anderson insured her boobs while filming *Baywatch*, I should take out an insurance policy for my hands.

Despite the incredible pleasures hands are capable of inciting, we devalue fingering as immature. It's what teenagers do before they can have "real sex." Giving a hand job is considered low and cheesy.

At the same time, we have more solo sex with our hands than any other kind of sex. That's not just because they're the only tools available—it's also because no other body part can match the dexterity, positioning capability, and pressure sensitivity of hands.

Don't Forget to Warm Up

Warm up your partner with external touch like we described in Chapter Six on foreplay. Give her vulva a pussy hug, tease her labia, pinch her labia gently around her clit—whatever feels good to her and helps her relax. Don't go straight into fingering her clit or sliding your fingers in her vagina (unless you know she likes that right away). Giving too much stimulation too quickly is equivalent to throwing on a light switch in the dark all at once: it can be a glaring change for the nervous system. Instead, think of increasing stimulation like a dimmer switch, gradually ramping up the intensity.

Clit Clocking

Like we talked about in Chapter Three, watching your partner masturbate is a great way to understand how she likes her clit to be touched. You can start with the same techniques to give her the same stimulation she gives herself and build from there.

Remember the clit clocking game from Chapter Three? Watch for how your partner moves her finger around the "clock face" of her clit. The most popular movements are side to side—three o'clock to six o'clock—and up and down—six o'clock to twelve o'clock.

The precise location matters quite a bit. Moving her finger from bottom to top, or six o'clock to twelve o'clock, gives her sensation across the head of her clit, while moving her finger from top to bottom actually sweeps the finger across the hood of the clit first with less sensation on the head (unless you pull it back). These specific locations create very different sensations in her body.

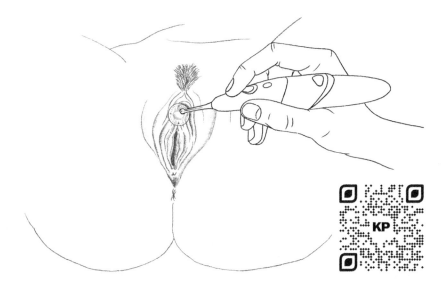

Get your own feel for what spots on the "clock" work for your partner by sweeping your finger in different directions to see what she responds to. Move your finger in big circles around the face, or small tight circles directly on the head of the clit. Keep your motions smooth and make sure you use plenty of spit or lube.

Different Strokes

You can try a variety of different kinds of touch around your partner's clit, but a few specific techniques stand out as being the most popular pleasures.

If your partner prefers sensation across her whole vulva, use your whole hand, with fingers flat and pressed together, to stroke back and forth across her vulva and clit. The subtle ripple between your fingers will give stimulation similar to a vibrator. You can increase the sensation by fanning your fingers out and moving your hand faster back and forth.

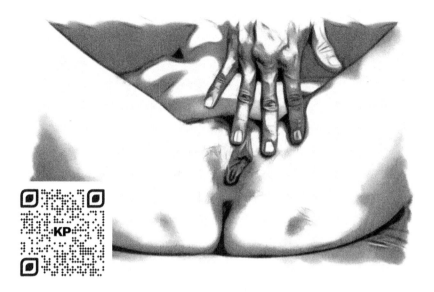

For another technique, make a loose fist. Place the flat surface of your fingers, between your second and third knuckles, against her vulva, and wiggle your fingers as you move your hand side to side.

This will stimulate her vulva and clit with a rippling sensation. You can do the same motion while also flexing your wrist up and down, which doesn't induce orgasm for many people, but does give a pleasurable mix of swiping-circular sensations.

As you continue to play with new types of touch, continue to watch for and ask for feedback from your partner. Tell them to let you know right away if something feels off or they don't like a particular technique. The faster they let you know, the quicker you can calibrate the kind of touch that feels amazing.

The more dexterity and body awareness you develop, the better quality of touch you'll develop, too—until your hands become a better sex toy than whatever is stashed under your bed. Your touch can be more precise, varied, and responsive than anything on the market.

Internal Touch

Before you slide your fingers inside your partner's vagina, tease around the vaginal opening to get the tissues warmed up to sensation. When your partner is fully aroused, she may be wet or she may not be; it depends on the person. One little hack I like for lubing my fingers is to create a little "dipping tray." I pour a little lube onto a part of their body where the lube can pool, like the hip crease or belly button.

When you're ready to slide your fingers in, use the technique described in Chapter Three: turn your hand palm-up so your fingernail presses against the bottom of her vagina, towards her anus. The bottom wall of the vagina stretches the most, and your lubed-up finger will slide in smoothly.

A technical note here: wash your hands and take good care of your fingernails. Keep them trimmed and nicely filed so you don't jab the sensitive spots in her vagina. Medical-grade gloves are great for fingering, because they create a smooth (and clean) surface.

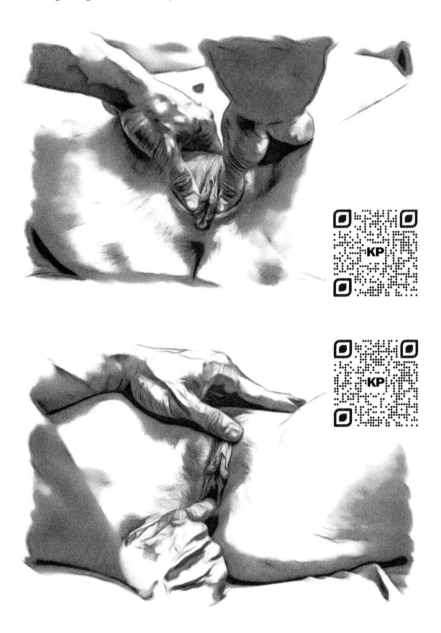

Once your finger is in knuckle-deep, keep your finger still for a moment to give your partner a moment to feel the sensation of your finger inside. If you want to insert two fingers, stagger your index finger on top of your middle finger so they create the least amount of surface space sliding into the vaginal opening.

Apply pressure up towards her belly button to map where her G-spot is. Start with a broad, sweeping motion from one side (one hip) to the other, making a half-moon shape, to get a sense of where she feels the most sensation. Only move your fingers in or out to adjust the depth, not as a back-and-forth thrusting motion.

When you have a sense of where the most sensitive spot is for your partner, you can focus your attention there. Press harder to see what range of pressure she likes—you might be surprised at how much pressure you can apply. You can also add friction, curling your fingertips back and forth. Try friction only and pressure only to see what your partner likes best.

To create maximum sensation on the G-spot, uncurl your fingers all the way so they press towards the back wall of the vagina. As you uncurl your fingers towards the back wall of the vagina, you're creating more range of motion. Then you can generate more force as you press back up against the G-spot, in a come-hither motion. You can create even more pressure by flexing your wrist as you curl your fingers. Then, extend your wrist as you straighten your fingers out again. Do this in a rhythmic motion. This might feel awkward and unnatural at first, but it will get easier with time.

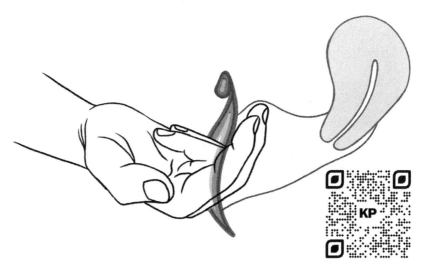

You can also curl your fingers upward in a walking motion like you're doing the moonwalk on her front vaginal wall with your fingers. This is a variation in sensation that some people really like. As you do it, pay attention to your fingertips, trying to feel the urethral sponge under your fingertips.

If your partner likes even more firm sensation in this area, you can use your other hand to press down on her lower abdomen from the front, pushing the front wall of her vagina back into your other hand.

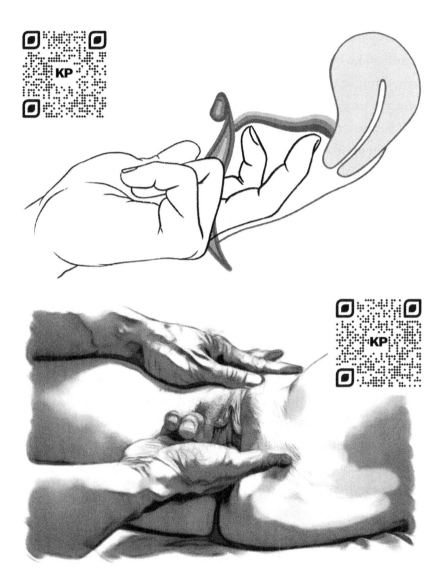

If you move your fingers with the right range of motion as you flex the back of your finger towards her anus, there is a moment when the G-spot separates from the pad of your finger. As you curl your finger up again, you will be pressing her G-spot back up towards her belly button. This is kind of like bouncing a ball on a paddle-board, and when you do this right, you get the satisfying feeling of a rhythmic bounce. You can actually feel the vaginal wall bouncing beneath your fingers, and the internal clitoris is right behind that wall bouncing along with it.

This motion of the internal clit activates more nerve endings. This kind of stimulation may or may not feel more pleasurable to your partner; everyone is different, and the range of sensation that feels good is unique. If your partner likes the sensation, you can firm up your wrist and use your whole arm to help you move your fingers up and down inside her vagina (more on this in Chapter Ten on squirting).

As you do this, you should be calibrating to find her "pleasure sweet spot" as we described in Chapter Four. The way to achieve this is to start off slow, increase the pressure and speed until it feels like too much, and then decrease the sensation slightly. For most women, their pleasure sweet spot is just under "too much."

Additionally, many women have never really had enough G-spot stimulation to be able to feel much, so when they do experience it for the first time, it often feels foreign and like they have to pee. The tendency she will have in these cases is to clamp down, trying to squeeze your finger with her pussy so she doesn't pee on you, or she'll try to control the sensation if it's overwhelming.

The solution is to coach her to relax and bear down on your fingers. If she doesn't know how to bear down, tell her to try and push your finger out with her pussy, or use the same muscle she would if she was trying to pee faster. Slow down and decrease the pressure, and then slowly build back up while she focuses on relaxing.

In addition to G-spot stimulation, you can explore deeper to see if your partner likes stimulation to the A-spot, P-spot, and cervix.

Reach your finger deeper in to find the A-spot, just in front of your partner's cervix, closer to her belly button. You may need your partner to hold the backs of her knees towards her chest in order to get your fingers deep enough, so her pelvis curls towards her belly like it would in the fetal position. You're trying to get her clit closer to her nose, so to speak.

Try moving your finger in circles with different amounts of pressure to see if your partner likes stimulation in the A-spot.

PRO TIP

A guiding idea when trying any of these motions is that you want to produce the most force with the least effort by recruiting larger muscle groups, leveraging joints and body position so you don't overtax smaller muscles to the point of exhaustion. My background in competitive swimming taught me if any movement does not propel you farther, faster, it's wasted energy. Efficiency of movement is the key to mastery. One of my favorite teachers, Tim Ferriss, calls this the "minimum effective dose." When you do this, you free up extra energy to accomplish your goals.

The P-spot is behind the cervix towards the anus. Turn your hand palm-down and use the pad of your finger to sweep half-moon shapes from one side to the other. Like you saw in Chapter Two, if your partner likes sensation from her P-spot, chances are good she also likes anal stimulation. Both P-spot and anal play stimulate the same nerves from different sides of the vaginal wall.

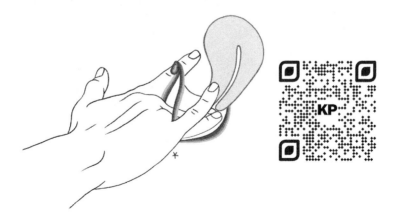

You can also play with the cervix, making circles around the donut. With big circles, you can continue to stimulate the A-spot in front and the P-spot in back. You can also make smaller circles on top of the donut, around the hole, with your fingers or a penis. You can also sweep the pad of your finger, the tip of your penis, or a dildo across the middle of the donut but be careful not to poke it or try to press your finger inside it—sharp stabs can cause cramps. Size queens who like to be pounded by big dicks may like a lot of cervical stimulation immediately. Others may need a lot of warm-up before stimulation to the cervix starts to feel good.

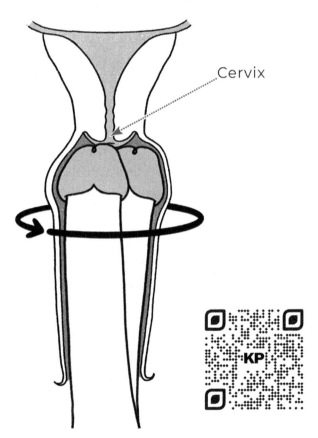

Cervix

An advanced trick for women who like a lot of stimulation to their cervix is to reach your finger deep towards the A-spot, with the pad of your finger pressing down on the cervix. Flick your finger to bounce the cervix up and down, almost like dribbling a basketball.

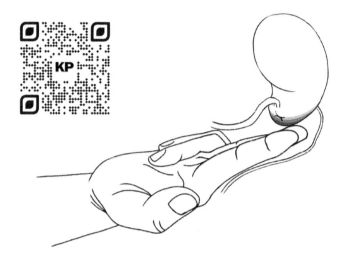

The A-spot, P-spot, and cervix are not star players for most women, but they can be nice for added stimulation when you're playing with the clit. These spots activate the hypogastric and vagus nerves, creating deep, radiating, visceral sensations.

The position of the cervix in the vagina varies from woman to woman. Also, the cervix ascends and descends in the vaginal canal at different points in the menstrual cycle. Getting to know where your partner's cervix sits in her vagina is important. If you're super comfortable with a partner, I recommend getting a plastic speculum and a flashlight and checking it out! You can buy a kit to do a self-exam, or examine your partner.[59] You can also get a pretty

59 The FWHC Store, www.fwhc.org/sale3.htm.

good sense of the location and position of the cervix with just your fingers. It's good to know what you're working with and form a 3D map of her anatomy.

PRO TIP

If you and your partner want to try stimulation of deeper areas of the vagina around the cervix for the first time, have her rub her clit so she gets reliable stimulation she likes as you try the new technique. Neurons that fire together wire together, so if your partner is warmed up and already experiencing pleasure, she's more likely to find a new sensation pleasurable, too. At some point, when she's warmed up, you can decrease stimulation on the clit and allow her to focus more exclusively on the new sensation. Once she gets more comfortable with this, you can try cervical or deep vaginal stimulation on its own, and see if she can learn to relax into this new sensation.

Because the cervix and deeper vagina are innervated by parasympathetic visceral nerves, the pathway to enjoying the sensation is often one of deep relaxation rather than tension, and it takes some practice to figure out. Sometimes getting out of old arousal patterns can create opportunities to lay down these new, more relaxed pathways to pleasure. Which of these techniques will work better depends on your partner's unique disposition.

Nail the Angle

When your partner masturbates, because her hands are connected to her shoulders (obviously), she can only touch herself from specific angles. For some women, trying to stimulate their own G-spot without a toy can be annoying, and even with a dildo it can be difficult to hit the right angle.

This is one reason partnered sex can be so much better than solo sex: you can position yourself in a variety of orientations, which means you can reach places and angles that your partner can't. As you explore your partner's clit, vulva, and vagina, note the angles that feel best to her. It's usually easier to find the right angle if only one of you is doing the adjustments. Both people trying at the same time tends to be confusing.

Your own body positioning is key. There's no reason to work against yourself; position yourself to create the movement and angle you want with the least amount of effort. Pay attention to the angle of your wrist and position your body to make movement as easy as possible. In general, the more you can keep your wrist in a straight line, the easier most movements will be. For a more in-depth illustration of different biomechanical angles, check out my instructional videos at *KennethPlay.com*.

Narrow and Broad Stimulation

Once you've determined which spots feel good to your partner, you can start to determine the type of coverage that feels good to her. How precise does she like the stimulation on this spot to be? Does she want it to be more broad? For instance, does she prefer a flat tongue covering more space, or just the very tip of the tongue stimulating a very precise location? Does she prefer you to stimulate her clit with the entire palm of your hand, or a fingertip?

Vibrators are designed with different types of stimulation in mind, from broad to narrow. Compare the Doxy vibrator, which has a big head to cover a broad space, with a Zumio vibrator, which is almost as fine as a pen tip. A Doxy gives lots of sensation across a wide surface area, while the Zumio can pinpoint specific nerve endings. Neither is better than the other; they're both excellent for different purposes. You can use your hands in the same way by sweeping your fingers across a wider area or pinpointing a small motion with a fingertip. Broad stimulation tends to create sensations that are more diffuse and spread out, while narrow stimulation tends to create more intense and focused sensation. This concept is beautifully covered in the OMG Yes course, in their module called "Broadening."[60]

When your partner starts reacting with pleasure, keep doing the action that drives them wild. Don't change the sensation too much. Shaking things up when they already feel good is equivalent to hitting one of the annoying pattern buttons on a vibrator—and hitting the reset button on her arousal. Just keep fucking doing what you're doing.

Dial in Pressure and Speed

After you've found the location and angle, it's time to find the threshold of sensation that gives your partner the most pleasure. At this point, she's already reacting to your touch—can you get her to react a little bit *more*?

---

60 OMGYes.com.

Play with giving your partner more or less pressure. An interesting feature about our complex network of nerve endings is that both light and strong pressure give higher (but different) sensations. You can see this effect by touching your finger to your lips: skim your lips very lightly with your fingertip, and then try pressing really hard. Both types of touch have unique benefits.

I usually start off very light and work my way into more and more pressure, asking my partner if more feels good. As we talked about in the communication chapter, it's a great hack to give your partner a contrast of two types of touch—hard and soft in this case—and ask which they like better. In the heat of the moment, picking an option is faster and easier than asking them to try to describe what they want.

Similarly, you can play with speed. Pick up the speed a little and see how she responds. Or give her a contrast—slow and fast—and ask which feels better.

Once you have all these factors aligned—location, angle, pressure, and speed—and your partner is giving you positive feedback, keep riding the wave of your partner's pleasure.

Timing and Endurance

It's really frustrating to dial in exactly the right kind of touch and see your partner go wild in ecstasy, only to tire out just as she hits the peak of pleasure. You can get everything right and still be stymied by your lactic acid threshold.

You build your endurance the more you do a specific action, but when fingering your partner there are many small muscles that have to coordinate, and if any one of them runs out of fuel, you'll have to stop and rest.

By scanning the QR code that follows, you can find resources on how to get fit for sex. One of the best ways to prevent exhaustion is to work out and train your muscles, so you can build your anaerobic threshold. That means doing high-intensity interval training, and training in the fifteen to twenty rep range with less than a minute rest time for about five sets. You're basically feeling the burn from the last couple of reps on your first set, and just continue to feel the burn all the way through.

Another way to prevent exhaustion is to switch hands quickly, so you can continue giving your partner the same stimulation while giving one hand a rest.

If your partner likes fast, vigorous sensation, you may only be able to keep it up for thirty seconds to a minute. Keep those techniques as your secret weapons in reserve. Don't bust them out when your partner is just getting warmed up. Wait until the moment when she's fully aroused and intense stimulation can have the most impact.

You can also bring in sex toys as labor-saving devices. Your fingers may tire as you stimulate deep spots inside your partner's vagina, but you can rock an nJoy Wand against her G-spot much more easily. You may not be able to flicker your hand over her clit for four whole minutes, but you can hold a vibrator on her vulva forever. A fun fact here: vibrators were invented in the Victorian era when doctors' hands were getting worn out from giving so many orgasms to their patients! In my view, sex toys make me into a bionic man; they don't replace me, they enhance my capabilities. I think men are just entering the Stone Age when it comes to sex—they're finally starting to learn to use tools!

I recommend starting with hands to get a practical understanding of your partner's body and her pleasure points first. When you add toys in after gaining knowledge first, the toys become an extension of you, and you'll know exactly how to use them.

Pleasure Stacking

As Dr. Pfaus and his research team learned, orgasm doesn't happen from a single type of stimulation alone; it's a "sum of the parts."[61] Orgasm is a multisensory experience. One of the best things about using your hands to explore your partner's body in manual sex is that you can discover new pleasures and combinations you (and she) may not have known before.

While you're using your hands to find the most sensitive spots and ways to dial in exactly the right kind of stimulation for your partner, you can also layer new sensations into her experience. Pleasure operates in a self-reinforcing loop: the more often your partner feels pleasure from a new sensation, the more pleasurable the sensation will become. You may start by combining clit stimulation (a star player) with G-spot stimulation (a rookie), and after a while, your partner might be able to cum from G-spot stimulation alone.

The easiest way to find new spots to include is with your hands. The sensitivity and dexterity of your fingers allows you to reach new places and get tactile data about how they feel. When you know your partner's genitals like the back of your hand, it's a game changer.

---

61   James G. Pfaus, Gonzalo R. Quintana, Conall Mac Cionnaith, and Mayte Parada, "The Whole Versus the Sum of Some of the Parts: Toward Resolving the Apparent Controversy of Clitoral Versus Vaginal Orgasms," *Socioaffective Neuroscience and Psychology*, October 25, 2016.

Fucking your partner without using your hands is like trying to navigate the world with a flip phone. Where the fuck are you going? Spend time mastering the three by six or so inches of space in and around your partner's vagina, and the increase in capability will be equivalent to getting a smartphone with maps and GPS.

11

Oral Sex

I f you've ever tied a cherry stem in a knot with your tongue, you know your mouth can be almost as dexterous as your fingers. It's also soft, self-lubricating, and warmer than your hand. Oh, and you can suck with it. Know why the Lelo Sila toy is so popular? Because sucking is a crowd-pleaser.

LELO

Having dexterity with your tongue is great, but you don't have to be able to tie a cherry stem to give good head. Between your tongue and your lips, you have great built-in tools at your disposal.

KP

Before we get tongue-deep, let's take a moment to talk about the smell and taste of pussy. I love washing my partner's body, and I like things to be clean and hygienic. But at the same time, sex is a very animal activity. Your relationship to those animal smells and tastes matters. If you expect your partner not to taste or smell like anything, her natural smell will seem "wrong." The same is true of your body, too—do you really think your cum tastes sweet, even if your partner says she likes it? For some people, reveling in these animal smells is hot, and for others it's not. Either way, connecting with our animal natures is a pivotal part of sex.

If I'm worried about myself or my partner's cleanliness and hygiene, I usually just hop in the shower and say something like, "I'm going to wash myself before you put your mouth on me." Most people will naturally follow me in there. As Gandhi said, "Be the change you want to see in the world."

The way someone tastes and smells varies quite a bit, not just from person to person, but from day to day. Pussy smells more of iron, for example, when your partner is about to get her period. You can develop your nose to detect subtle changes in her body. I recommend *The Vagina Bible* by Jen Gunter MD, for both women and men to get a better sense of what different scents mean, and which ones can be indicative of genuine problems, rather than normal fluctuations.[62] But having said this, a good rule of thumb is to be willing to experience your partner's smell and taste without expectation; just learn what her unique scent is like. If you like it, go for it. If you don't, I don't know what to tell you, buddy; be willing to be generous sometimes anyway.

---

62   Jen Gunter, *The Vagina Bible: The Vulva and the Vagina: Separating the Myth from the Medicine* (New York: Citadel Press, 2019).

Face Fucking

It may seem like a counterintuitive place to start, but one way to get a partner warmed up is to have her sit on my face. It's a great mindfulness hack for my partner, because it flips roles on the Wheel of Consent. I'm no longer touching my partner for her pleasure; she's now touching me for her pleasure, using my tongue as a tool to get herself off.

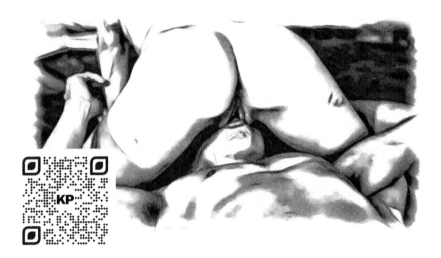

All her attention goes to the sensations in her clit and how she wants to move her body across my tongue and lips. Meanwhile, I don't have to move; I can just lay there with my tongue out, and as my partner moves on top of me, I learn a lot about what angle, pressure, and speed she likes as she pleasures herself.

On top of all of that, face fucking helps my partner get into her body and feel the relationship between her own movement and pleasurable sensations; she shifts from passive receiver to active lover.

Encourage your partner to be active and move her hips back and forth or rotate her clit on your tongue. As for you, you can either stick your tongue out and lie it flat against your lower lip and chin so she can glide along it, or try a more complex technique. In this move that I call "The Pfaus," after Dr. Pfaus, you curl your tongue into a circle or U shape and she can glide her erect clit back and forth into it almost like a cock would go into a vagina. Dr. Pfaus says this hack brings out the inner assertiveness of women on top, encouraging pelvic thrusting in women who might never have tried this before. In his words, "The immediate empowerment that comes with the immediate pleasure is often the spark of a revolution."

For many women, flipping from a passive role to an active one is unfamiliar. This makes sense when you consider how men and women are conditioned differently for sex. From puberty, men grow up masturbating in active ways. We use our hands and our hips, and we're used to moving our bodies to generate sensation until we cum.

Women, on the other hand, are not only often shamed for masturbating, but many of them imagine the majority of their sex life will be spent lying on their backs being fucked. Add to that the cultural script that women aren't supposed to touch their own clits during penetrative sex, and it's easy to see how many women arrive at partnered sex with the idea that they're not supposed to generate their own pleasure and sensation.

No wonder it seems men are able to cum more easily than women—they're generating their own sensation and responding to their own pleasure feedback loops. Because they're taking an active role in their own pleasure, they can create the sensations they need for orgasm. They expect to cum each time they have sex. Many women, on the other hand, are conditioned to passively accept the stimulation they get, and if their partner doesn't know how to play their instrument, they expect to walk away disappointed instead of satisfied.

Face fucking subverts all that shit. Encourage your partner to sit on your tongue and ride herself to orgasm. You'll not only learn how she likes to grind and move her body, but you'll help her take an active role in her own pleasure. You'll also take something she may have been shamed for—humping and moving her body in a way that feels good—and making it sexy. It's the equivalent of throat fucking for men, and we all know how good that feels.

How to Give a Good Licking

When you're ready to start oral sex, don't go straight for the clit or the vaginal opening. Kiss her vulva all around to build anticipation and get your partner really turned on. Think of sex like a good movie: you're waiting for the right moment, waiting for enough tension to build up, to kick into action.

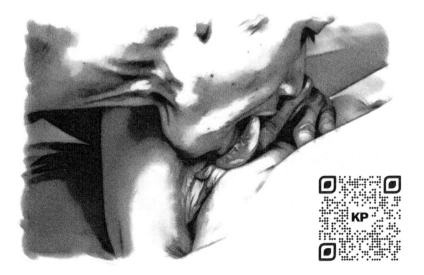

Start with one long, flat, consistent stroke from the bottom of her vulva all the way up until your tongue touches her clit. Then, with your tongue still in contact with her vulva, reverse the direction and go all the way back down. Drag the moment out for dramatic effect.

I like to rub her clit with my fingers first before oral sex, so I have a good idea of what kinds of touch, friction, and pressure she likes. Just like you can use flat fingers for a broad sensation or one fingertip for a focused sensation, you can use your entire tongue or just the tip to stimulate your partner's clit and other parts of her vulva.

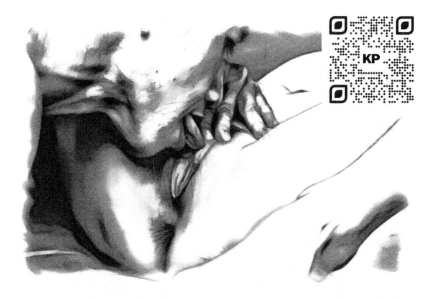

You can continue giving your partner big, long licks with your whole tongue, sliding your tongue from the vaginal opening all the way up over the top of the clit, and back down. Keep continuous pressure and contact, like a violin bow sliding back and forth across the strings. The more surface area you create with your tongue, the more friction you can give your partner across a wider area of her vulva.

To give more precise sensation, use the tip of your tongue. Just like you would with your fingertip, you can use the tip of your tongue to flick across the clit head using side-to-side or up-and-down strokes, depending on what direction your partner likes best. With constant pressure, you can also trace circles with the tip of your tongue, sliding around the clit head and across the hood.

Training Your Tongue

The tongue tends to get tired when you're being precise, and it may take a bit of conditioning to get your tongue in shape for long oral sessions. Think of it like a workout and give yourself breaks by going back to a flat tongue or using your fingers to pinch-hit. Don't forget about your lips: you can use them to keep providing sensation to your partner even if your tongue gets tired.

Like we talked about in the previous chapter, you can also wait until your partner is highly aroused to start using the tip of your tongue, so you're able to give her focused sensation when it has the highest impact. Whether you're already athletic with your mouth or barely scratching the potential in your tongue game, you can improve your endurance and dexterity with training. The more you eat pussy, the more those tongue muscles get trained!

Pleasure Sucker

To build your skills at sucking, pucker your lips to make a fish face and practice sucking the tips of your fingers. Adjust the tension in your lips until you have a good amount of suction. You'll be amazed at how hard you can suck. Essentially, you're using your mouth to create a vacuum, and you can create different sensations by moving the vacuum around your partner's clit and vulva.

Wrap your lips around your partner's clit to create a good seal. Once you've created enough of a vacuum, you can vary the sensation by changing the amount of suction, creating a pulsing sensation. This is not very different from sucking on a nipple like you are trying to get milk out of it. Imagine you can suck something out of the clit. Suction toys are a big deal in the sex tech community, carving out a whole new niche of toys that are super popular. One of my favorites is Sila from Lelo, a sonic massager and suction toy in one. Suction is super effective, and some women prefer this sensation over vibration because it feels more natural.

You can also add stimulation with the tip of your tongue so that you can suck and lick at the same time. Try holding a good amount of suction and giving the clit fast licks with the tip of your tongue. In my experience, that's the most orgasm-inducing move.

Use Your Head—and Your Whole Body

You don't have to perform oral with your mouth alone. You can stick your tongue out flat and keep it still and use the texture of your tongue to give your partner stimulation while you move your head around. You can also pucker your lips to create a softer texture.

Shake your head side to side or nod up and down. Try different speeds and pressures to see what your partner likes. You can also combine the directions by moving your entire body while you also move your head: nod your head up and down while you move your body side to side.

You can create different experiences and sensations by trying different body positions. For example, when you're eating out your partner while facing her between her legs, and you nod your head, you're creating a specific pattern of pressure from six o'clock to twelve o'clock on the "clock face" of her clit. Rotate your body into a sixty-nine position, and keep nodding your head, and you've now got the same movement pattern reversed: you're now giving your partner stimulation from twelve o'clock to six o'clock, going over her clit hood and head in the opposite direction. You get the same direction of sensation if your partner is bent over and you lick her from behind.

If your partner is flexible, try putting her in a position like bridge pose in yoga. Have her lay on her back with her knees bent and feet flat, and then ask her to roll her hips up towards the ceiling. She can hold her hips to support them, or you can prop her hips up with pillows. This position makes it easier for you to sit up so you can lick her, and it's also super hot because your partner is vulnerable and exposed, and the pressure of her shoulders against the bed feels a little like bondage.

The point is to experiment. Play with different shapes and orientations. Turn the puzzle pieces of your bodies, and you'll find different access points for sensation.

12

Squirting

W hen I first got into the sex party scene, it seemed there were always one or two guys in the room who were capable of making every woman squirt. Watching couples play, I was fascinated by how a particular type of stimulation could erupt in waterworks. I was obsessed.

Immediately, I got into my learner's mindset and began to nerd out. I walked up to the men who were able to help their partners squirt, and I peppered them with questions. I asked the women who'd squirted what their experience was like, and what worked and what didn't. Some women described squirting as a pleasurable experience. Others equated it to a party trick. Either way, I wanted desperately to know how to do that trick. I read everything I could get my hands on about what squirting was and how it happens.

There's probably no other human on the planet who did as much thinking, researching, and experimenting with squirting as I did.

From all my questions, I'd gathered some of the most effective techniques that tended to work for most women. I was puzzled to see that it was hard to nail down a reliable method. Not everyone responded the same way to the same stimulation. I finally realized that my own actions were only half of the recipe—squirting depended on the relationship between my partner and me, and I learned how to coach my partners to optimize their experience. Like dancing, while one person is leading and the other is following, both are active roles that depend on being in tune with oneself and the other dancer. In each session, my partners and I learned to work together to make squirting happen.

At a party, one of the organizers who I'd become close to approached me and asked if I would teach a squirting class. At first, I was honored—as a previously sexually insecure kid, it was nice to receive a little ego stroke. But that confidence boost lasted for about half a second before nervousness set in. I'd been a personal trainer for many years by then, but I'd never taught a class in an educational setting, and never with people who were naked.

Of all the couples who came to the class, some of them had tried different techniques to squirt but they hadn't worked. Some of the women had squirted before, but they didn't know how to teach their partners how to help them make it happen.

I coached the couples through the techniques I'd learned, and they followed along in real time. As we got to the final steps, the men's arms started to work furiously, their partners relaxed and let go, and suddenly, all around the room, the women began to squirt.

It was synchronized like the fucking Bellagio. I loved it. I realized hands-on sex education is magic. When you're learning to ride a bike or perform a new style of dance, you need to practice live. The same goes for sex. I'd trained thousands of people in fitness, and I knew that it was possible to change someone's life with hands-on experience. I realized I could do the same thing with sex.

Fast-forward to today, and I've partnered with Dr. Zhana to create the largest survey ever conducted on squirting, with seven thousand participants and counting.[63] The largest survey done previous to ours had fewer than four hundred respondents. There's a lot we're still learning about squirting, and a lot we're still learning about sex. Use the QR code that follows to see the results of this groundbreaking project!

While there is raging debate on what squirting is and isn't, scientists have been able to clear up a few common misconceptions. No, the fluid that sprays out when your partner is squirting is not the same as pee. Nor is squirting directly connected to orgasm; some people experience orgasm while squirting, but it's also possible to squirt without cuming. It's not a sexual function that everyone enjoys or needs to do. Let's take a closer look at how it works.

The Science of Squirting

Where does all that liquid come from, and what exactly is it? There have been only a few small-scale studies done to look into this question, so the answer isn't conclusive yet. But researchers

---

63   Zhana Vrangalova and Kenneth Play, "Squirting Research Project," squirtingsurvey.com.

have identified two types of liquids that come out when someone is squirting.

The first is a milky white substance, similar to the watery part of semen, that comes from the Skene's glands. These glands surround the urethra and are similar to the prostate in men, because they develop from the same tissues in embryo. The Skene's glands are inside the urethral sponge, but one study found that only 66.7 percent of women actually have them—there is a lot we have yet to discover.[64] The actual function of the fluid produced by these glands may be to lubricate and protect the urethral opening. The glands are small, and the amount of fluid they produce is small, too—about the volume of a shot glass.

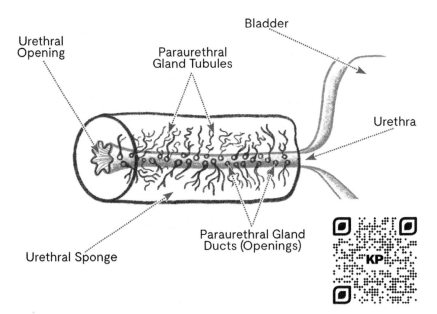

64 Emily Wernert, et al., "The 'Female Prostate' Location, Morphology, Immunohistochemical Characteristics and Significance," *European Urology*, 1992, 22:64–69.

But if you've seen squirting on porn, you know it's possible to squirt way more than a shot glass worth of liquid. Some people can fill up a Gatorade bottle. Larger amounts of spray come from the bladder. But squirting is still possible even when the bladder is emptied right before sex, and we think the bladder can fill up rapidly during arousal. It's possible that this mechanism relates to the same process whereby the genitals fill with blood during arousal. So, while squirt may be mixed with pee if there's some urine left-over in the bladder, chemical analysis has shown that the liquid that fills up the bladder isn't pee; it's a clear, odorless fluid that contains prostate-specific compounds, as well as glucose, which isn't present in urine.

The fluid from the bladder is mostly water, with some of the same milky substance from the Skene's glands. One hypothesis is that while fluid from the Skene's glands can drain out onto the vulva when the area around the urethra is stimulated, these glands can also drain out of the urethra next time you pee, if not released during sex.

While many of us are accustomed to thinking that fluid ejaculating out of someone's body is a sign of orgasm, it's not a given with squirting. In my own observations, less than half of women squirt when they're having an orgasm. It's possible for the sensations of squirting to trigger orgasm, or for an orgasm to trigger squirting, but the two phenomena don't always go together. Scan the QR code that follows to go to Dr. Zhana's video on the science of squirting, if you'd like to learn more.

The Emotional Side of Squirting

Squirting comes with unique sensations; some people like the feeling of squirting, and some people don't. The experience of squirting for the first time can be very emotional because it's a loss of control that some people haven't experienced before. From what I've observed with my partners, one out of eight or so women has an emotional release when they squirt for the first time.

In various schools of psychological thought, there are theories that our physical experiences help us process our emotional experiences. A new physical experience like squirting seems to unlock some of the connections our partners have between their physical and emotional experiences around sex.

A partner who I helped squirt for the first time told me a story afterward that moved me. She said that even as a young kid, she knew she was very sexual, and she built up a lot of hype around her first time having penetrative sex. When she lost her virginity, she remembered the sensation of her partner's penis inside of her feeling like she might have to pee.

Her instant reaction was, "Oh shit, I don't want to pee on my partner." She said she instantly felt shame and developed a response in her body: her muscles clenched to hold back pee. Her reaction became subconscious after a while.

She said that when I stimulated her to help her squirt, it was the first time she let herself let go of all the tension she was holding. The release made her cry. I listened and held her for a while after our session.

After my experience with this partner, I realized there were probably many women who held themselves back from certain sexual experiences because they were ashamed or afraid of letting go. Oddly enough, my journey of mastering squirting helped me understand how important it is to coach a partner on letting go.

> **PRO TIP**
>
> When someone is having an emotion around sex, don't make it about you. Your partner's emotional response might be from her interaction with you on that particular day, but it also might be about her history or her trauma. When a partner has an emotional response, what they're feeling most likely comes from a range of stuff. If you start thinking it's all about you, suddenly your partner has to deal with you instead of with her emotions. Give your partner time to process. Hold space for her, listen, and simply acknowledge her experience.

As we've discussed in the section of Chapter Six titled "Letting Your Body Guide You," this association between letting go emotionally and G-spot stimulation is not some sort of woo-woo notion. The nerves that connect to the G-spot run through the viscera of the body, where we experience emotions, and being able to fully feel sensations in the deeper parts of the vagina depends on your partner's ability to allow herself to feel the emotions that come up in her body as well. Ultimately, experiencing the depths of pleasure is dependent on experiencing deep feeling, period. I see my role in this as encouraging and allowing my partner to experience anything that comes up. It's also very moving to hold space for this kind of experience.

Early on in learning to help partners squirt, I would get frustrated when I couldn't "figure it out." My ego got involved, and as a result sometimes my partners were disappointed that their bodies didn't perform. I quickly learned to let go of my attachment to outcome with squirting. I never wanted my partner to feel like they were broken because squirting didn't happen. Instead, I now use squirting as an opportunity to connect with my partner and help her let go, whether it ends in waterworks or not.

Involuntary Reflex versus Voluntary Control

From the study with Dr. Zhana, and from my own experience with over a thousand partners, I estimate that most women are able to squirt—maybe around ninety percent. That doesn't mean every partner *wants* to, nor does it mean squirting is easy to do the first time. It requires your partner to have a degree of mastery over her own body.

When I made my educational video on squirting, I actually made a small mistake: I picked a coteacher who has absolute control over her squirting response. In the video, I'm not struggling because my partner knows how to squirt voluntarily. We're both confident we can show the viewer how it works, but with many partners, there's a lot more trial and error to get just the right stimulation and just the right amount of muscle control.

If someone pokes the space between your eyes, you'll automatically blink; that's an automatic reflex. But you can also consciously control your reaction if you focus on not blinking when you're poked. Similarly, squirting is an involuntary reflex that can be brought under conscious control.

Remember the pelvic muscles from Chapter Two? Well, one of these muscles, the bulbocavernosus, is a sphincter muscle, which is closed while in its resting state. When we become aroused, this muscle opens and relaxes. We bear down on this sphincter the same way we bear down when we need to release the anal sphincter.

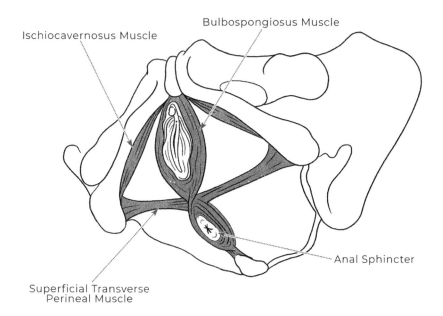

This mechanism is brilliantly explained by Stacy Lindau MD, from womanlab.com, who says, "Bearing down is a conscious act that overcomes the normal, contracted, closed state of the anal sphincter. We bear down using a trick of physiology called a 'valsalva' maneuver to generate enough pressure from inside our body to overcome the pressure in the anal sphincter muscle."[65] This same process works when it comes to the bulbocavernosus muscle.

---

65   Stacy Lindau, "Part 1: Your Vagina Has a Sphincter!" womanlab.com, 2018.

Another mechanism that prevents fluid from being released during sex is the swelling of the urethral sponge. The urethral sponge surrounds the urethra and swells up to prevent fluid from being released from the bladder during sex, but under pressure from the pelvic muscles pushing outward, fluid can still be released from the bladder. For squirting to occur, bearing down must happen strongly enough to bypass both the tonically closed state of the bulbocavernosus muscle as well as generate enough pressure to move liquid through the urethra while the urethral sponge is swollen around it.

G-spot stimulation of a certain variety can cause this bearing down reflex to happen involuntarily, *and* your partner can also learn to control the response of these muscles to tighten or relax them. Some women just happen to naturally respond to sexual stimulation by bearing down, whereas others need to learn to do this maneuver. Voluntary squirting can happen when your partner is able to control these muscles to bear down and push the fluid out of her bladder. I played with two girls at a party once who were proud of their squirting ability and ran around the party squirting people in the mouth like they had a pair of water guns.

Some women experience involuntary BC contractions when they orgasm, and some people push out when they cum. The ones that push out when they cum tend to squirt each time they cum, not because they're doing it consciously, but because their body reacts to orgasm by bearing down. If you've ever slept with a partner whose body seemed to push your cock out when she orgasms, that's this muscle at work.

The take-home idea here is that urethral and vaginal sphincter muscles have to open up in order for squirting to happen. This can occur for a variety of reasons: arousal, bearing down consciously, or bearing down involuntarily. If these muscles are closed because she isn't aroused, or she isn't sure how to let go, squirting isn't likely to occur. The name of the game is making her feel safe and relaxed enough that she can let go. Literally.

Coaching Your Partner to Squirt

If your partner isn't already familiar with the way her pelvic floor muscles work, you can use a dildo to practice. After your partner is fully warmed up, insert the dildo into her vagina (with plenty of lubrication, of course). Ask her to squeeze her pelvic floor as if she's trying to hold back pee, to pull the dildo up inside her. Then ask her to bear down to push the dildo out in the same way she would push out a tampon.

The benefit of using a dildo for this exercise is that both you and your partner get a visual and experiential understanding of how these muscles work. Your partner can learn to actively work the conscious connection with her pelvic muscles. You can also hold a mirror up so she can see what she's doing. This added visual feedback can help her develop a relationship to her body and to develop more control over her pelvic floor.

Then, insert your finger into her vagina so you can feel the action of these muscles from the inside. Press your finger on her G-spot and ask her to squeeze her pelvic floor muscles as if she's trying to pull your fingers further in. You'll feel how her vaginal wall contracts, and she'll feel how the sensation changes as she squeezes.

Then, with your finger still inside your partner's vagina, ask her to bear down, as if she's trying to push your finger out. You'll feel her vaginal wall press out against your finger, and she'll feel how the sensation changes. She can voluntarily bear down to create more pressure on her own G-spot. Usually, bearing down makes G-spot sensation feel really good, while squeezing inwards interferes with pleasure. The increase in stimulation and the action of pushing out on the pelvic floor are the actions that help your partner squirt. As a guy, if you don't know the difference between neutral, squeezing, or bearing down, it's hard to coach someone to let go. Knowing how these muscles work is essential.

Not everyone needs internal stimulation to squirt; some people squirt just from clitoral stimulation. But if your partner has never squirted before, in my experience, G-spot stimulation is one of the most effective ways for a beginner to explore.

Bearing down usually feels good to most women, but it can also trigger a sensation like they have to pee. If I notice my partner tensing up, I ask her, "Does that feel a little weird, like you have to pee?" So often, my partner replies, "How did you know?"

I tell my partner the sensation is totally normal, and I ask her to relax and notice what it feels like. I coach her to let her body get used to the sensations. I take it slow, letting her awareness build. Rushing a partner at this stage can cause her to associate her awareness of the peeing sensation with negative thoughts and shame; I want to help her reprogram that pattern. If she's worried about peeing and making a mess, I tell my partner it's her job to make a mess—with a smile on my face.

On that note: always keep a waterproof cover on your bed. You can also lay down a towel or puppy pads, not just to protect your sheets, but to give your partner the peace of mind that she can make as big a mess as she wants.

While it's great to encourage your partner to relax into the sensation, you also have to pay attention to her feedback. Don't push her to stay with the experience if she's uncomfortable; being pushy will make your partner feel pressured, and it will make you feel like shit. If your partner doesn't like spicy food, you wouldn't force her to sit down with you and eat spicy Indian curry. It would be just as crazy to keep pushing something she doesn't like in bed.

Optimal Positioning

For most people, squirting requires vigorous, high-velocity stimulation. You won't be able to provide your partner with high-intensity stimulation for more than a minute, so before you go for broke, it's important to get your partner thoroughly warmed up and aroused. Finger her in order to map where her G-spot is most sensitive.

To stimulate the G-spot vigorously, you'll need a full range of motion with your fingers inside your partner's vagina. Rather than using just your fingers or your wrist to create the motion, you'll use your whole arm—so it's important to get into an ergonomic position. With your partner lying on her back, position yourself on your hands and knees across her, with your body perpendicular to hers.

Lift her leg that's closer to your hands over your shoulder, and plant that hand on the bed to stabilize yourself. You now have full access to your partner's vagina. With your free hand, slide your fingers in and press your fingertips up against her G-spot.

Keep your finger hooked up towards her G-spot, and rock your palm up and down, using your whole arm to travel as far as you can down towards her anus and as far up as you can towards her G-spot.

Remember the bouncing sensation we talked about earlier in the G-spot section? This is like a more intense version of that. You want to hit the G-spot with as much velocity as you can. By keeping your palm in contact with her vulva, you'll also give her clitoral stimulation to increase her pleasure.

You're trying to mimic the rapid movements of a Hypervolt massage gun, but internally on her G-spot. Remember that the visceral nerve runs through her G-spot, so this kind of vigorous stimulation typically feels like a radiating, whole-body sensation.

Once you've found the right range of motion, it's time to go for it: increase your speed until your partner responds with pleasure. When she seems to be close to orgasm, that's your moment to go as fast as you can.

Give your partner a heads-up that you're going to go fast and give it your all; you don't want to surprise her with a sudden burst of higher intensity. As your partner gets close to squirting, you'll be able to hear the fluid building up; it creates a juicy squishing sound as you move your hand. In my experience, when the sensation feels good to my partner and I'm going all out, squirting is usually triggered in about fifteen seconds.

This body position has become my signature move. Once I worked out the most reliable technique to help my partners squirt, I created a video showcasing this crazy body position on PornHub so others could learn how to do it. The video didn't just show the mechanics of the technique; it also showed how my partner and I related to each other. The video took off, and it now has over 7 million views and climbing. I was shy about posting that video and putting my teaching out there, but it ended up being the video that launched my sex ed career.

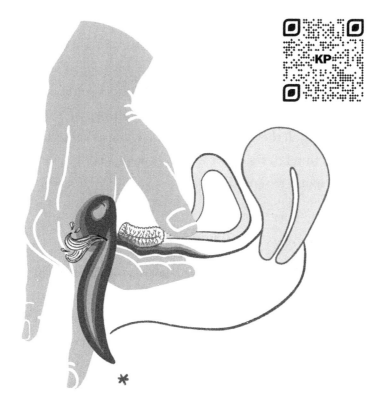

*

That video resonated with people not just because it demonstrated squirting technique, but because it showed the blend of elements that makes for really good sex: knowledge of anatomy, communication with a partner, proper positioning, and confidence in calibrating the exact stimulation that can trigger pleasure. My job was to bring all these elements together, and as a result, my partner was able to relax, focus on what felt good, and let go so her body could respond to sensation.

Playing with Toys

I mentioned before that toys are labor-saving devices. The squirting technique I just described is strenuous, but you can take some of the effort off by using an nJoy Pure wand. The shape and weight of the nJoy make it one of the best fucking sex toys ever made—in fact, it's so legendary that every sex educator seems to have one. The nJoy is made of stainless steel, so you can use it to create a lot of pressure, and it has a curved shape that allows you to use it like a rocker to stimulate the G-spot.

Make sure to warm the toy up to body temperature first, either by holding it in your hands or resting it on your partner's body where the weight of the toy can build her anticipation. Once it's warm enough, you can lube the toy up and tease your partner at the same time: Drip lube onto a spot of her body that can serve as a dipping tray—it could be the crease of her hip or the divot of her belly button—and slide the toy around in the lube using smooth, fluid motions. You can use the head of the toy to tease your partner's vulva and clit to get her used to the feel of the toy.

Insert the head of the toy inside her vagina to press against her
G-spot, and rock the other end rapidly up and down. The curved
shape turns the toy into a sexual teeter-totter, while the large surface space on the head of the toy can give your partner a lot of pressure over a broad area.

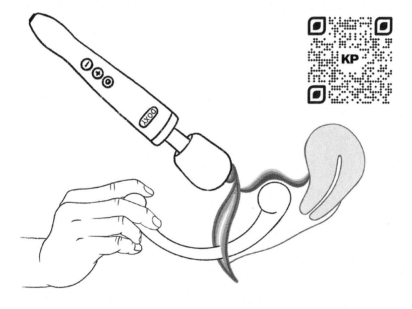

You can rock away at the nJoy wand and use one of my favorite
vibrators, the Doxy, to stimulate her clit at the same time. Start with
the Doxy on its lowest setting, gradually ramping up the speed to
intensify the sensations your partner is feeling. As she gets more

aroused, you can ask your partner to hold the Doxy and keep stimulating her clit while you use both hands to rock the nJoy.

Ground Her Experience

Squirting can be a full-body, intense experience, so help your partner's system calm down afterward. Give steady, grounding touch to her body. If you've used toys, remove them slowly and smoothly. Place your whole palm over her vulva in a pussy hug and breathe with your partner.

It's nice to have a towel or baby wipes on hand to gently wipe your partner down. Tell her how beautiful she was to watch and thank her for sharing the experience with you. Tell her she doesn't have to manage anything, she can just relax and soak up the experience. "I've got you" is a good phrase for this moment.

13

Vaginal Penetration

ize matters, but not in the way you think it does.

We talked about this in the sex myths section in Chapter Two, under "Myth #1, Bigger Is Better," but we're going to take an even deeper dive here, because men write to me all the time expressing the same crippling insecurity around the size of their own cocks that I felt around mine. Despite the many studies I could provide to show their penis size falls well within average (over a dozen studies are cited in a single *Medical News Today* article),[66] somehow the science isn't enough to change their genital self-esteem. Why is this?

---

66 Markus MacGill, "What Size Is the Average Penis?" medically reviewed by Joseph Brito III, MD, *Medical News Today*, January 4, 2021.

Like me, you may have spent much of your adult sex life worrying about the size of your cock. Some of that worry stems from comparison with porn stars and cultural scripts about what it means to be a man. But there's another factor involved in our genital self-esteem: deep down we all want to feel like our penis is the magic stick—that it is the best tool to give women orgasms. We want women to worship our cock like it is the holy grail of penises. Just being "normal" isn't what really moves us. We want to experience ourselves as truly worthy of admiration, adoration, and awe. If you're with a long-term partner, you may even want to be her GOAT (greatest of all time).

How do you do that with the equipment you have?

Well, firstly, you have to be willing to acknowledge that the pain you are experiencing around an imaginary problem is doing way more harm than good. One of the most entertaining dynamic duos in Hollywood is Kevin Hart and the Rock. If you see them next to each other, the contrast in height and size is shocking. Because of the porn industry, we think most men are like the Rock in the dick department and that Kevin Hart is the sad minority. But Kevin Hart is actually closer to average height than the Rock. If we all compared our height to the Rock, thinking we're way too short, everyone from Kevin Hart to guys that are six feet tall would be walking around with a huge Napoleon complex! But that is what we do with our dicks.

The secret I've found, through my own personal life and the lives of my clients, is that most women would strongly prefer to be with an incredibly confident Kevin Hart than a cripplingly insecure Rock. What women truly want isn't the big dick, it's the big-dick energy, and Kevin Hart has that big-dick energy. Confidence and competence have way more mating value than the things we think we need to possess in order to have that competence and confidence. So, I want to get real with you here and give you the actual info you need to develop both of these things.

Now, the first thing you need to understand to develop genuine genital self-esteem is how women's sexual preferences actually work. As we addressed in the myths section, most women actually prefer an average-sized cock for long-term sex,[67] even if they'd want a slightly larger one for a one-night stand.[68]

The reasons for this aren't random; most women have an average-sized vagina, and people generally want something that fits with their body. In the graphic that follows, Dr. James Pfaus, Chelsey Fasano, and I created an illustration of the actual data around genital sizes. Statistically, 95 percent of people are within the dimensions bracketed on the ruler. As you can see by the chart, that means that most penises will fit with most vaginas, especially when vaginas are properly aroused and lubricated. The pleasure gap is not a size gap, it's a skills gap.[69]

---

67   Brogan Driscoll, "Penis Size Guide: Women Reveal Ideal Length and Girth in Easy-to-Follow Guide," *The Huffington Post*, December 11, 2015.

68   Nicole Prause, et al., "Women's Preferences for Penis Size: A New Research Method Using Selection among 3D Models," *PLoS One*, 2015, 10(9).

69   The following graphic represents statistical analysis done by Dr. James G. Pfaus, created from the data in the following sources:
      Kurt T. Barnhart, Adriana Izquierdo, E. Scott Pretorius, David M. Shera, Mayadah Shabbout, and Alka Shaunik. "Baseline Dimensions of the Human Vagina." *Human Reproduction* 21, no. 6 (June 1, 2006): 1618–22.
      Debby Herbenick, Michael Reece, Vanessa Schick, and Stephanie A. Sanders. "Erect Penile Length and Circumference Dimensions of 1,661 Sexually Active Men in the United States." *The Journal of Sexual Medicine* 11, no. 1 (January 2014): 93–101.

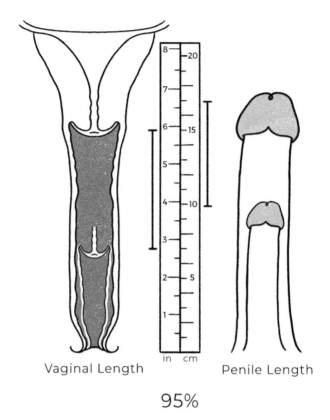

Vaginal Length　　in　cm　　Penile Length

95%

Bruce M. King, "Average-Size Erect Penis: Fiction, Fact, and the Need for Counseling." *Journal of Sex & Marital Therapy* 47, no. 1 (January 2, 2021): 80–89.

Paula B. Pendergrass, Meyer W. Belovicz, and Cornelia A. Reeves. "Surface Area of the Human Vagina as Measured from Vinyl Polysiloxane Casts." *Gynecologic and Obstetric Investigation* 55, no. 2 (2003): 110–13.

K. Promodu, K V Shanmughadas, S Bhat, and K R Nair. "Penile Length and Circumference: An Indian Study." *International Journal of Impotence Research* 19, no. 6 (November 2007): 558–63.

David Veale, Sarah Miles, Sally Bramley, Gordon Muir, and John Hodsoll. "Am I Normal? A Systematic Review and Construction of Nomograms for Flaccid and Erect Penis Length and Circumference in up to 15,521 Men: Nomograms for Flaccid/Erect Penis Length and Circumference." *BJU International* 115, no. 6 (June 2015): 978–86.

There's an important lesson in this study. What we think we want—or what looks good in an ad or from across the room—isn't necessarily what we actually like.

A funny example that illustrates this point is what has happened with iPhones in recent years. There was a trend for a while in which iPhones were getting bigger and bigger. Particularly in the US, a larger phone seemed like a good idea because of the "bigger is better" myth that we apply to almost everything—hamburgers, cars, soda pop, you name it. But what actually happened was people

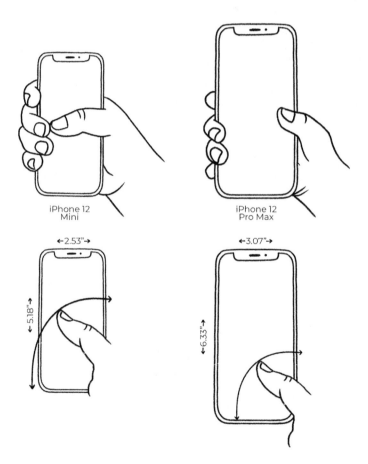

iPhone 12
Mini

iPhone 12
Pro Max

←2.53"→

←3.07"→

← 5.18"→

←6.33"→

stopped buying them because no one could hold them anymore. iPhone ended up going back to making the iPhone mini, because people wanted to be able to comfortably hold the thing in their hand!

What actually works, and what is satisfying to interact with, depends on the size of your hand compared to the size of the iPhone, and how the two interact on a day-to-day basis. User-friendliness is huge. So the question is: how do you make your *cock* user-friendly?

To get super real: you're gonna need to use different tactics, depending on the size of your penis. How did I figure all this out? Like most things in life, it was the result of experience. I got to know women with all shapes and sizes of vaginas, and men with all shapes and sizes of dicks. I spoke to and had sex with a variety of people.

I played with women who had short vaginal tunnels, who liked short penises. I met women with narrow vaginal openings who liked slim penises. I had manual and oral sex with women who didn't like penetration at all. I pulled out big dildos for size queens who loved to have their pussies stretched and their cervixes pounded. I fingered women who only wanted gentle touches on their cervix, and I stroked women who didn't want their cervixes touched at all.

Once, when I was fucking a partner who had a short vaginal tunnel, I hit her cervix and she yelped in pain. I immediately backed off and had to be careful the rest of the time we were playing. With my average-sized cock, I'd never experienced that before. I suddenly had compassion for those with big cocks. While I constantly worried my cock was too small, the well-endowed guys had to worry just as much about what to do with their cock that was too big.

None of us is one-size-fits-all. I loved my cock so much more from that moment on. Because it was average-sized, most of the time I could pound as hard as I wanted to and not hold back.

Instead of trying to compensate for what I thought every woman wanted, I started looking for lovers who were the right fit for me. Once I busted the myth of "bigger is better," I realized there was nothing to compensate for in the first place. The moral of the story is that I started to get to know all the different vaginas out there.

Beyond Size

At sex parties, I watched how these different women with different vaginas interacted with different men with different-sized cocks. What I figured out is that knowing how everything works together is more powerful than any one size or shape of vagina or penis. In martial arts, you're not going to fight the same way if you're huge or small. Both can be equally good fighters, depending on their ability to use their particular body type in the way it works best. In the same way, different sex advice is necessary for different cocks.

If you're a guy with a penis length that's 4.75 inches or less, you're actually in the same group as about 25 percent of men (different studies have slightly different numbers, but most are around this percentage).[70] In this case, you should find partners who are compatible with you who have vaginas that are on the smaller side as well, or people with bigger vaginas who enjoy a gentler feeling of penetration. There are actually a fair number of women with tiny vaginas who are overjoyed to find a partner whose penis doesn't hurt them. These women find penetration painful with average-sized penises. Because of this, when you find the person who is

---

70   Markus MacGill, "What Size Is the Average Penis?" medically reviewed by Joseph Brito III, MD, *Medical News Today*, January 4, 2021.

compatible with you, she will be equally as relieved to have found you as you will be to have found her.

If you want to be with women who have larger vaginas or really want to be stretched out, learn to fuck someone well with a dildo of their liking, or how to fist them, and learn to be confident as fuck while doing it. The truth is that most women would prefer to be with a man who's an amazing lover with a smaller penis and willing to fuck them with whatever toy or number of fingers they want, than some overconfident asshole with a big cock who doesn't know how to do anything but pound away. Remember that unshakeable confidence? Using sex toys with that attitude is sexy as fuck to the majority of women. If they like anal, you can double penetrate them with a dildo, which feels amazing to women who like being filled up.

If you're a guy with a medium-sized cock, within the 4.75 to 6.25 inch range, you are in the majority, with about 50 percent of men sharing your size. While there are differences in preference within this group as well (some women prefer 6 inches, some 7 inches, some 4.5 inches), there are some general rules of thumb to follow when it comes to figuring out your best tactics.

Firstly, recognize that you are in the majority and will be compatible with most women's vaginas! Secondly, stop obsessing about your cock size and whether it feels good to her and start thinking about how to improve your technique. Focus on how you use that penis and how you do *all* the other parts of sex. The main pitfall for you is underestimating what you have and putting way too much emphasis on your penis—at the cost of focusing on what's mutually satisfying.

If you're a guy with a larger dick, 6.25 inches and up, you're in with around 25 percent of other men. Porn-star-sized penises are very rare: only 2 percent of men have a penis that is 8 inches or longer in length.

In your case, the main danger is in *overestimating* how magical your dick is. A lot of guys with large penises skip foreplay and then try to pound away at vaginas in a way that is just downright painful without a warm-up. They try to emulate porn and are confident they can recreate the scenes they've seen where a large penis used as a jackhammer is the main focus of the show.

In real life, if this is the way you are fucking, what you are really stroking is your own ego. For the majority of women, even those that like big cock and love cervical stimulation, foreplay and clitoral stimulation is going to be super important, maybe even more so for you because of your size.

If you're a guy that is doing all of this and still finding that women are in pain because of your size, or you can't fit inside them all the way, you probably just haven't found the right vagina. There are deeper and wider vaginas out there, and women who enjoy intense stretching sensations. A guy I know even advertised on dating websites to find women with larger vaginas, after finding that so many women were in pain because of his size. The secret for those of you with this problem is that these women with larger vaginas are looking for you too—you just might need to be more explicit in your search to find them.

You can also use tools to increase your partner's comfort and pleasure. Buy an OhNut, a wearable donut for your dick that makes sex less painful if it's going too deep.[71] And don't forget: lube is your best friend; it should be in your everyday carry.

---

71 OhNut.co.

No matter what size cock you have, there are certain principles that apply to everyone, and these are arguably the most important of them all. Be a caring, kind person, who values her pleasure and her happiness. Make her feel safe and cared for. Learn how to give her pleasure with other things besides your dick. Read erotic cues and learn to be a good dance partner in sex. Don't be boring. Be willing to learn, give and receive feedback, and approach each woman's body as unique.

Learn to use your cock in a way that feels good to her, through learning about her body and asking her questions about sex. Figure out how to make her cum, a lot! When you pull together all the details covered in this book, you'll end up taking her beyond satisfied. And the more she cums, the happier she'll be, and the more she'll associate you with pleasure, safety, and happiness. *That* is when she will start worshipping your cock like you always wanted it to be worshipped.

That is the real secret to genital self-confidence. I can tell you over and over that you are enough, but at the end of the day, I'm just a dude you don't know, speaking to you through words on a page.

Confidence and self-esteem are earned. If you want to feel like your dick is the magic stick and make her adore your cock, you just have to make her associate you and your cock with reliable pleasure, orgasms, and happiness. At the end of the day, what this boils down to is reliably making her feel good. This is achievable for everyone through sexual skill acquisition, and learning to be a good and decent human being who is worthy of that kind of admiration. If you take the time and make the sacrifices to be that guy in bed and in life, you can get what you've always wanted. You can earn those feelings of being worthy of awe, and make her view your cock as a magic wand, no matter what size dick you have. And if you're into being a slut, you'll have a line of women who'll want to come back for more.

Your Soft Skills Are as
Important as Your Equipment

I'm going to tell you a story to really bring this point home. A couple of years ago, I met one of my lovers, Astrid. She was a super hottie with an unbelievable body who had been a stripper for most of her life and fucked almost exclusively huge black men with porn-star-sized dicks, many of whom were actual porn stars and professional athletes. I was pretty convinced that I wasn't her type, but I thought it was worth a shot anyway. Why not?

At this point, I was already super confident and had nothing to lose. What ended up happening is something that surprised even me. We became friends and bonded over shared interests, and during our friendship she showed me a picture of one of her ex's dicks. The guy had a cock the size of a soda can. At this point I was thinking, "Oh fuck, this is never gonna work." But we continued to be friends and really connected in many ways.

Then, one night we ended up in bed together. Even though I had a lot more confidence, the insecurity I had about my penis size came back to haunt me all over again, and the wave of fear rushing down my spine was all too familiar. I felt like a teenage boy all over again. But, instead of drowning in my insecurities, I reminded myself of what I had learned over the past decade. I decided not to be the one to reject myself before she rejected me, and I decided to be sure as hell to give it my best.

Then, I did exactly what I'm telling you to do: over the next few months, I provided her with reliable pleasure, was super confident and caring, and learned her body. We explored things together. Sometimes we played with the nJoy 11, one of my favorite toys for size queens. I helped her have her first anal orgasm with my dick, and she learned things about her body she didn't know. I held her when she cried, cooked her good food, and gave her lots of orgasms. To both of our great surprise, as she continued being with me, she ended up having vaginal and cervical orgasms with my penis. She turned into one of my regular lovers and was incredibly enthusiastic about being with me. But something even more surprising happened that taught both of us a lot about sexual preference.

Over the course of a couple of years, her preferences changed. She now goes on dating websites looking for Asian guys, and has learned to love my size in a way that she never really thought would happen. Why is this?

Listen up, because here comes the secret sauce: a large part of sexual preference is what we've learned makes us feel good. When we have positive experiences, we associate that person and all their physical characteristics with the positive experience. We go through pleasure conditioning. When something gives us pleasure, we start to associate that thing with pleasure. We learn to prefer and learn to be attracted to what consistently feels good.

This is not just a theory; it's backed by scientific research. Dr. Pfaus explained to me that there are oxytocin receptors on the clitoris and cervix that respond to oxytocin release by the pituitary, which is triggered by bonding. This oxytocin pathway responds to conditioning and causes us to prefer and want what we associate with pleasure.[72] Even rats operate on this basic premise, seeking

---

72   Conall E. MacCionnaith, et al., "Fos Expression Is Increased in Oxytocin
      Neurons of Female Rats with a Sexually Conditioned Mate Preference for an
      Individual Male Rat," *Hormones and Behavior*, January 2020, 117.

after the rat partners that are associated with the best sexual experiences, which alter oxytocin expression in the brain.[73]

The above story is an extreme example, and it's not to say you should chase after someone if you're not their type, trying to change their mind. The reason I'm saying this is to impress upon you just how powerful being a reliable, competent sexual partner who cares about their lovers is. It can do mind-blowing things. As James Clear, the author of *Atomic Habits* would say, when something is satisfying, we tend to make a habit out of it.[74] You can be her habit. And when someone associates you with repeated pleasure and consistent happiness, your cock is usually the lucky recipient of all that gratitude.

There are tons of guys out there that are amazing humans but are stuck in total despair because they think their penis is the reason they aren't enough. At the end of the day, figuring out how to be a man that is worthy of admiration is a learnable skill for anyone, as long as he's willing to do the work to become a good lover and a good person.

Never Take a Good Warm-Up for Granted

So, now that we've gotten the psychological parts of penetrative sex sorted out, what about the physical? The first step to good penetrative sex is a good warm-up.

I recently hopped on as a guest to a coaching call for women, led by a fellow sex coach, Alexa Martinez. The women wanted to know

---

73   Amanda Holley, et al, "The Role of Oxytocin and Vasopressin in Conditioned Mate Guarding Behavior in the Female Rat," *Physiology and Behavior*, May 2015, 114: 7–14.

74   James Clear, *Atomic Habits: An Easy and Proven Way to Build Good Habits and Break Bad Ones* (New York: Avery, 2018).

how they could enjoy penetrative sex more. I mentioned offhand that it helps to have a few warm-up orgasms, and midway through my mansplaining, I realized many of the women's jaws had dropped. I stopped and asked them what they were thinking.

"*Warm-up orgasms?*" one woman said. "I usually don't even cum once."

Like I said in Chapter Six, most women are multiorgasmic. The reason many women haven't experienced multiple orgasms is usually not biology. Barring a medical condition, the reason many women haven't had multiples is because they don't know how to coach their partners to pleasure them, and their partners don't know what they're doing.

Even so, only about one in six women gets off from penetration alone. Most women prefer a blend of external and internal stimulation—penetration plus clit rubbing, for example. The more aroused your partner is before penetrative sex, the more likely it will be pleasurable for her. Everyone hates premature penetration.

As people get more relaxed and aroused, their bodies change. The genitals get more engorged and swollen. My favorite time for penetrative sex is after my partner has had a couple of orgasms: their vagina feels different to me, more squishy and engorged, and the sensation tends to get better for them, too.

Take Turns

One of the features of penetrative sex is that the positions that feel great to one partner don't always feel good to the other. For example, one of the most pleasurable positions for a lot of guys is to fuck their partner with her knees bent in towards her chest. But for women with low hip flexibility, this position can get uncomfortable.

Also, for many women, it's easier to cum if they straighten out their legs. But if she straightens her legs out to relieve the muscle tension or to get into a more orgasm-friendly position, her pelvis tilts back into a position that's not very penetration friendly. Her body almost literally kicks the guy's cock out. Interestingly, bondage can be a great engineering hack for this problem: it gives the muscles something to flex against.

If you've experienced this challenge, there are a variety of ways to work with it. You can turn your partner facedown and prop her belly and hips up with pillows so they're elevated. Pillows, cushions, and furniture can become handy props to support your partner in different positions. You can even bend her over the kitchen counter or the dining room table. One of the exciting puzzles of penetrative sex is finding the positions that are optimized for what each partner is feeling.

But think back to Betty Martin's Wheel of Consent. We're used to moving our cocks for our pleasure, which puts our partner in the receiving position. If we want to optimize penetrative sex for our partner's pleasure, we can also encourage her to touch us and move for her pleasure.

Many women are not familiar with what it's like to fuck their partners for their own pleasure. They may have no idea what feels good to them, or what they want to do. Set up a play lab to test different positions and angles so you can both discover what feels good to your partner.

If I'm fucking a new partner who isn't used to directing her partner for her pleasure, I ask her to move in the way that feels good to her. Pay attention to the angles she uses. If you're fucking in missionary position, your cock most likely goes pretty straight into her vagina. But if she lifts her knees towards her chest, the angle of her pelvis tilts, and so does the angle of your cock in her vagina. Your thrusts (or hers) put more pressure on one side of the vagina than another. She can twist her hips to put more pressure on other sides of the vagina. She can raise and lower her legs, or you can raise and lower her hips. When you find an angle that works, you can start to calibrate with smaller adjustments, getting more and more precise on the angle that works best for your partner.

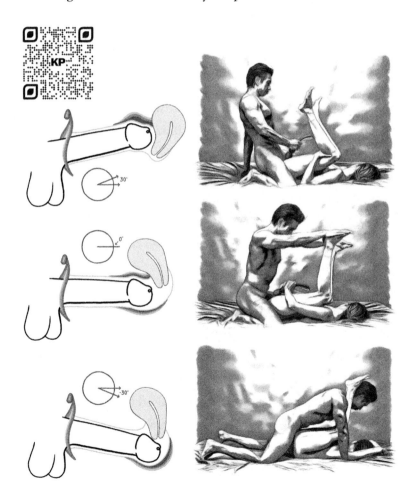

When you spend time taking turns to calibrate the angles that work for your partner and the angles that work for you, you'll dial in the positions and transitions that are hot to both of you.

The Positions

Each penetrative sex position comes with unique sensations and different kinds of access to your partner's body. As you get into position, take some time to look at your partner's body, connect with her, and think creatively about what each position allows you to do.

With each position, add in clitoral stimulation. Ask your partner to rub her own clit however it feels good, or you can use your thumb to stroke her clit as you thrust. You can also bring in a vibrator for her to hold or for you to hold.

Missionary

With your partner on her back, you have access to stroke her belly and play with her boobs. You can playfully slap her thighs if she likes a little impact. Because you're face-to-face in missionary position, you can look your partner in the eyes and connect with her before you begin.

One of the most ergonomic positions is to have your partner hold the backs of her knees with her knees bent and her legs wide. This gives you full access to her vagina, and it tilts her hips in a way that feels good to most people. You can accentuate this tilt by putting a pillow under her hips.

Tease your partner's vulva and clit with the head of your cock. When you're ready to penetrate your partner, hold the head of your penis and push it down against the bottom wall of her vagina as you slide in. This is the same technique you learned in Chapter Seven to insert your fingers: the bottom wall of the vagina is the most stretchy, and pressing down into it makes insertion easier.

To adjust the angle, have your partner let go of her knees. Take hold of her feet and slowly rotate her legs down so she can feel how the change in her hips changes where your cock puts pressure on her G-spot internally. Find the angle that feels best to her.

Adjust the distance between her legs, too. She'll feel different sensations from having her knees wide versus having her thighs together.

Then try adjusting your own position. You can be upright, kneeling with both knees on the bed, holding her feet or her hips. You can also bend over and plant your hands next to her shoulders, with her feet over your shoulders. Try positioning yourself in a lunge, with one foot planted on the bed and one knee down. Another idea, called the Coital Alignment Technique, or CAT for short, is great for clitoral stimulation. Climb on top of her so that your pelvis is higher than normal and then use your pubic bone to rub against her clit while you are fucking, doing more of an up-and-down grinding motion than in-and-out. You can also move from side to side in this position, massaging the A-spot, P-spot, or cervix, while grinding against her clit simultaneously.

Side Angle

Having your partner lie on her side is a great way to put her in a comfortable position while still giving you access to play with your partner's boobs, slap the side of her thigh, or caress her body. This is also an easy position for her to play with her own clit with toys or a hand. With her hips turned to the side, she gets different kinds of stimulation than in other positions. Have her split her legs so her bottom leg is straight and her top leg is bent at the knee towards her chest.

When you enter your partner from this position, press the head of your cock towards the bottom of her vagina, which in this position is to one side.

Tilt her body towards her back or more towards her chest until you both find the angle that feels best. Like in missionary, you can hold her top hip steady as you thrust, or you can bend over and place your hands on the bed at either side of her waist.

Adjust your own position to find the most comfortable angle. You can stay on all fours with your torso parallel to hers, or you can move both hands to one side, so your torso is positioned diagonally to hers. In either of these positions, with the right hip movement and a bit of attention to where your penis is inside her vagina, you can hit the G-spot and move up to the cervix and back down, finding which spots she enjoys most. I find it most pleasurable to keep my torso straight, but by trying the variations you and your partner may find a new sensation you love.

Doggy Style

In doggy style, your partner is on her hands and knees. Her back is arched, her knees are wide apart, and her butt and vulva are on full, beautiful display. Take a moment before you enter your partner to stroke her body and appreciate her. Have her look back at you to connect—it's super hot.

As you enter your partner in this position, push the head of your penis up towards her anus, again where her vaginal wall is most stretchy. She can stay on her hands and knees with straight arms, or she can lower her chest towards the bed, keeping her hips high. Your partner can adjust the height of her hips by widening or narrowing her knees.

There are a lot of possible variations with doggy style, depending on how strong and flexible you and your partner are. One of my favorite variations is to have my partner take her chest all the way down to the bed and reach her arms back towards me. Then I take hold of her wrists with a firm grip, and I lean back. As I pull on her arms, my partner's chest lifts off the bed, and I counterbalance by leaning farther back.

If your partner's shoulders are flexible, you can have her reach both arms behind her back to hold her own wrists. You can hold her forearms or wrists as you thrust, and the position creates a light bondage experience for your partner.

Cowgirl

In cowgirl, you lay on your back as your partner rides your cock. This is a great position to get comfortable and relax as your partner moves in the ways that feel best to her. Let her guide your cock to enter her.

Your partner can fuck you while she's on her knees, or she can squat over you with her feet on the bed; both variations create different sensations. You can watch her touch her clit and pay attention to how she moves her fingers as she thrusts.

She can ride your cock by moving up and down, or she can keep her hips pressing down on you as she tilts her pelvis back and forth. If she needs help figuring this one out, you can actively move her thighs or pelvis back and forth while pressing your pelvis into her, so she can grind against you in a way that feels good for her.

One of my favorite hacks is to wear the NŌS cock ring, which provides amazing clitoral stimulation for her, hands free. This way she can hold onto you, or the bed, to support herself, while still getting clitoral stimulation. It's also super hot when she is riding you to get herself off. It's pure erotic gold, just being the witness of that. And sometimes, if you time it right, it can be a good way to facilitate a simultaneous orgasm for both of you. Use the QR code that follows to check out the NŌS.

You can take a more active role in this position, too. Have your

partner lay her chest against yours, hold her hips, and plant your feet on the bed. Use your legs to lift your hips to pound her.

In another variation, hold hands with your partner and place her hands on either side of your head, so your arms are bent at the elbow with backs of hands on the bed. Then lift your hips a lot, until your partner is on hands and knees and your hips are high in the air. You can thrust by lowering and raising your hips.

In a similar variation, have your partner squat over your cock with her feet on the bed. Ask her to press her hands on your chest and straighten her arms. Hold underneath her hips to support and lift them a little, and then thrust your hips to pound her.

If you're able to install a strap above your bed, like a TRX suspension trainer, she can much more easily ride you while holding onto the strap above.

Reverse Cowgirl

Have your partner turn to face away, and let her hold your penis to insert it in herself. She can stay upright, or she can give you a fuller view of her vulva by holding your ankles and tilting her butt back.

She can give herself stimulation by riding up and down, or by undulating her body to tilt her pelvis back and forth.

Think like a Mechanic

You can experience variations in each of these positions depending on who is moving: one partner, the other partner, or both at the same time. Some positions, like reverse cowgirl, make it easier for one partner to move actively while the other partner stays more passive. In doggy style, you have the option for either or both partners to do the moving. You could fuck her; you could stay still while she fucks you; or you could synchronize your movement so you're both thrusting.

Encourage your partner to move in the way that feels really good to her. Add stimulation to her clit when possible. Cowgirl is a great position for your partner to experience external and internal sensation, because she can ride your cock and rub her clit on your pubic bone at the same time.

When you find positions that work for both you and your partner, you can play with pounding harder or faster. Some positions create new challenges as you increase the velocity. Pounding away in missionary position can cause your partner's whole body to slide away from you one thrust at a time, and you can lose your leverage point. Hold her hips to keep her in the same spot. You can also wrap a pillowcase or a T-shirt around your partner's hips to create a handle to hold her closer to you.

When you're fucking harder and harder in doggy style, your partner's legs might spread farther apart, which changes the height and angle. Communicate with your partner to understand whether she's adjusting to change the sensation, or whether her legs slipping is incidental. You can give commands for her to lift her hips or hold her legs closer together. Turning on a little more of your director side can be incredibly sexy and damn useful.

Sometimes the movement between you and your partner is intuitive, and everything seems to click. Other times, you'll need to communicate more to dial in the right position, angle, and speed. Take note of the conditions that reliably give your partner pleasure. You can come back to these to keep her arousal up in between new positions and sensations.

One of the most pleasurable things about penetrative sex is that both partners are getting sensitive areas stimulated at the same time. Penetrative sex allows each partner to shift fluidly between giver and receiver at different times. When you spend time calibrating the sensations that feel best to each partner, you can intuitively find a flow between different positions and learn to dance with your partner.

PRO TIP

Physical health is erotic wealth. This statement could not be more true than when it comes to penetrative sex. This is where your flexibility, mobility, strength, and aerobic endurance all come into play in the bedroom.

When everything comes together well in penetrative sex, it can be one of the most intimate sex acts. It can be one of the kinkiest power play realms, one of the most romantic connected experiences, and everything in between. So, remember, it's more than just biomechanics. With practice, it can be an expression of the different pleasure styles, a place where different sides of you can come out to be seen, met, and played with.

14

Anal

*I*n *porn, you can find videos of people getting cocks pounded* in their asses with no warm-up and (apparently) no lube; they go seamlessly from vagina to ass to mouth as though each one is a spotlessly clean, unrestricted tunnel.

But anal sex in porn is about as close to real-life anal sex as the stunt driving in *Fast and Furious* is to real-life driving. It's possible to do both acts—obviously the drivers and porn actors are able to pull off their respective feats—but what you don't see behind the camera is the immense amount of prep work, training, and multiple takes needed to do the scene safely.

When it comes to anal sex, it's important for your education to precede your experience. You have to be aware of the health hazards anal sex presents, most importantly to the receiving partner, and you have to know the techniques that keep the receiving partner safe from illness, tears, and anal fissures. The consequences of diving in to anal without a proper education are severe. If you fuck up anal sex the first time with your partner, you'll likely ruin your chances to try it again.

So before you ask your partner if you can fuck her in the ass, think about how you'd feel if the roles were reversed. Imagine your partner has no idea how to do anal sex, and she goes out to buy a thick dildo to fuck you in the ass. She might feel confident trying it out on you because she's seen it in porn—but do you want to get in that car with her behind the wheel?

Despite the risks, people have been fucking butts since forever ago. Anal sex is a little taboo, and at the same time it takes a lot of trust between two partners to do it well—both these factors make anal really sexy. Some people think anal sex feels better than vaginal sex, but of course every person's preference is subjective. The anal sphincters are tighter than vaginal muscles, but only at the opening. Past the sphincters, it's actually roomier inside a butt than inside a vagina, and the sensations are different with anal than with penis-in-vagina sex.

For the receiver, anal sex can be pleasurable when it's done at the pace the receiving partner needs. Remember the P-spot from Chapter Two? If your partner liked getting fingered on the P-spot in her vagina, you can give stimulation to the other side of the same tissues with anal sex. Some people have orgasms from anal stimulation alone, though it's a great idea to layer anal stimulation with other sensations you know your partner likes, like clit stimulation.

Asking for It

One of the most frequent questions I get as a sex educator is, "How can I get my partner to do anal with me?" My answer is: be good at everything else. Never pressure a partner into anal (or any sex act, for that matter). When you nag your partner to do something you want but she doesn't, you show a lack of respect for her boundaries and you damage the relationship.

Instead, focus on building skill and trust with your partner so they're willing to be more vulnerable. If you fuck up cooking an egg, no one will trust you with a filet mignon. Anal sex is earned.

In addition to building your skills and demonstrating care for your partner, you can use your request for anal sex to practice good communication with your partner. Share why anal sex is hot for you. Tell your partner you want to talk about the possibility of anal sex, but you don't want to do it if she's not excited by it. You don't want your partner to simply tolerate anal sex for you; the risk of having an unpleasant or even painful experience is too high. Lay out clearly that if your partner wants to try anal sex with you, either of you can stop at any time for any reason without consequences.

Before you explore the pleasures of anal sex, you need to know how to do it in a safe and healthy way.

A Healthy Butt Is a Happy Butt

First off, a caveat: we're not going to cover absolutely everything you need to know for Olympic-level ass play. There are great resources for how to keep yourself and your partner healthy and safe, and you need to do your due diligence to keep learning before you try more advanced techniques.

But to get you started, let's go over the basics.

The first obvious risk is that the ass is literally sometimes full of shit. As a result, it houses specific bacteria that are safe and healthy in the ass, but which can cause infection if they're spread to other areas of the body. When engaging in anal sex, you have to be very careful of cross-contamination. Don't massage your partner's asshole with your fingers and then use the same hand to finger her pussy. Have gloves on hand. You can easily finger your partner's butthole with a gloved hand and then peel the glove off to touch other parts of her body with your clean hands.

Of course, shit happens—literally. Porn often sets people up with an expectation that assholes are clean and they smell like flowers. But porn stars often have enemas or colonics in addition to fasting the day before and the day of a shoot, so there is no chance of poop being in their colon in that moment.

Since most people don't go to these lengths in real life, it's important to be realistic: this is where poop comes out, and if you want to engage in anal sex, you have to develop a relationship with mess. Don't shame your partner if your fingers or your cock come out with a little poop on them. Have a plan to handle it.

You can keep puppy pads, towels, gloves, condoms, and lube nearby, as well as a basket in which to throw anything that gets dirty. If shit happens, just clean it up. Deal with it like you don't give a shit.

If I can tell my partner is embarrassed, I'll often respond with a gentle joke like, "Would it make you feel better if I poop on myself?" Usually, my partner laughs and we go take a shower. In short, if you don't want to deal with shit, don't do anal.

Another risk in anal sex is that while the vagina and the mouth create their own lubrication, the anus doesn't. You need lube, not just to help toys and fingers and your cock slide more easily into your partner's ass, but to protect those delicate tissues from tearing.

Butts have two sphincters that act as gates to the rectum. One is external, and it's possible to control it voluntarily when you clench or relax your anus, which is a helpful feature that keeps you from pooping unexpectedly. The second sphincter is internal, and its action is involuntary.

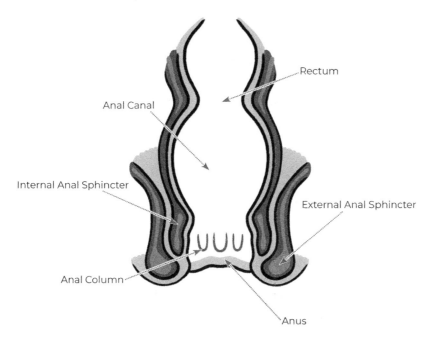

The second sphincter is controlled by the autonomic nervous system, the same thing that controls your heartbeat, breathing, and digestion. You can control your heart rate and breathing voluntarily by learning to relax and calm yourself, but not directly like you would your arm or leg muscle. Similarly, you can't force yourself to be sleepy. In order to sleep, you have to learn to relax in a dark, cold room, and your body naturally drifts off.

The same is true of the action of this second sphincter—the only way to control it is through indirectly relaxing it. These gates are right next to each other, one after the other. Don't pry open either sphincter with too much force, or you can damage the tissues.

Lube helps reduce friction on those tissues. Because the anus doesn't self-lubricate, you have to continually reapply lube during anal sex. A good warm-up is also necessary to help your partner relax and soften the involuntary muscles around the anus. If you want to fuck your partner in the ass, start with warm-up orgasms from fingering, oral, or vaginal penetration. Then slowly progress towards penetration with the tips that follow.

How to Prepare for Anal Penetration

How much prep and cleaning your partner wants to do is up to her. Prep can range from washing the exterior with soap and water to douching or doing an enema. (Toilet paper doesn't cut it; if you want to have anal sex often, invest in a bidet.) We won't get into instructions for that here, but you can find resources at the QR code that follows.

A sensual shower like the kind described in Chapter Five is a great

way to clean your partner and build intimacy. Plus, washing your partner and sliding your hands over her soapy skin is sexy and romantic.

Start with a good warm-up to relax and arouse your partner (and possibly give her a few orgasms). Don't make anal the first activity; give yourselves lots of time to have other kinds of sex first. Remember that arousal doesn't just soften and swell tissues; it will also help your partner feel less inhibited. When you're ready to play with your partner's butt, explore and go slowly.

A rim job is an excellent way to warm your partner up to anal touch because it prepares her psychologically for anal play. If you show you're willing to lick her anus and put your face on it, she can relax knowing you're comfortable playing down there.

Beyond warming your partner up, you want to help her create positive associations, both with sensation on her anus and with how she feels about the experience emotionally. The ass is a vulnerable body part for most people, so show your love and admiration for your partner's butt.

Put a puppy pad and a dark towel down on the bed to make any messes easy to clean up. Have baby wipes at the ready. With gloves on, lubricate your hand and use your fingers to massage your partner's anus around the opening. Let her get used to the sensation of your fingers and encourage her to finger her own clit while you stroke her ass.

If she's really feeling uncomfortable, it might help for her to put her own fingers in her ass while you play with her clit, and then swap. Wear gloves for anal play, so you can remove them when switching to the vulva and clit. Sometimes intense sensations can be more enjoyable when we feel in control of them and are aware of what's going on.

Especially if it's your partner's first time receiving anal stimulation, ask her to take the lead on telling you when to advance. When you demonstrate that you're willing to wait on penetrating her with your cock, you show your partner that you can put her well-being and her body above your desire. Honestly, if you can't demonstrate that basic principle of sexual etiquette, I recommend you don't fuck anybody, anal or otherwise. Show your partner that you can keep your word.

Start Small, Stretch It Out

As your partner pleasures her clit and vulva, let the pad of one gloved finger rest over the opening of her anus. Breathe, wait, and feel for her anus to pucker slightly as it relaxes. That's how you know your partner's body might be ready for insertion. That little pucker is the first gate opening. Always tell your partner what you're about to do so she's not surprised by a finger sliding up her ass. Take a moment before each step to check in. Don't persist through pain; if your partner tells you it feels painful or irritating, ask if she wants to stop and always be willing to pull back.

> **PRO TIP**
>
> Here's a great hack for anal insertion used by medical professionals in the emergency room. When your partner wants you to insert a finger, ask her to try to gently push your finger out as you smoothly slide your finger in. While this hack may seem counterintuitive at first glance, think about what happens to the muscles of the anus when you're pooping. As you push out, the muscles relax and open wider.

Have your partner bear down to push out while you slide your finger to one knuckle deep. See how your partner feels, and if she wants more, repeat the hack to slide your finger in deeper. You never have to insert a finger or a toy all at once. If your partner wants, insert in small stages. Start small so there's no struggle for your partner the first time she feels new sensations in her anus.

Anything inserted in the butt—whether fingers, a toy, or a penis—feels better when angled upward towards the belly button at a forty-five-degree angle. This forty-five-degree angle rule was popularized by Gigi Engle, an amazing sex educator colleague of mine, author of *All the F*cking Mistakes*.[75]

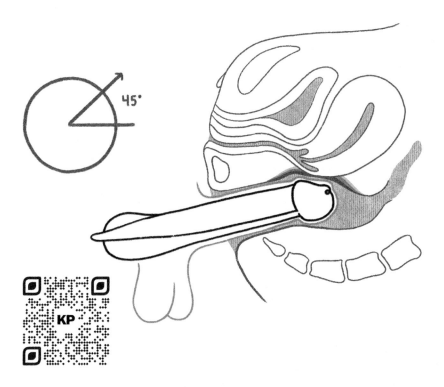

---

75   Gigi Engle, *All the F*cking Mistakes: A Guide to Sex, Love, and Life* (New York: St. Martin's Press, 2020).

This insertion angle makes it so that pressure is applied to the G-spot, clitoral bulbs, or A-spot and cervix, depending on how deep you go. By doing this, you create stimulation of the vagus, hypogastric, and pelvic nerves all at once. This is a game of calibration. It might not be exactly forty-five degrees for every person; you might need to experiment with angles around that range. But when you hit the right spot, it will feel different to the receiver, and should make this act way more pleasurable.

Here's a second trick: ask your partner to squeeze your finger as hard as she can. Have her squeeze until she gets tired of holding the tension, and then ask her to relax. When the muscles release, they usually open up even more.

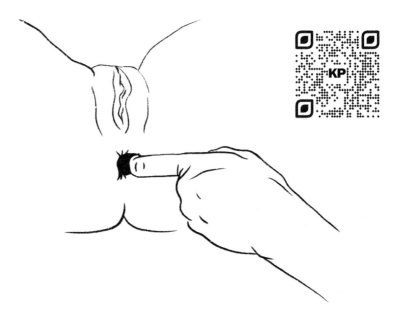

You can also help your partner stretch her anus just like an athlete would stretch a muscle by using PNF stretching (proprioceptive neuromuscular facilitation). This type of stretching was designed to relax muscle and increase tone or activity. This is the reason I love this hack for helping with anal play: it helps your partner develop the distinction between a clenched and relaxed anus, while increasing flexibility. With your finger inserted in her anus, ask your partner to squeeze your finger, and press your finger up towards her G-spot.

Keep pressing as she squeezes her anus for five to seven seconds. When she relaxes her muscles, continue to press up even more to stretch the tissues if that feels comfortable for her. Then turn your finger so you can press to one side and repeat the exercise. Turn your finger so it presses down towards her spine and repeat. Do the exercise one more time to stretch the final side.

With your finger fully inside, take time to feel the different textures of your partner's anus and the gentle S-curve shape of her anus. You can flex your finger up to massage her P-spot and G-spot. Don't slide your finger in and out; just flex up towards her G-spot. Calibrate to find the level of pressure that feels good to your partner. I go over this stretching technique extensively in my Sex Hacker Pro course.

As your partner relaxes, you'll feel her anus relax, too. Continue to lube up your finger periodically. After your partner gets used to the sensation of your finger in her anus, you can try other kinds of stimulation. Your partner might like more friction from moving your finger in and out, or she might like the sensation of twisting your finger back and forth. You can add in a vibrator or any other kind of stimulation your partner likes so that you're layering something she already finds pleasurable with the new sensation. If your partner wants to, you can help stimulate her clit and G-spot to orgasm, so she has the experience of linking orgasm to anal stimulation.

Once one finger is comfortable for your partner, you can see if she wants to try two fingers. Bring her to another orgasm with that level of stretch and stimulation, and then try actively stretching her anus a little more. Continue to check in about what feels pleasurable and back off if anything hurts.

When your partner is ready for you to pull your finger out, ask her to push your finger out as you slide it out. Just like inserting your finger, when your partner bears down the muscles relax and open up, making it easier to slide your finger out.

Whether you go to penis-in-anus penetration from there is dependent on the size of your cock and the comfort of your partner. One of the beautiful features I realized about my average-sized cock is that it's anal friendly. Guys who have larger cocks will likely need to do a lot more warm-up and play with toys before their partner can increase their capacity. Don't go from two fingers to the size of a soda can. Use toys to stairstep up with two or three stages in between.

If your partner isn't ready to try having your cock in her ass, invest in toys. You can get anal training kits with different-sized butt plugs from small to large. Always make sure to buy toys with flared bases for anal play, to make sure you don't accidentally get a toy stuck in the anus. Your partner can wear a butt plug in her anus during vaginal sex to get used to the sensation. Silicone lube can't be used with silicone toys, so be sure to buy the appropriate lube. Consider buying a dildo that's the size of your cock and give it to your partner to masturbate and practice with on her own. When she's able to fit the toy cock in her butt, she'll be able to look at your cock and think, *Game on.*

Advanced Anal Fingering Techniques

I want to share with you two backdoor techniques you've probably never heard of but that will most likely blow your lover's mind.

Warning: this is not a basic bro technique. Before you try this, make sure you have a certain level of mastery over the other techniques in this book, a good understanding of anatomy, and a solid level of comfort and communication with your partner. If you skipped the anatomy and neuroscience section, go back and read it before proceeding.

The first trick is an extension of what I call my "signature move," the squirting technique you learned in Chapter Twelve. The principle is exactly the same, but instead of inserting your fingers into the vagina, you insert your fingers into the anus. You're aiming to stimulate all the nerves of the G-spot, vagina, and anus altogether. If you do this right, you can induce squirting because it will also stimulate the urethral sponge.

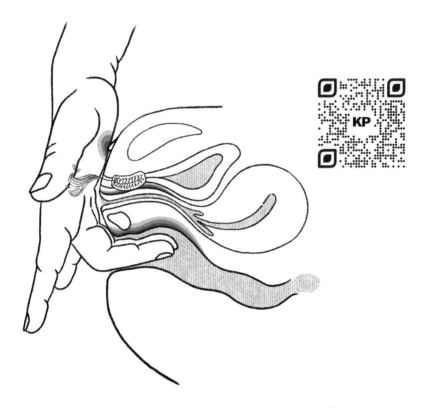

Finally, if your partner likes this so far and you feel she'd enjoy some more intense sensations, I have a move I jokingly call "release the Kraken." To do this successfully, you'll need a partner who is willing to fully trust and surrender to her own bodily functions, because this technique—and the pleasure and orgasm it produces—causes a lot of involuntary gaping and contractions anally and vaginally. When done correctly, it will cause her pelvic floor to push and pull in ways that are beyond her conscious control. If you've been holding a fart in all day, it's bound to come out. I highly recommend an enema beforehand if you're not into scat play or super comfortable with your own or your partner's poop.

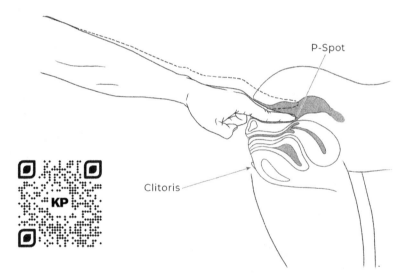

To do this, your partner should be in doggy style, and your fingers will be inserted as deeply as they can go. You should already be stimulating her, and she should be on the verge of cuming. A vibrator on the clit works well with this trick. When she's about to cum, straighten your arm and move your hand up and down at a forty-five-degree angle as fast as you can. Speed and pressure are key. Done right, all the involuntary pelvic floor contractions this causes, from gaping to strong squeezes in, feel absolutely amazing, and the pleasure will radiate all the way through her body, via visceral nerve fibers. This also induces a deep feeling of surrender to both her own body and to the person facilitating the experience. For people that like kink play, this provides the same feeling of intense sensation and intense intimacy.

Going All In

When you and your partner are ready to have penetrative anal sex, be sure to warm her up just as thoroughly as you did for the exploratory exercises. She may not need you to help stretch the tissues, but she'll benefit from stimulating her clit with her hand or a vibrator while you finger her anus and get her aroused and familiar with anal sensations.

Wear a condom. Just like you don't want cross-contamination from anus to vagina, you also don't want to get poop in your pee hole because it can cause a urinary tract infection. Be sure to lube up your cock and condom from the head all the way down the shaft. Silicone lube lasts longer for anal sex, and it provides a slicker, smoother sensation.

Position your partner lying on her side with her bottom leg straight and her top leg bent at the knee. This makes for an easy, straight line to enter her anus, and it also ensures that when you lube up, the lube doesn't drip down to cross-contaminate your partner's vulva.

Don't do anal in the dark. Be sure you can clearly see your partner's anus so you can confidently slide your cock in. You also want to make sure you're fully aroused and hard; it won't be as comfortable to try to put your penis in your partner's anus if it's soft.

Hold the head of your cock and align the angle so your pee hole is in a straight line with your partner's anus. This is like threading the eye of a needle—alignment matters. You don't want to angle your cock up or down as that will likely be uncomfortable for your partner. Ask your partner to push out as you slowly slide in, and check with her to see if it feels comfortable. Don't fuck vigorously right away; stay still as your partner pleasures her clit and gets used to the sensation of your cock inside her.

When your partner is ready for you to add a bit of movement, keep your cock straight and gently move in and out. Lube up your cock by dripping lube on the shaft as you pull your cock out, and then you can seamlessly slide your cock back in. (Porn stars use a lube shooter to squirt lube into the anus to make lubing up easier.) Make sure the lube doesn't drip down from your partner's anus to her vulva—this is a particular consideration when you're fucking her ass doggy style.

If you're switching back and forth between anal and vaginal sex, wash your cock and pelvis with soap and water in between. You can make the transition faster by wearing a condom for anal sex, and you can take off the condom when you want to go back to vaginal sex. Wipe your pubic bone down with a baby wipe before pressing yourself up against your partner's vulva.

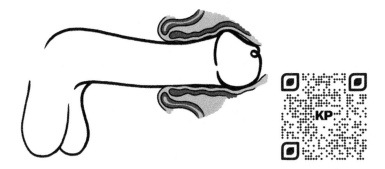

Positions for Anal Sex

You can do anal in any of the positions that you do vaginal sex in. But there is one in particular that is great for beginners. The cowgirl position covered in the previous chapter gives your partner more control over the depth, angle, speed, and sensation of anal sex. This gives the receiving partner total control of what can often be a very scary act, making it much less intimidating. Encourage your partner to take the lead and move her body for her own pleasure. She can reach back to hold the shaft of your penis while she guides the head of your cock into her anus.

In another variation of the cowgirl position, your partner can anchor her hands on your chest and lift her hips slightly to give you room to pump up and down. Plant your heels and use your legs to lift your hips and thrust. Your partner can then move from an active role to a passive one as you move your hips to stimulate your cock and her anus. Go slow with this variation, as it can be very intense for the receiver.

Double Penetration

Another reason to gift your partner a dildo to masturbate with is that you can use it for double penetration. She can insert the dildo inside her vagina while you fuck her butt, and you can both experience a new range of sensations. You can also hold the dildo against your pelvis while you fuck her with your dick, turning you into an anime tentacle porn fantasy with multiple penises.

I love the feeling of double penetration, because the toy creates more pressure against my partner's anus. Many people like the "full" feeling that comes from having a toy and a cock in them at the same time.

Pulling Out

The head of the cock is usually the biggest part, so getting it in and out of the external sphincter is usually the most intense part for women. Communication around pulling out matters. In the same way that you checked in with your partner to see how far to advance, check in with her again when you're ready to pull out. Ask if she's ready, and if she is, tell her to push you out with her muscles as you pull back. If you notice a little poop on the condom, handle it right away. Use baby wipes to clean yourself and your partner off, take off the condom, and wash your hands and your cock with soapy water.

Don't stay in bed after anal sex; get up and shower. Offer to shower together or give your partner space to shower or use the bathroom alone. If your bathroom is close to your bedroom, go into the other room, tell her you're going to get her some water and make her a snack, and give her some space to clean up or use the toilet alone. Tell her to meet you in the kitchen afterwards. Sometimes anal will make her have to poop or fart and she might want some private time. Both partners should pee after sex to lessen the chance of getting a urinary tract infection.

Embrace the Sillier Moments of Sex

Feedback is critical with any style of sex, but particularly with anal. As you communicate with your partner, try new things, and adjust to each other's needs, you may bump up against awkward moments. As Reid Mihalko says, "Embrace the awkward."

Porn edits out the awkward missteps and little negotiations that are a normal and necessary part of sex. Check in with your partner when you notice hesitation or resistance. Stop and ask what is most comfortable with her and send a clear message that you don't want her to grit her teeth and endure sensations that aren't pleasurable. The best way to understand how truly vulnerable anal sex is to receive is to receive it yourself. As I mention in the section of Chapter Six called "Letting Your Body Guide You," experiencing anal play on your own butt is the best education in general you can get on how it feels to be penetrated in a vagina or anus. Too many straight bros equate anal play with being gay. Guess what? Being gay, by definition, means you are having sex with a man, not engaging with a part of your body. Even if you never try anal more than once, even knowing a little of what it feels like can transform your understanding.

When you're trying this out, if you have mishaps or adjustments, you can embrace these moments as opportunities to connect with your partner, laugh, and reset. Anal sex is an incredible trust exercise. Stay present with your partner in these human moments, and you might even deepen the intimacy of your connection.

15

Introduction to Kink

This is a letter I received from a lover after our first encounter at my birthday play party:

I have no words. Thanking you isn't enough. Songs barely capture it, and I've been singing all morning. The facts are clear, you made me touch my clit in front of that whole room, while throat fucking me. You made me wait to orgasm, you counted down from twenty, and I was quivering, so happy, so alive, so embarrassed. I came three times with your cock in my mouth. You called your friend over and talked about something, ignoring me while I kept squirming.

You asked to play with me. You asked permission and I gave it. Something in your eyes said you would follow through. The air was hot and thick, I was watching your girlfriend get fucked in a cage. She was sucking a curvy brunette's toe. I could not look away.

Then I was on a mattress and your mouth was on my thighs, pussy, clit—you told me I was pretty and a good slut, and I lost it. I could feel the people, the eyes, hear the moans, make out the blur of gorgeous bodies. Heat was spreading, wanting to cum and cum for you, and all the men lurking. Then you put your fingers inside me and I squirted. Christ! I don't know how many times it happened. Your wrist was drenched.

You tied me to a chair, a throne in the middle of the room. I was bent over and spread, my glistening pussy exposed. You pulled out the nylon rope and I whimpered. I almost cried from excitement and fear. My thighs were quivering. You spanked me, then you traced your fingers up my thighs. My lower back. Told me I was a good girl and you would be back.

I waited. Staring at the chair. Spread so wide. Feeling all the glorious space and eyes on me. I was burning up in shame and joy, my breath came heavy and hot.

I shook my head from side to side, giggling, shaking, my shoulders ached. My pussy flowed.

Waiting.

Then, I heard you. I peeked over my shoulder at the crowd, at the toys, tools. I wanted to see them but couldn't quite look at them.

It begins.

A crop, I think? You explain the rules, and I fall into your hands. There's something with leather, pretty and purple, it has tails and fringe. I'm too ashamed to look at it, if you catch me, if the crowd sees me yearning for it, I can't bear it. This is what I have always wanted. This is what I've always been afraid of. Look right through me and see the inner slut. The cock-craving whore. I'm mewling, and trembling, my insides melty.

You spank me, flog me, brush my back and I am crying, I am yelling, I am wailing.

Thank you, sir!

You tell me to stay here. To not check out, to feel it all. To stay in my sub space.

This is sub space? Wow...I am truly enough. I am nothing. I am yours. I am a slut. I am dirty mucky shiny joy.

There are no words. I sob. You have cracked me open. Everything I was afraid of. Everything I've dreamed. I am so full and then you fuck me. I cum and cum and cum and cry. I was so scared. I am so happy.

My knees cave and you tell me to kneel and rest. You untie me and ask if I'd like aftercare. I would. You get me water. We cuddle and watch your girlfriend get fucked doggy style a foot from my head. Her ass is fucking gorgeous. A couple above me looks down at me, she tells me "that was beautiful." I nod and cry happy tears.

Thank you, sir. I will never forget this.

That letter above is real. But I wasn't always like this. Throughout my adolescence, I was every girl's best friend, never the guy she wanted to fuck. I was an empathic listener, never an animal. I was agreeable, never commanding. When I started going to kink parties, I realized I was turned on by the thought of being a dom. This not only came as a surprise, but it was a scary, uncomfortable discovery. I'd suppressed the animalistic, domineering, aggressive parts of my personality for my entire life. To express those parts of myself sexually, I was going to have to dig them up from where I'd buried them long ago.

Growing up, my parents didn't have the best relationship. My dad didn't treat my mom well, and after all the shit she went through, my mom's opinion of men soured. "Never be like your father," she said, and I took it to heart. Subconsciously, I thought it was my duty to make it up to women in general for the hurt my dad had caused my mom.

I made it my mission to be really nice to women. The core of this mission was the unconscious belief that I was undeserving of relationships and sex with women. This core belief created a slew of insecurities about the size of my penis and my social awkwardness. In so many ways, I worried about not being good enough, and I disowned the parts of myself that were "not nice."

Watching porn, I was triggered by the behavior of male doms because what they did to their partners initially looked like abuse to me, but at the same time I was turned on. It was very confusing for me. But when I went to sex parties, I saw the same behaviors in real life, and I talked to the women who were being dominated about how they felt and what they liked. I started to understand the pleasure they took in kink play, and I began to see more nuance in their scenes.

When I looked closer, I realized the kink scenes at sex parties were beautiful performances where both partners showed a mastery of intensity and gentleness at the same time. I remember one scene in particular in which I watched a dom skillfully lock a collar around his sub's neck with care. The locking of the collar was a ceremony that marked the start of the scene, and it shifted the energy of both partners.

The dom began to direct his partner, ordering her to put her hands behind her back so he could wrap her arms in an artful tie. He put a blindfold on his partner and teased her, caressing and spanking, mixing sweet touch with sharp pain, reward with punishment. I recognized the skill and competence the dom demonstrated. My perception of dom behavior started to shift. I realized he wasn't being *aggressive*; he was being *assertive*. With the dom in control, the sub was able to totally surrender. Every action the dom took, he did for the sub's pleasure and his own pleasure at the same time. The scene unfolded in a spellbinding dance between them.

After watching that scene, I wanted to learn more about kink. I read books and took a beginner bondage class with Tender Flame. The rope technique itself was relatively easy, but I was more struck by the way Tender Flame talked about the beautiful power dynamic that happens between two partners in kink play.

For me, kink became a way to access my primal erotic drive in a way I'd never allowed myself to explore before. Pleasure is sweeter in contrast to pain. When you are sitting in the sauna for too long, the cool air feels like heaven when you finally get out. When you're starving, food tastes amazing. As Janet Hardy puts it, kink is negotiating primal urges with civilized agreement.

The sex-positive community puts it another way: kink is a way to threaten your partner with a good time. It excites our fear and perks up our instinctive sexual urges in a consensual environment. Before kink, I didn't have a great relationship with power. Kink gave me a new set of balls I didn't have before.

There are entire books written on every facet of kink, from power dynamics to rope bondage to spanking and impact play. If you're unsure where to start, my mentee Quinn Felthorn has created an awesome beginner's guide to kink that will help you dip your toes into the water with a competent teacher. Scan the QR code that follows for a list of books and other resources, including Quinn's, that

will help you get started on your kink education journey.

In the following sections, I'll give you an overview of different kinds of kink so you can start to play with the basics and know where to look to learn more.

The Kinkster's Glossary

Kink fantasies are among the most popular fantasies among Americans. In one survey, a full 50 percent of men *and* 50 percent of women reported having dominance and submission fantasies.[76] A

---

76   Justin J. Lehmiller, *Tell Me What You Want: The Science of Sexual Desire and How It Can Help You Improve Your Sex Life* (Boston: Da Capo Lifelong Books, 2018).

lack of knowledge and skill with kink lowers your probability of being a good lover. You don't have to be a master with rope to satisfy a kinky partner; a few basic skills and the right mindset will take you far.

That said, you can't just watch *Fifty Shades of Grey* and then pop over to Home Depot to get a bunch of rope to tie your partner up with. Your education needs to precede your experience to ensure physical, mental, and emotional safety for your partner and for yourself.

In addition to skill, you and your partner need to establish clear consent to keep a scene pleasurable. Let's start by defining some basic kink terms, so you and your partner can share the same language as you negotiate what kinks you want to explore.

BDSM

This is a two-for-the-price-of-one acronym that stands for *bondage and discipline*, *dominance and submission*, and s*adism and masochism*. Essentially, BDSM is an umbrella term that denotes power play and sensation or pain-based play.

- *Bondage* is physical restriction with rope, belts, or other restraints.
- *Discipline* is psychological restraint through orders, rewards, and punishments.
- The *dominant* (dom/domme) in a scene is the person who has authority.
- The *submissive* (sub) in a scene is the person who obeys authority.
- A *sadist* enjoys inflicting pain with consent.
- A *masochist* enjoys receiving pain with consent.

People sometimes conflate some of these terms, assuming that all doms are sadists and all subs are masochists, for example. But it's possible to be dominant and masochistic—a dom could order his sub to inflict pain in exactly the way he wants it.

Dom and sub can be set roles in a partnership, where one partner is always the dom and the other is the sub, or partners can switch roles for different scenes. Because the most common scenario is for the guy to be a dom and the woman to be a sub, many of my examples focus on that dynamic. But of course, you and your partner get to design your own power play and roles to fit the sexual fantasies you want to explore.

Scene

When kinksters agree to play with a specific scenario, they clearly outline the *scene* they want to do together. Thinking of sex in terms of scenes helps to put boundaries around the time both partners will spend in their respective roles. The ceremony I saw with the dom putting the collar on his sub marked the beginning of their scene, and helped them both shift into gear. When the scene is over, both partners transition out of the roles they took during play so they can debrief about how the scene went and care for each other as needed.

Tops and Bottoms

A *top* is the person doing the action in a scene; the *bottom* is the person receiving the action. In a rope scene, for example, the bottom is the person being tied up, and the top is the person doing the tying.

Safe Words

Safe words are determined in advance by both partners to give clear cues for when the action needs to slow down or stop altogether. The color system is a popular method because it's easy to remember: "green" means continue, "yellow" means slow down, and "red" means stop what you're doing. When a scene gets intense, it can be difficult for the receiving partner to try to describe directly what they need. Safe words are a faster and easier way to alert the top if something is wrong or the bottom needs a check-in or aftercare.

When a sub or a bottom is immersed in an intense experience, they can lose the presence of mind that would normally allow them to advocate for themselves. In addition to safe words, build in passive ways to check in with your partner. If you've tied up your partner's wrists, for example, you can ask her to squeeze your hand to check her circulation. If she doesn't squeeze your hand, that's a passive check-in. Stop to see why she didn't respond. If you're giving your partner a "good girl" spanking, you can pause and ask, "Who's a good girl?" If your partner doesn't respond, that's a check-in. Slow down to see if everything is working for her.

Hard Limits and Soft Limits

As we negotiate kink scenes with our partners, it's important to detail exactly what each partner wants to do, and what they want done to them. Within those negotiations, we each define our limits or boundaries. There are *hard limits*, which are the activities we absolutely do not want to do, and there are *soft limits*, which we might be willing to do under the right conditions.

While kink allows us to uncover and play out our fantasies, it's equally important that we get clear on the risks we're not willing to take. If your hard limit is being cut with a knife, you shouldn't do knife play. You could take every precaution to mitigate the possibility of being cut, but when it comes down to it, you'll have a knife against your skin. Get clear about what risks are too high for you and ask your partner to describe where her limits are so you'll know if a fantasy you both want goes too far.

Physical Safety

Practice basic safety precautions as you experiment with different forms of play. Don't try to use a whip on your partner if you've never cracked one before. If you want to play with knives, take a class to learn how to handle them. Most importantly, don't try out a new skill all at once; work your way up to it. Get comfortable spanking with your hands, for example, before using a paddle.

If you're venturing into impact play, your hands can be some of the best tools to start with because they give you immediate feedback on how hard you're hitting. Read up on what parts of the body are safe to hit and which parts are high risk, like the joints, kidneys, spine, face, and other sensitive areas. You can find great free resources online to learn about safe ways to play with impact sensations.

There are also great resources available on rope safety, and I cover some of the basics in our video course. If you want to tie your partner up, be sure to learn how to tie without restricting circulation or creating nerve damage. Beginners should never wrap a single thickness of rope around their partner's limbs—that's how you create a tourniquet. Use multiple wraps on every tie.

PRO TIP

Just like any other form of sex, you'll need to calibrate the level of intensity with any new sensation you introduce to your partner. Start with light sensations to let the body warm up. When you're ready to ramp up the intensity, communicate with your partner to find the best level of sensation for their preference. If you're spanking your partner, for example, you can ask her to rate the pain of a single hit on a scale from one to ten. Then ask what number she likes it at. If she says she likes to be hit at a seven, practice dialing in the amount of force you use until you know what a seven feels like to her.

Boy Scouts and sailors sometimes get themselves in trouble with rope bondage because they're confident in their knot-tying skills. Learn the ties that are recommended for bondage. Make sure your knots can't tighten down on themselves.

Bondage can be a decorative art, and it can be a physical restraint. There are many ways outside of using rope to create restraint for your partner. For example, one quick hack is to take a pillowcase off a pillow, have your partner hold her arms behind her back, and slide the pillowcase up her arms to secure them. Pull the ends of the pillowcase above her shoulders and then spread her arms to her sides. Then lay her down on her back so her body weight is holding her arms in place like a strait jacket.

But when it comes to rope, learn the fundamentals—a single-column tie, two-column tie, chest harness, and hip harness—and you'll be able to create a wide variety of bondage scenes.

Most importantly for practicing any form of bondage: always have safety shears available, like the kind EMTs use to cut clothes and seat belts, so you can cut your partner free quickly if any problems arise.

Emotional Safety

Getting clear on your limits requires self-awareness and good communication. In Chapter Four, we went over a list of questions for you and your partner to ask as you negotiate the kind of sex you want to have. One of those questions is particularly important for kink: how do you want to feel during sex?

Like in all sex, erotic context in kink can make the difference between a scene that fully enacts a fantasy and one that falls flat. Your partner may want to be spanked, but does she want a "good girl" spanking or a "bad girl" spanking? As the dominant, you would speak differently to your partner and change your body language depending on which scenario is hot to her. Some people like to be tied up because of the physical sensation of restriction and compression; for others, bondage makes them feel strong and athletic; and still others like rope play because of the sense of helplessness and surrender they feel. As you and your partner discuss what you want to do in a scene, be sure to talk about why you want it, so you can each deliver on your partner's fantasies.

Know your triggers and ask your partner about hers. Some people love choking while others are triggered by having a hand on or near their throat. If a hand on the throat is a trigger for your partner, it's much easier to talk about that during negotiations than to accidentally throw your partner into fight-or-flight mode by reaching for her neck in a passionate moment.

In the course of kink play, it's possible you or your partner might stumble upon limits you didn't know, or traumas that have been repressed until you try a particular kind of play. Kink pushes our limits, both in terms of physical sensation and emotional headspace. Plan frequent check-ins when trying new scenes so you can see whether your partner's experience or expectations have shifted. Be willing to stop the action at any moment to care for your partner's needs.

The reward for all this negotiation and careful navigation isn't just great sex—it's also greater intimacy. You can set yourself up to be an amazing lover to your partner simply by understanding her fantasies in nitty-gritty detail. Getting into kink can be like opening a Pandora's box for some people: they've craved a certain fantasy for so long, but never had a partner who was willing to listen. Once they get used to opening up about their desires, many people find there are more and more possibilities they want to try. When you listen to what turns your partner on and negotiate how to bring her fantasies to life, you'll increase your chances of blowing her mind.

Commit to Your Role

Kink is a game of trust, communication, and mutual satisfaction. It's also fundamentally an exchange of power. Whether you're practicing discipline or impact play, there's always a leader and a follower, regardless of the specific scene.

Being a good dom is actually about being a great leader. Doms need to be trustworthy and competent. They have to be willing to make difficult decisions. They know how to get others to willfully submit to their commands. Submissives, meanwhile, need the skills of surrender. They are self-aware and know how to communicate their boundaries clearly. Leading and following are essential skills, and in kink we get to eroticize and play with both roles.

To pull off the fantasy, each partner needs to commit 100 percent to their role. It's annoying when a dom half-asses dominance. Same for a sub who refuses to relinquish their director side. Stay in character. If you're playing a serious, threatening dom, don't crack a goofy joke in the middle of the scene.

Adopt your character not just through your voice and words, but your physical postures as well. You can communicate power by the way you place your partner and yourself in relation to each other. Have your sub kneel with her hands behind her back. You can then stand up straight to tower over her, or walk slowly around her, or pet her on the top of her head, or use one finger to lift her chin to look you in the eyes. Each of these actions creates a physical language to establish power. This doesn't just happen during sex— watch movies featuring medieval Chinese kingdoms or Chicago mobsters, and you'll see the same physical expressions to convey dominance. Humans have been practicing BDSM in the bedroom and in empires throughout history.

Use play labs to practice new kink skills, experiment with new facets of your personality, and get familiar with new sensations. If you've practiced tying your partner up during a play lab, you'll get over the initial clumsiness. Then, during sex, you'll be able to tie up your partner with the confidence and competence your dom character requires.

Committing 100 percent of your attention to the scene also means being fully present in the moment and adapting to what comes up. Find ways to check in with your partner while maintaining the mood. Be willing to stop or change direction as the play evolves and you both discover more about each other.

Lastly, the foundation for a healthy kink dynamic is for both parties to want each other to succeed and win. Even if the sub enjoys being bratty or provoking the dom, she ultimately still desires her dom to succeed in being dominant—she wants him to find the strength to continue in his role. Even if the dom is pushing the sub to her limits, he still wants her to find the strength to remain in the submissive role. That's what makes kink wonderful. If you don't genuinely want your partner to succeed in their half of what is happening, don't even play. It's disastrous to engage under any other circumstances, and doomed from the start.

How to Give Commands

When I first started getting into kink, my background as a personal trainer served me well because I was used to directing people to do specific actions. I quickly discovered I didn't need an elaborate script to be an effective dom; I could drive my partner wild simply by giving clear, direct commands.

To turn on your dominant side, start by telling your partner what to do. Use simple language, as if you were talking to a five-year-old. Of course, your partner is far more sophisticated than a five-year-old, but if you focus on using simple, directional language, you'll be able to give clear, assertive commands that any partner will be able to understand. "Rest your head on my thigh. Take a deep breath in. Relax your body. Now pick up the riding crop with your teeth."

For some submissives, the exciting part of power play isn't the submission so much as the struggle. Your partner may fight you for power. In the kink community, we call these submissives *brats*. Brattiness can be confusing at first: if your partner agrees to submit to you, why are they giving you so much shit? Under the surface, the brat is testing your competence with power to make sure they can trust you with power. This is a natural human behavior. Smart, competent, powerful people still desire to be led, but they need to know you're capable of controlling the situation when shit gets difficult. Brats test these boundaries by rebelling against the dom, or trying to humiliate them. You have to be unfazed. If you get butt-hurt about it, you've lost the game. If you are able to put your partner in her place—not by being aggressive, but by being assertive—you'll have won her trust.

Beyond establishing the power dynamic, the purpose of giving instructions and orders is to help the submissive get in her body. You can tell her what to do and how to move, and you can also tell her what to pay attention to. "Follow my finger as I trace your body." Some commands, like "Don't you fucking cum," can cause your partner to focus on the sensations that might make her cum on accident if she loses control.

When you've established the power dynamic, you can also play with objectifying your partner, depending on her fantasy and her preference. Taking a sense of ownership can be hot when you've set the right context. When your partner becomes your fuck toy or your slave, she gets to witness your desire for her. You can mix objectification with praise: "You're so beautiful. I love when you act like a little slut for me."

Objectification can take a lot of different forms. Some people want to explore taboo, and it's hot to be called a street whore. For others, the helplessness of a hostage or a victim is sexy. Some people want to be worshipped like a goddess or praised like a good girl. Often these different characters are in contrast to how they feel in real life. Someone who is normally a control freak might need to be tied up and made helpless in order to drop into their body and surrender. There are a million variations, and a million reasons why different people find these different contexts hot.

For some people, humiliation can be a powerful tool to bring out their inner slut. When the dom sets the power dynamic of the scene, they also set the psychological frame for control. I like to play with a sense of ownership over my partner by saying things like, "Look at you, getting so wet from your spanking—you can't even control how slutty your pussy is." As the dom, I pretend to take responsibility for the sub's sluttiness. The sub can then give herself full permission to be slutty and erotic, because she's not in control of her body's response; she's able to unleash her own restrictions.

Play with combining different flavors. You can mix slutty words with loving touches, assertive postures with gentle teasing, powerful moves with skilled precision. Contrast is thrilling and sexy. By combining different elements, you can demonstrate your ability to bring forward different aspects of yourself with grace and control. I can tell you from experience: when you learn to bring out the dom within you, it feels deliciously empowering.

Ramp Up the Intensity

In Chapter One we looked at the role of the parasympathetic (rest-and-digest) and sympathetic (fight-or-flight) systems when it comes to arousal and orgasm. Kink gives us an expanded tool kit to influence these systems. I mentioned earlier that kink is a way to threaten your partner with a good time—and a well-timed threat can become a tool to put your partner's system on alert and kick it into orgasm.

Here's an example of a sequence that works well to play with sympathetic arousal, endorphins, and orgasm:

Start the scene by blindfolding her. Tie her hands together in front of her, between her legs. Put a vibrator in her hands set on the lowest level and have her hold it on her clit while you spank her slowly, mixing in caressing with the spanking.

Keep the vibrator on low, mixing in some light to medium spanking, and wait for her to really drop in and relax into the sensations. Once you feel like she is fully aroused in a spellbinding erotic experience and has really dropped into the sensations of her body, you switch gears.

This is where 100 percent of your presence is required to make this the most delicious part of the scene. When she's ready, tell her you're going to spank her ten times really hard, and you want her to count them out loud. Anticipation is one of the most underrated sex hacks to multiply pleasure.

Here you're using an anticipation hack to capture her attention, where she has a job to do and must stay engaged. Tell her, "I want you to do your best to relax into the pain." When you start spanking her hard like this, the pain will trigger her into fight-or-flight mode, and right after she reaches spank number ten, as she utters the sound of relief, turn the vibrator up to four.

She will feel the intensity of the pain, the intensity of the pleasure, and will be totally tuned in to her body's sensations. She's likely to have some super intense orgasms at this point and be completely overwhelmed with pleasure. You can encourage her to scream and let everything go in this super intense experience. If you want to make it even more extreme, pull her hair while she's cuming!

You can create variations on this sequence with any sensation your partner likes. The key is to follow where your partner's nervous system is on its cycle between rest-and-digest and fight-or-flight and create sensations that help her system along.

Great sex actually involves the mutual activation and balance between sympathetic and parasympathetic systems. In other words, there's a balance between relaxation and tension. Finding out how to be alert and relaxed, or excited and yet super chill at the same time, is a recipe for the best sex ever. Using kink techniques skillfully can give you more control over these systems in yourself and your partner. In some ways, sex hacking is about accessing "super user" level.

For example, when you take your iPhone to the Genius Bar to get fixed, the employees can plug your phone into a particular program and get "super user" access to shit you normally don't have control over. By accessing the internal system, they can fix, change, and upgrade your phone in ways you can't with normal user access.

Similarly, there are ways to get access to your internal system— or your partner's—through sex. Kink is one way to get deep into someone's mind and body and access their primal desires and subconscious urges. When you're playing with kink, you're playing with aspects of your partner that are normally hidden deep inside their psyche. These parts are off-limits in everyday interactions, restricted by the need to be domesticated, civilized, and safe. The level of intimacy kink play entails is therefore super vulnerable—imagine the damage someone at the Genius Bar could do to your iPhone. That's why this process requires so much negotiation and so many safety precautions. You're giving someone access to parts of you that normally cannot be touched.

How to Surrender Responsibly

In the submissive role, it's important to know your boundaries. You have to know yourself well enough that you aren't relying on the dom to read your signs; you need to lay out your own limits and communication style for the dom beforehand. In order for the dom to step fully into their role, they have to trust the submissive to speak up as soon as something feels off. Don't expect a dom to read your mind; speak up.

We talked about the five-second rule in Chapter Four, and that rule is especially useful in kink. Be willing to tell your dom to slow down or stop as quickly as possible. Be cautious and go slow. Don't endure anything that isn't a turn-on for you.

While the guideline to know your boundaries and speak up when they're crossed is a simple one, it can be a hard guideline to practice. I was once doing a workshop demo with a live audience in which I was the sub and my partner was the dom. The scene became uncomfortable for me, but I decided not to speak up in the moment. I'd agreed to help teach this particular technique, and I felt pressure with the audience watching. I should have stopped the scene and described why it wasn't working for me, but I chose to endure. The scene affected me deeply because I didn't speak up when I reached my limit, but I'd also failed to model stopping a scene to adjust.

You can't fake trusting your dom. In order to surrender, you have to be authentic about how you feel and what's coming up for you moment by moment. Many people underestimate how much training it takes to be truly present and authentic throughout a scene. As you experiment with kink, you may have regrettable experiences where you should have spoken up but didn't. Look to these experiences to learn what you need next time to feel safe, communicate with your partner, and fully experience pleasure.

One of the most beautiful aspects of playing in a submissive role is that it can be a vehicle for overcoming your own self-limiting beliefs. We often put limits on our own pleasure based on what we believe we deserve. We stop ourselves short. When you trust your dom, and you're able to surrender to their control and authority, you allow them to coach you into deeper pleasure. It's magical when someone believes in you more than you believe in yourself, and your dom can push you to surrender to more pleasure than you let yourself experience on your own.

Kink Aftercare

In Chapter Five we looked at the importance of aftercare, and all the same principles apply when it comes to kink. Because kink can be more intense physically, psychologically, and emotionally, ask what kind of aftercare your partner might need while you're negotiating before the scene. How your partner wants to be treated afterward often depends on the content of the scene you both want to play out. If the play involved your partner being dominated, she may want to be held afterward—or she may want to be covered with a blanket, given a glass of water, and left alone.

Kink can brush up against your partner's triggers and even activate old trauma. You can take all the possible precautions and still make a mistake that sends your partner into a difficult emotional space. The intensity of kink can make it hard for your partner to regulate her emotions if she gets triggered. Try your best to listen to her reaction. Even if your partner blames you for something you disagree with, don't get defensive. Care for your partner until she gets back to her baseline and make a plan to talk later.

Your partner may not know what she needs after trying power play or impact play for the first time. Be patient and understanding as you each figure out the best way to care for yourselves and each other.

The All-Important Debrief

No matter how clearly you negotiate with your partner, chances are high that your first kink scene (or your twentieth, or your fiftieth) won't go perfectly. You might make a mistake like forgetting your partner told you not to put your hand on her throat. Some mistakes are easy to blow off in the moment, and some mistakes can have big emotional consequences. Be willing to have a conversation with your partner after each kink scene to uncover what you each liked and what you plan to do better next time.

If a scene activated old trauma in your partner, be calm and kind as you unpack what came up for her and why. Don't shame or blame your partner, even if she lashed out at you. Ask instead whether she wants to avoid those triggers, or set up safer conditions to explore them.

This conversation shouldn't happen during aftercare—that's a time to help both partners come down from their sex high. Have a conversation an hour after the scene is over, or maybe even the next day over coffee. Ask your partner: How did that go for you? Did the scene accomplish what you wanted it to?

The more effective you get at these conversations, the better your scenes can be—and the more fully you'll be able to play out your partner's fantasies and your own.

Kink can ultimately be a tool for developing our human potential. Great kinky sex requires authenticity, physical engagement, strong boundaries, and compassion. With good communication and boundaries in place, kink offers a beautiful container to play with surrender, control, and eroticism. Many people tend to lean towards being dominant or being submissive, but it's a good idea to practice both so you can develop the skills and experience that each side offers. By learning to be a great leader and a great follower, you learn to be a better collaborator—and you open up incredible new possibilities for your life and your sexuality.

16

Aftercare

W*hen the thrill is winding down*, it's important to give your partner a smooth landing so they can safely get off the ride. During orgasm, we can often bring our partners to a deeply emotional state of surrender. They trust us enough to let go. After we orgasm, we get a big oxytocin release. Oxytocin is a powerful bonding chemical, and like it or not, it tends to make us feel intensely connected to our partner after sex. If the sex is good, we're literally high on brain chemicals. It takes time to transition back to a normal state. In this transitional state, we can give aftercare to our partners in a variety of different ways, which we'll describe next. Aftercare is a great time to create deeper loving connection with a partner. It's also the worst time to be an asshole.

A brief side note here: the intense emotional connection that tends to happen after sex can cause some people to freak the fuck out. Unfortunately for a lot of men, even though our neurological wiring is the same as women, and we are set up to connect deeply through sex and bond in the post-orgasm afterglow, social scripts can prevent this from happening.

Culture encourages men to be emotionally steady and constantly in control, which is impossible when romantic feelings get involved. This kind of vulnerability is foreign to many men, and when they don't know how to handle it, they often end up pushing the woman away, both physically and emotionally, after sex. This can look like falling asleep, running away, or immediately turning on the TV. Disengagement is easier for some men than embracing the vulnerability inherent in these moments.

I'm actually one of them: my internal desire to disengage is super high after sex because of my avoidant attachment style, which I'm not proud of. I have to keep my emotional brain from hijacking me into shoving my partner's clothes and some cab fare into her hands and asking her politely to be on her way. Nature can be shitty like that. While my automatic response may be to detach, my value is to care for my partners, and when it comes to aftercare, I make conscious choices to align with my values.

Even with the most casual of sexual encounters, our partners still deserve respect and care. Being purposefully uncaring is not the most ethical way to prevent her from catching feelings, if she is in fact even in danger of that. There are more appropriate ways to establish boundaries than by being an asshole. Having proper post-sex etiquette is extremely rare these days, but very important.

Sex is one of the most vulnerable experiences we can share with another human, and the nuances of how we treat our partners after sex matter. In the transition period after orgasm, as we start to down-regulate from our love chemical high, we begin to form the narrative of what happened. The neurons that fire together wire together, so the experience our partner has after sex will color their perception of the sex itself.

Check in with your partner to see what she needs. Offer her a glass of water, see if she needs to use the bathroom, or if she just needs a moment to rest and cuddle. I love to cook for my partners as a way to nourish them and transition from sexual partner to gracious host.

Sensual Shower

One of my favorite ways to care for my partner after sex is to take a sensual shower together. I love washing my partner's body, and a shower gives an opportunity to combine lots of different sensations: the smell of the shampoo, the temperature of the water, and the feel of touch on wet skin.

Adjust the water temperature to your partner's liking, and you can stand behind her to let the warm water fall on her chest while you caress her. Ask if she would like you to wash her hair, and you can use it as an opportunity to give her a scalp massage. Give head scratches and a little gentle hair pulling; just be sure to gently pull large handfuls rather than small locks, which can give a sharp twinge. Connect with your own senses as the giver, feeling the texture of her hair. When it's time to rinse, tilt her head back so shampoo doesn't drip into her eyes. Work conditioner into her hair and let it sit as you wash the rest of her body.

I have bars set up high in my shower, on commercial suction cups, so I can stretch my partner's arms overhead and have her hold onto the grips. Then I wash her body, sliding my hands across her arms, torso, hips, and legs, and because her hands are anchored, she can really let go and let me do the work.

Sometimes, after a kink scene where she feels a lot of humiliation or degradation, it can be a super loving gesture to get on your knees and wash her feet. You can say words like, "Thank you for sharing that part of yourself with me; I really appreciate it."

You can reapply conditioner to her hair right before rinsing it out, just to bring the smell back to your partner's experience. Bonus points if you have a warm towel to wrap her up in as soon as she steps out of the shower.

If you want to build intimacy with a partner that you have romantic feelings for, this is a wonderful way to do it. Washing someone is an act of incredible sweetness, nurturing, and care that is usually not displayed by men. It can be an incredibly touching act for women to receive.

The Goddess Bath

I love to create a special pampering session that allows my partner to fully relax and revel in a sensory experience. The Goddess Bath takes a bit of prep work and some creative supplies, but it's well worth the effort.

This experience was shared and inspired by Omorphy, who captured his incredible process in the photo series "Bath Disturbed."[77] He taught me how to make the person who models for him feel like they themselves are a beautiful piece of fine art.

---

77 "Bath Disturbed," *Omorphy Photos*, OmorphyPhotos.com/bathdisturbed.

With this experience, I share the ultimate integration of my favorite philosophies of peak experiences, curation, and pleasure. The Goddess Bath is a ritual that incorporates all of the senses and is meant to pamper your partner.

To begin, you'll want to gather several sensual elements for the experience:

- A bouquet of flowers picked or bought with your lover in mind—think of her favorite flowers or her favorite colors
- Bath bombs to give fizzy or foamy effects to the water
- Biodegradable glitter, color tablets, or other body-safe products to decorate the water
- Sensual foods for her to enjoy, like chocolate, honey, macarons, small candies, or fruit
- Candles to create soft lighting and fill the air with a scent she likes
- Optionally, you can have a camera on hand to take pictures of her in the midst of the beauty you create

Fill the bathtub in advance, and check that the water temperature is good. Light candles around the bathroom to create a soft, warm lighting effect. Play music in her taste that will enhance the mood. Have the vase of flowers and the other supplies to decorate the water close to the tub.

Then, when you're ready to bring your partner into the bathroom, adorn her in a sensual robe and a silky blindfold. Tell her you're excited to share an experience you've curated just for her.

Walk your partner into the bathroom and slowly remove her robe and caress her body. Explain that you want her to just enjoy this experience, luxuriate in the sensations, and focus solely on herself.

Walk her over to the tub and let her touch the water. Tell her you'll help her in. Lightly caress her body as she settles in and give her time to acclimate to the water.

Dip your finger in the honey and give her a taste; use your fingertip to tease her lips. Feed her a chocolate and invite her to savor the flavor. Then give her a kiss with your own lips.

Remove her blindfold and show her the beautiful bouquet of flowers, letting her know you picked these out just for her. Select one flower and pull it from the bouquet. Let her smell it and feel it. Trace the petals across her skin, encouraging her to take a deep breath and just focus on the sensation of the flower. By encouraging her and guiding her focus, you give her a sense of grounding and meditation that lets her drop fully into the moment, release any hypervigilance, and open her body to pleasure.

If you're using a bath bomb, drop it into the water and let it swirl and fizz. Then begin dropping flowers and petals into the water, telling your partner that the art you're creating in the water is inspired by her.

Use high-contrast flowers of different colors and vary between scattering petals and dropping in the whole head of a flower. Rose petals create a beautiful effect because of their size.

If you're using glitter, pour a little bit into your palm and blow it across the water. Don't sprinkle it, or it will simply sink.

Take your time and enjoy the process of scattering the petals. Don't rush—this is a mindful experience of beauty and creativity.

Know your partner's favorite color and pick up a bath color tablet in that shade to have ready in your hand. Then ask your partner's favorite color and create magic as you draw the color across the water.

Offer to take a photo of how beautiful she looks. Tell her that she is a work of art, your goddess and your muse.

If there's room, get into the tub behind her and give her a massage, connecting to your partner skin-to-skin. You can also wash her hair and body.

Hold her against you and continue to caress her. Let her know you want her to just receive this gratitude; it doesn't have to be reciprocated.

When you're both finished, help her out of the tub and dry her off, telling her how beautiful she is and how amazing it was for you to pamper her this way. Thank her for allowing you to experience this with her.

Afterward, spend some time simply cuddling or having some quiet time to highlight the moment. Let her enjoy the relaxation without feeling she has to immediately be responsible again.

The definition of a peak experience is one that is unexpected, novel, pleasurable, and multisensory. The use of surprise, blindfolds,

chocolate and honey, colors, temperature, and more qualifies it as a peak experience. The effect of the bath is a "heartgasm"—the deep delight of being spoiled, worshipped, and cherished as a muse. You'll be crafting an overwhelmingly delicious encounter that will leave her in awe.

Notice What You Love, Love What You Notice

This appreciation exercise is adapted from *horizontal with lila*, a podcast and blog by Lila Donnolo, and it's an excellent way to verbalize your appreciation of your partner.

By hand, write out one thoughtfully chosen compliment for each of the categories that follow. (This only works if your praise is genuine!) You can bookend your compliment with this simple sentence frame: "I notice _____ and I love it."

- Your body
- Your work
- Your art
- Your energy
- Your emotions
- Your values
- Your ideas
- Your aspirations
- Your fantasies

If you're giving these compliments to a long-term or live-in partner, you can also add compliments about your life together, such as:

- Our family
- Our kids
- Our home

Read these compliments to her in a shower of admiration. Accompany each compliment with a physical gesture, such as a teasing kiss.

Afterwards, give the handwritten compliments to your partner so she can reread your tribute to her whenever she wishes to. Bonus points for making the presentation special—you can nestle the compliments in a mason jar full of LED twinkle lights, slip it inside a wallet full of cash, or frame each compliment with hand-drawn illustrations. The best time to do this is in the goddess bath experience, while you're in the bath with her.

Casual Intimacy Etiquette

Especially because the sex afterglow is stewed in bonding chemicals, it's important to continue to communicate clearly about what you want, especially if you're with a new partner. One of the side effects of giving a great, curated sexual experience is that the experience feels really special to the receiving partner—and may cause the receiver to assume their personal, romantic connection is as special as the sexual connection. For people who are dating around, this can be problematic: your partner can feel attached when you don't.

I play with lots of different partners, and I usually only play with the same person once or twice. I have to carefully and kindly set clear boundaries with my partners. I make sure to tell my potential partners clearly at the beginning that I love playing with new people, and I don't fall in long-term sexual relationships very often. People who don't want that type of connection can then choose not to sleep with me. It's important to be clear about those boundaries after sex as well; sex is an emotional experience and can cause people to feel differently after it's over.

Check in with yourself and your desires and do your best to communicate what you feel as the afterglow subsides.

17

Bringing It All Together

The 90-Minute Orgasmic Experience

One of the privileges that I get working with Pamela Madsen at Back to the Body Retreats is that I get to experience accelerated learning in the realms of female pleasure. I've seen women from all walks of life, who have all sorts of different sexual desires and challenges, experiencing sexual arousal. On an average day, I did four 90-minute sexological bodywork sessions. From this type of back-to-back practice, I was able to metabolize a ton of information in a concentrated manner and test out a lot of theories in real life.

What have I learned, after curating over 1,000 90-minute orgasmic experiences?

What I learned from all of this concentrated time in the midst of female sexual pleasure is that most women are capable of expanded, extended pleasure that is greater than what they could ever imagine. Researchers Masters and Johnson laid out a sexual response cycle with four distinct stages: excitement, plateau, orgasm, and resolution. This simplified model doesn't paint a complete pleasure picture, especially for women. There is a way to extend pleasure towards a prolonged orgasmic state, instead of a momentary peak followed by an immediate crash.

There's a certain pattern and framework that I've found works to help women access this physical and psychological state. I've found that it usually takes around ninety minutes, which also happens to be the average length of a movie. Maybe Pamela just stumbled upon this by accident, or she happens to be a pleasure genius. Like a movie, this amount of time is enough to develop plots; introduce enough characters, scenery, and plot twists; and leave you enough time to avoid feeling that the end of the movie is rushing to a conclusion (like the last season of *Game of Thrones*).

An important ingredient in evoking this type of experience is your partner's psychological arousal. What is her flavor of turn-on? Is it kinky, sensual, romantic, mystical, animalistic, or some combination thereof? Some people's sexual fantasies involve vampires and werewolves; some are as romantic as a cheesy rom-com; some are as primal as two wrestlers in a jujitsu match. We talk pleasure personalities in the next chapter, but basically, a kiss is not just a kiss. A kiss while your partner is tied to the mast of a pretend pirate ship is very different than a kiss while you two are walking in a field of flowers together on a sunny day. Know the erotic context and characters that your partner likes.

The key to facilitating this experience is that for ninety minutes, you set aside time to focus exclusively on giving to your partner. But it's not just about giving her a massage or providing sexual touch. Think of this more like curating a nine-course meal, where you pick the perfect restaurant, atmosphere, outfits, and plan all the details of dining out. You could even imagine that it's like a surprise birthday dinner where you think carefully about who to invite, what gifts she might like, and all the nuances of what makes her happy. You might even try to think of things she would never expect.

This experience is about pairing what you are good at doing as a giver with the things they specifically like as a receiver. It's a place for you to play with expressing your eroticism with the intents to find what delights her and satisfies her, expanding her sense of what's possible. In the following paragraphs I'll offer a guide on what has worked for me during this 90-minute experience. However, it's not meant for you to follow exactly, but to use as a framework for creating your own menu. Sex is always best when you're expressing yourself rather than imitating others. Additionally, it's best to have a plan but also go with your intuition as you go. You'll know the most by reading your partner in the moment and adjusting your plan to her reactions.

The first step to creating this experience is figuring out what she likes. Even if she's a long-term partner, you may not know exactly what gets her going. You can either ask her directly about her fantasies, or show her clips from different movies, or even porn, and see what she reacts to most strongly. Ask her what kind of erotica she reads, and read some of her favorite chapters. In his book *Tell Me*

What You Want, Dr. Lehmiller talks extensively about fantasies and desires, and how to talk about them with your partner.[78] I highly recommend reading his book if you want to know all there is to know about fantasies.

Then, you could tell her something like, "I think it would be fun to explore each other's fantasies. I want to create a night that is all about you. But I want to talk about all your preferences and boundaries now so we don't kill the mood on the night we do it." Then talk about any special wishes she has, any hard limits she has, and a time and place that you can both agree on doing it. Tell her that it's all about her pleasure, and you want her to be totally selfish and let go of thinking about reciprocating. You can give her the option to plan it all out in advance, or leave room for surprises and spontaneity. You should also let her know that if you try anything out that she doesn't like, she can always say no in the moment, and you will take a different direction or end the night, whichever she prefers. Ask her if you can count on her to let you know if things come up that she doesn't like or want.

When the night comes, make sure to set the mood. Remove all distractions, including dirty laundry, nosey roommates, or anything else distracting. Set up lighting and music as well as any toys or supplies you'll need in advance. I find that ritualizing the experience works well, so I like to incorporate something that helps her transition out of her ordinary state of mind. Have her take a shower, tell her to open the box on the bed. The box on the bed should have some lingerie for her to wear, and a note to tell her to change into them

---

78   Justin J. Lehmiller, *Tell Me What You Want: The Science of Sexual Desire and How It Can Help You Improve Your Sex Life* (Boston: Da Capo Lifelong Books, 2018).

and wait for you on the bed. If she's kinky, it could just be a collar. You could leave the toys you intend to use out in plain sight nearby. This way she has a moment to herself to build up anticipation.

Once she's on the bed, start with seductive touch, like a gentle hair stroke. If she's kinky, grab her hair and pull. Or you could put on her favorite song and dance with her. Compliment her on specific things you like about the way she looks, or what you love about her personality if you know her better. For instance, you could tell her, "The way you look right now makes it really hard for me to not just throw you on the bed."

Start going into foreplay with kissing and touching. You could play with feathers, a pinwheel, sensual massage, or any other kind of touch she likes. Treat her entire body as an erogenous zone. Make her aware of the entirety of her skin and all of her five senses. Tease her and increase anticipation by getting closer and closer to her pussy without touching it directly. Then begin massaging or lightly touching parts of her vulva, but make her clitoris wait. You want to allow the clitoris to be engorged before you even touch it. According to OMGYes research, 65 percent of women enjoy this "hinting" around the vulva before diving in.[79] This part is all about building anticipation, introducing eroticism, getting the person into the moment, and making her feel deeply desired and wanted. You want to get her body to yearn and give it permission to engage sensually and sexually. Kinky or not, giving her simple instructions on how to focus on the moment, her body, and her senses is usually

---

79   Debbie Herbenick, et al., "Women's Experiences with Genital Touching, Sexual Pleasure, and Orgasm: Results from a US Probability Sample of Women Ages 18 to 94," *Journal of Sex and Marital Therapy*, 44:2, 201–212

very helpful. Say something like, "I want you to take a deep breath in, feel the temperature of the room, and as I touch you, focus all your awareness on your body and how it feels right now."

PRO TIP

At a sushi restaurant, when they serve omakase, chef's choice, they start with the most delicate flavor so they don't overwhelm the palate too quickly. This same principle applies to sexual pleasure. You want the first orgasm to be induced by the lightest touch possible so that you can keep building to more and more sensation. If you start off with a vibrator at the highest setting, there's nowhere you can really go from there.

Eventually, start moving towards the clitoris gently. Calibrate touch with that person by noticing her erotic cues in response to your touch. Think about adjusting pressure, location, and speed according to what she is enjoying in that moment. Begin with a consistent rhythmic touch, let the pleasure build, and continue to stimulate her in a consistent way until she has her first orgasm. But you don't need to rush this first orgasm either. It's not about how many orgasms she has, it's about the quality of the overall experience and allowing pleasure to build up. At a certain level, counting orgasms is for amateurs.

From there, you want to rotate areas. Bring in other members of her soccer team, like we talked about before. Rotate stimulation like circuit training, giving her as many different types of orgasms as possible and layering sensations from multiple areas. Once she's in an orgasmic state, it gives whole new pleasure potential to areas that previously may have not felt good. The more aroused she gets, the more you can try different areas and more intense types of sensation that she might normally find foreign or overwhelming. For instance, you could start with gentle teasing with fingers and tongue, progress to fingering and more intense oral stimulation, and then progress to vaginal penetration while she rubs her clit. Then you could put a ball-gag in her mouth, a butt plug in her butt, and a vibrator on her clit. At the end she might be tied up while you fuck her ass and introduce the Zumio vibrator to her for the first time on her clit.

Ideally, by the hour mark, the woman should be in an intense orgas-mic state, where the refractory period between orgasms shortens and she is experiencing rolling climaxes, described by Pamela Madsen as the erotic trance state. Keep her in this state for as long as possible by continuing to rotate playing with various erogenous zones.

Within this sequence of events, it's good to introduce one new thing that she's never experienced before. Either a new toy, a new sexual experience, or some kind of unexpected plot twist she would never expect. Adding novelty in with reliable pleasure is usually a great mix for most people. Creating a new reference point by build-ing on what already works and adding some surprising elements is ultimately what takes her beyond satisfaction.

Keep in mind that usually the set point for how much pleasure a woman thinks she can have is not biological. It's just a point that she has psychologically gotten used to stopping. It's usually not about the body's capacity, but rather how much she believes is pos-sible, thinks she deserves, or has gotten used to having. If you keep going after she thinks she has had all the pleasure possible, you can show her what she is truly made of.

Your partner might be quite emotional during this experience. Many women cry and release a lot of emotions during intense, mul-tiorgasmic sex. Encourage her to let go and feel it all fully. Don't make it a big deal. This type of deep feeling is where deep orgasms come from, so it is really a good sign.

When you are nearing the end of this experience, try to create a smooth landing. She might have the urge to "get it back together" in some way, and go back to "board meeting" mode. She may hurry to clean up cum, wipe away tears, make the bed, or do other tasks to clean up. She might hop into service mode, trying to do something for you. For some, this is a psychological defense against allowing themselves to receive this fully.

Take the pressure off by assuring her that you have taken care of everything, and her job is to relax. Tell her things like, "I want you to leave all the management to me. I got this." Let her know that when she's ready, you can take a shower together (or take a walk, cuddle, drink a glass of wine, take a bath, etc.). Light some candles or whatever else you believe will create a relaxing environment. Believe it or not, having your shit together so that she can fully relax at this point is the sexiest thing you can do. This should be about a transition into luxury and relaxation.

Conclusion

Before joining a sex-positive community, Hacienda, I'd internalized a few myths that were destroying my sex life. I believed I wasn't good enough, physically or socially, for a fulfilling sexual relationship. I believed men were selfish assholes and it was my job to make up for it. I believed I was unworthy of love. These beliefs came from core wounds I got in childhood as an immigrant Asian kid with a skinny-fat build, an average-sized cock, and the lack of a good male role model.

None of these myths were grounded in truth; they were bugs in my internal operating system. Throughout my twenties, I kept repeating the same old pattern of relationships, falling for people with whom I had to prove my worth to earn their love. I went to transformational workshops to dive into my shit and build my confidence.

But it wasn't until I found a sex-positive community that I started to make a permanent, positive impact on my sense of self. Seeing the self-awareness, skill, and compassion within my partners in the sex party scene helped me start to debug my mental software. Sex, I realized, was about far more than physical pleasure. It gave me a portal to develop meaningful, mutually satisfying relationships with women—and with myself.

Now, in my relationship with my fiancée, I feel like an equal. I recognize my worth, and I know I have something to give instead of something to prove. I no longer feel insecure, and I'm not constantly trying to compensate for perceived shortcomings. Through sex, I learned to be authentic and ground myself in my own confidence instead of comparing my average-sized cock to another porn star's.

Great sex can be the key to lasting confidence, not because you can make a girl cum twenty times, but because to have great sex you have to be authentic, present in your body, and connected with your partner. You can build the skills to please your partner and elevate your external game, but the real boost in fulfillment and confidence happens when you elevate your internal game. You earn your self-esteem by investing in yourself.

Beyond being good in bed, when you're able to express yourself and demonstrate your competence, you earn genuine admiration from your partner. It may be my own overgeneralization from being a fatherless child, but it's a powerful feeling to be known not just as a good lover, but as a good man.

Throughout this book, you learned detailed instructions for how to get better at the technical skills of sex. Competence is important. But the more important parts of this book, the ones you'll find yourself returning to again and again, are the soft skills that help you connect to yourself and your partner. To create mind-blowing sex, you have to connect with your partner and understand what she needs to be satisfied. Otherwise you're just another vibrator—and honestly, most vibrators probably do a more reliable job of delivering orgasms.

We're living in an age where many people are faking it—faking orgasms, faking connection, faking intimacy, faking pleasure. When you learn to deliver the real thing, it nourishes you and your partner to the core.

In an interview, Bruce Lee once described how he experienced this kind of authenticity as an actor and a martial artist.[80] He said, "Honestly expressing yourself...it is very difficult to do. I mean, it is easy for me to put on a show and be cocky and be flooded with a cocky feeling and then feel pretty cool...or I can show you some really fancy movement. But to express oneself honestly, not lying to oneself...now that, my friend, is very hard to do."

When you can combine sexual skills with great communication and your own authentic sexual expression, sex can be deeply satisfying. And the confidence you gain from being able to deliver so much pleasure to your partner and to yourself—that confidence is lasting because it's *real*.

Sexual mastery is transferable to every other area of your life. Put a nice suit on a competent dom, and he'll know exactly how to be assertive in the boardroom. Learn to wholeheartedly submit to a lover, and you'll be able to better handle moments when you feel out of control.

---

80   Black Belt Simon, "Bruce Lee's Lost Interview in the Pierre Berton Show 1971," November 27, 2020, YouTube video, 24:47, https://www.youtube.com/watch?v=fEDfznOP82o.

I'm calling on all of us to elevate sex from the dirty underground to the art form it truly is. Collectively, we can bring sexuality out of the dark ages and shift the shame, negativity, and stigma that surrounds sex. I want people to realize it's not only essential, but super sexy, to be sex educated.

To do that, we need each other's stories. We need to hear each other's experiences and trade sex hacks so we can become great lovers and great people. In any great endeavor, it takes the exchange of ideas between people, cultures, and leaders to elevate the pursuit further.

We can't do it alone. We must take sex out of isolation, and share information and support as freely as we share which protein shake to drink, or how to increase strength on the bench press. We should trade sex hacks like people trade recipes. To remove the stigma of sex education altogether, especially for men, it is essential for *real* progress to occur. Visit my website at *KennethPlay.com* to learn more skills, connect to our community, and share your experience.

There's more we can learn from each other, and mastering sex can be a vehicle to mastering yourself. I've shared what I know with you now, and I hope I've given you the tools to begin your own exploration and develop things that are even better than what I could have imagined. And I hope you'll share that with me and others.

Great lovers are made, not born. Through learning and exploration, it's possible to be not just great in bed, but extraordinary. You can transform your sex life beyond what you thought was possible. Beyond mind-blowing, beyond connected...beyond satisfied.

Acknowledgments

Thank you to Andrew, the founder of Hacienda. In my late twenties, when my fitness startup failed, I was completely lost and on the verge of being evicted. Andrew bailed me out, took me in, and asked me to support his mission to share a sex-positive culture with the world. He gave me a job and a purpose, working towards a vision we both share. Andrew remains one of the most generous, giving, kind, and supportive people I've ever met.

Hacienda's fearless leader, Beth, is the best project manager I've ever worked with. She bought into my vision for a high-tech, interactive guide, and managed all the complicated QR codes to make this book as user-friendly as possible. She's also one of my closest friends who always believes in my ambitions and backs me with love and action plans.

To my family at Hacienda, you've seen me through all the phases of my career, and you were there for me. Thank you for believing in my crazy dreams.

I'm grateful for collaboration with Dr. Zhana, my "work wife." She's a researcher with a PhD in sexuality, whereas I'm just a guy in the community who throws sex parties. Dr. Zhana taught me that sex can be taken seriously and is worthy of rigorous scientific study. I'm honored to help with her relentless pursuit to debunk the myths about sex that harm so many people. When I described myself as a person who bounces from one shiny thing to another, she helped me see my novelty drive isn't a defect, but a personality trait. Dr. Zhana has been not only a scientist but a relationship and sex coach for me, helping me with issues I struggled with in myself.

In addition to a "work wife," I'm honored to also have a "work mom" in Pamela Madsen. I met her at Sex Geek Summer Camp, then became her host and pool boy at her "Back to the Body" sensual retreats for women, where Pamela quickly realized I had a lot more to give. She took me under her wing and taught me how to connect with women—how to understand their different needs and desires, follow their arousal, and connect to their sexuality and their humanity. Thanks to Pamela I traveled the world and got thousands of hours of hands-on experience. But more importantly, Pamela and the women I worked with helped me see the core thread in all of us: that we all want to be seen, loved, validated, celebrated, appreciated, adored, and given pleasure.

Thank you to Reid Mihalko, who created the first Sex Geek Summer Camp and showed me it was possible to make a living as a sex educator. Reid's mentorship shaped the early days of my career, and he was there to help me navigate some of the most painful and difficult spots.

Tim Ferriss gave me a framework to think about life hacking, and his work guided and shaped my perspective on how to improve sex.

From his books I learned that it can be an adventure to offer yourself up as a human guinea pig and share what you learn. When I met Tim, he was writing *The 4-Hour Body* and he needed a gym in which to shoot photos; he chose mine. Later, at the party for his book's release, I remember thinking, *Shit, will I ever write a book in my life?* Here this book is, a decade later. If anyone calls it "the 4-hour sex book," I'll have Tim to thank.

Bruce Lee taught me that when everyone thinks you're weak, that's the time to show your strength. Growing up in Hong Kong, it was pivotal to watch a martial artist from my own country challenge the stereotype of Asian men as the underestimated, inferior "sick men of the East." Bruce Lee didn't just share his skills in martial arts; he also brought pride back to his people. For so many men out there who feel being Asian is inferior, I hope to bring justice and pride back to our sexuality, in the same way Bruce Lee showed us it was possible to have pride in our nationality. Most people know Bruce Lee as a martial artist, but it was his philosophy that profoundly influenced me and this book: learning principles, ego consciousness, how to honestly express yourself. His philosophy is, surprisingly, very useful for sex.

Thank you to my business mentor, who saw there was a book in me and encouraged me to write it. When I objected that I could never write a book report in school and could barely string a text message together, my mentor said, "I know a guy who can help people exactly like you." He set me up with a meeting with Tucker Max. By the next morning, I was at Tucker's house workshopping this book.

Thank you to Tucker Max for building the company that made this book possible. Tucker listened as I described the crippling sexual insecurity I'd felt in my early adulthood, and how I'd realized that being vulnerable about the size of my penis had helped me build my entire career. "I don't see another motherfucker willing to be you," Tucker told me. "Your vulnerability is your biggest market advantage." Tucker understood what I was trying to teach, and he saw the value in my message. If it wasn't for him starting Scribe, you wouldn't be holding this book.

Thank you to Emily Gindlesparger, who used her way with words to translate my spoken thoughts. It was intimidating to explain female pleasure to a female scribe, and I appreciate how deeply she listened and crystallized my ideas on the page. This book had to go through her to be birthed.

It has been incredible to have world-class help at every step of the book process. Thank you to Kayla Sokol, my publishing manager; Erin Tyler, my cover designer; and everyone else on my team for your incredible help. Imagine having a car concept and being able to take it to a Ferrari factory to be built—that's what making this book has been like with Scribe.

Thank you to Robert Bienstock, who was one of my clients as a personal trainer. When I told him I wanted to pursue a new career direction, he paid for my early education at Sex Geek Summer Camp to get me started.

Peter Shankman and Calvin Corelli, among other personal training clients, became business mentors for me. Before creating my Sex Hacker Pro course, I was lost on how to find the right business model and make it work. I'm grateful for their encouragement for me to build a course. They helped remove the "starving" from "starving artist," and showed me how to turn my passion into an abundant career.

One of my dearest clients and friends, Chris Wink, trusted me as his coach and completely transformed his sex life. But beyond keeping this newfound knowledge to himself, he shared my work generously with many of his close circle. Many men are ashamed to talk about sex with each other, but Chris broke down all that stigma, and was truly shameless about the power and importance of sex education and female pleasure.

Thank you to my family, and specifically to my mom, who took the chance to immigrate to a foreign country where she didn't speak the language, raised her two sons on minimum wage, and gave us the opportunity to live the lives we choose. To quote Jimmy O. Yang: "Most Chinese parents would say pursuing your dreams is how you become homeless." Yet here I am, an Asian immigrant who decided to pursue the weirdest career in the world, and I'm making it. My mom's acts of courage gave me a real opportunity to follow my dream.

Thank you to Karen, the love of my life, my ride-or-die fiancée. She has always been willing to help me at the drop of a hat, whether coming over to help make a sex swing unicorn prototype at 3 a.m., practicing positions before I have a shoot, listening to my ramblings, or even just brainstorming ideas and coining phrases like "play lab." She also gives me the gift of the space and time that I needed with lovers and colleagues and the long hours that I needed to write this book.

I find myself teetering sometimes with insecurity and Karen knows how to encourage me when I feel less than I truly am. She's been there for me in every sense, bringing me up when I was at my lowest, and talking me through some really rough times. Her honesty has been at times brutal but fair, and that's why her support has meant so much to me. She has always urged me on and told me I have something worthy to give to the world, and has given her undying support, even when my dreams seemed crazy to me.

Thank you to my current and former team members, Quinn, Rene, Arnaud, and Clara, who believed in my vision. I came to Arnaud with an idea for a master class in sex ed, and he made it happen. Quinn helped me build the course initially, Clara helped with art direction and branding, and Rene has taken all of it to the next level. In working and living together, Rene learned to manage the chaos of my life as we executed the vision for Sex Hacker Pro and this book.

Thank you to my collaborators: Wednesday Martin, Sarrah Rose, Alexa Martin, Erika Lust, Whitney Miller, and Bryony Cole. I have learned so much from working with you.

Melissa Vitale, the most badass publicist ever, helped put me on stages I never dreamed of.

Honz dedicated countless hours to the illustrations in this book. When I told her the scale and complexity of the illustrations I wanted to create—including anatomically accurate diagrams and more drawings of genitals than any illustrator has probably ever drawn, she hopped on board with enthusiasm and was willing to upgrade her own skillset in the process to achieve the goals I set for us.

Thank you to my teachers: Destin Gerek, Bob, Om Rupani, Betty Martin, Mal Harrison, and Dr. Emily Nagoski. I stand on the shoulders of giants who have done so much work for the industry.

Thank you to the amazing authors, researchers and scientists whose work I drew on to create this book. Though many have influenced me, there are a few that have been especially helpful and generous with their time: Drs. Jim Pfaus, Barry Komisaruk, Nan Wise, and Laurie Mintz. I appreciate their input and hope I do justice representing their ideas in my book.

Before I met Dr. Jim Pfaus, I read one of his more famous pieces of scientific literature, "The Vagina Strikes Back," which I loved so much I'm getting it framed for my wall. Little did I know I'd get to work with him. For months during COVID, Dr. Pfaus donated his time to fact-check this book and deliver advice 24/7, and forward his ample supply of research. When we wanted to compare penis and vagina sizes to determine genital compatibility from actual math, Dr. Pfaus was the researcher we called, and he helped us show that the orgasm gap is a skills gap not a size gap.

Finally, Chelsey Fasano has been my collaborator on this book—but more than that, she's been a cocreator. If you watch geese fly in a classic V formation, you can see the flock sometimes trades out the point goose in front. The leader falls back, and another goose seamlessly takes the lead. When this project got overwhelming for me, Chelsey was the leader I could swap out at the top of the V to hold things together and guide me and the book to new heights. Chelsey has been the perfect copilot, workshopping my ideas with me, helping me express them, and taking over the Word document to write much of this book. Although I'm the author who brought Chelsey onto this project, it's as much her book as it is mine. There aren't many people in the world who can nerd out about sex for as long as Chelsey can. She elevated my standards from a Pornhub star sharing his opinions on squirting to a teacher sharing research-backed work with perfect citations. One day Chelsey will write a wonderful book about the convergence of meditation, tantric practices, and neuroscience, and I can't wait to read it. She's the one to watch out for.

To the tens of thousands of my students and clients across the globe, and to the millions of people who have watched my videos, your willingness to invest in your sexual mastery and your care for female pleasure inspires me to do this work. Especially to those of you who have overcome seemingly insurmountable sexual insecurities, or nearly given up on sexual pleasure: your transformation inspires me every day.

Printed in Great Britain
by Amazon

48358849R10229